# STAR WARS

# DARTH VADER

## THE SHU-TORUN WAR

# DARTH VADER

## THE SHU-TORUN WAR

Writer **KIERON GILLEN**

### ANNUAL #1

Artist **LEINIL YU**
Inker **GERRY ALANGUILAN**
Color Artist **JASON KEITH**
Cover Art **LEINIL YU**

### ISSUES #16-19

Artist **SALVADOR LARROCA**
Colorist **EDGAR DELGADO**
Cover Art **KAARE ANDREWS** (#16-18) &
**MARK BROOKS** (#19)

Letterer **VC's JOE CARAMAGNA**
Assistant Editor **HEATHER ANTOS**
Editor **JORDAN D. WHITE**
Executive Editor **C.B. CEBULSKI**

Editor in Chief **AXEL ALONSO**
Chief Creative Officer **JOE QUESADA**
Publisher **DAN BUCKLEY**

For Lucasfilm:
Senior Editor **FRANK PARISI**
Creative Director **MICHAEL SIGLAIN**
Lucasfilm Story Group **RAYNE ROBERTS, PABLO HIDALGO,
LELAND CHEE, MATT MARTIN**

Collection Editor JENNIFER GRUNWALD
Associate Editor SARAH BRUNSTAD
Associate Managing Editor ALEX STARBUCK
Editor, Special Projects MARK D. BEAZLEY
VP, Production & Special Projects JEFF YOUNGQUIST
SVP Print, Sales & Marketing DAVID GABRIEL
Book Designer ADAM DEL RE

DISNEP LUCASFILM

STAR WARS: DARTH VADER VOL. 3 — THE SHU-TORUN WAR. Contains material originally published in magazine form as DARTH VADER #16-19 and ANNUAL #1. First printing 2016. ISBN# 978-0-785-19977-9. Published by MARVEL WORLDWIDE, INC., a subsidiary of MARVEL ENTERTAINMENT, LLC. OFFICE OF PUBLICATION: 135 West 50th Street, New York, NY 10020. STAR WARS and related text and illustrations are trademarks and/or copyrights, in the United States and other countries, of Lucasfilm Ltd. and/or its affiliates. © & TM Lucasfilm Ltd. No similarity between any of the names, characters, persons and/or institutions in this magazine with those of any living or dead person or institution is intended, and any such similarity which may exist is purely coincidental. Marvel and its logos are TM Marvel Characters, Inc. Printed in Canada. ALAN FINE, President, Marvel Entertainment; DAN BUCKLEY, President, TV, Publishing & Brand Management; JOE QUESADA, Chief Creative Officer; TOM BREVOORT, SVP of Publishing; DAVID BOGART, SVP of Business Affairs & Operations, Publishing & Partnership; C.B. CEBULSKI, VP of Brand Management & Development, Asia; DAVID GABRIEL, SVP of Sales & Marketing, Publishing; JEFF YOUNGQUIST, VP of Production & Special Projects; DAN CARR, Executive Director of Publishing Technology; ALEX MORALES, Director of Publishing Operations; SUSAN CRESPI, Production Manager; STAN LEE, Chairman Emeritus. For information regarding advertising in Marvel Comics or on Marvel.com, please contact Vit DeBellis, Integrated Sales Manager, at vdebellis@marvel.com. For Marvel subscription inquiries, please call 888-511-5480. Manufactured between 6/8/2016 and 7/11/2016 by SOLISCO PRINTERS, SCOTT, QC, CANADA.

10 9 8 7 6 5 4 3 2 1

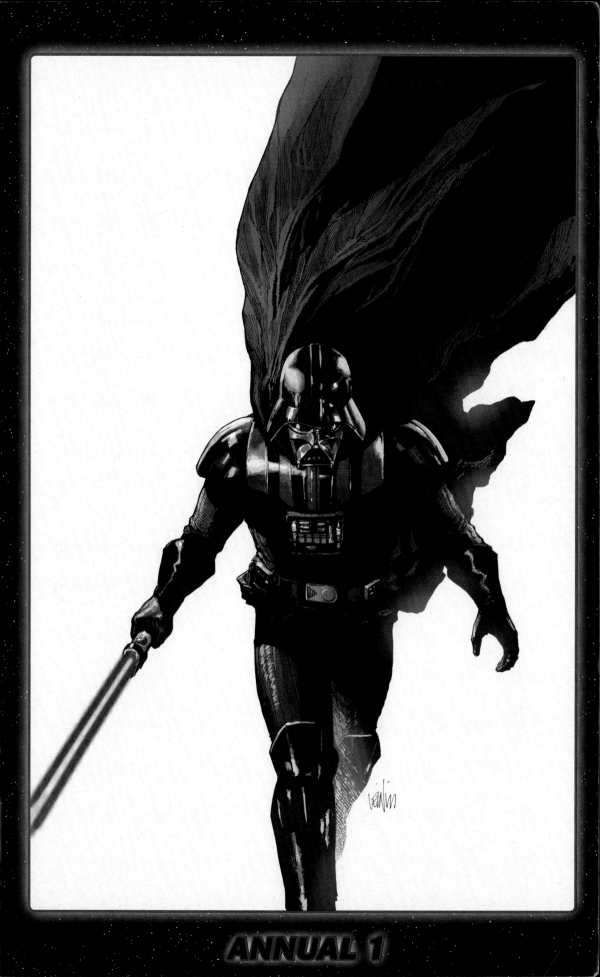

ANNUAL 1

# DARTH VADER

*It is a time of unrest. After the fall of the Republic, the Galactic Empire took over with an iron fist. Yet the Empire does not stand unchallenged as the rebels continue to fight back.*

*The destruction of the Death Star has ignited faith that the Rebellion will prevail, but the Emperor is determined to eliminate any and all threats. As more and more planets fall under Imperial control, Lord Vader travels to Shu-torun with a message to reinforce their cooperation....*

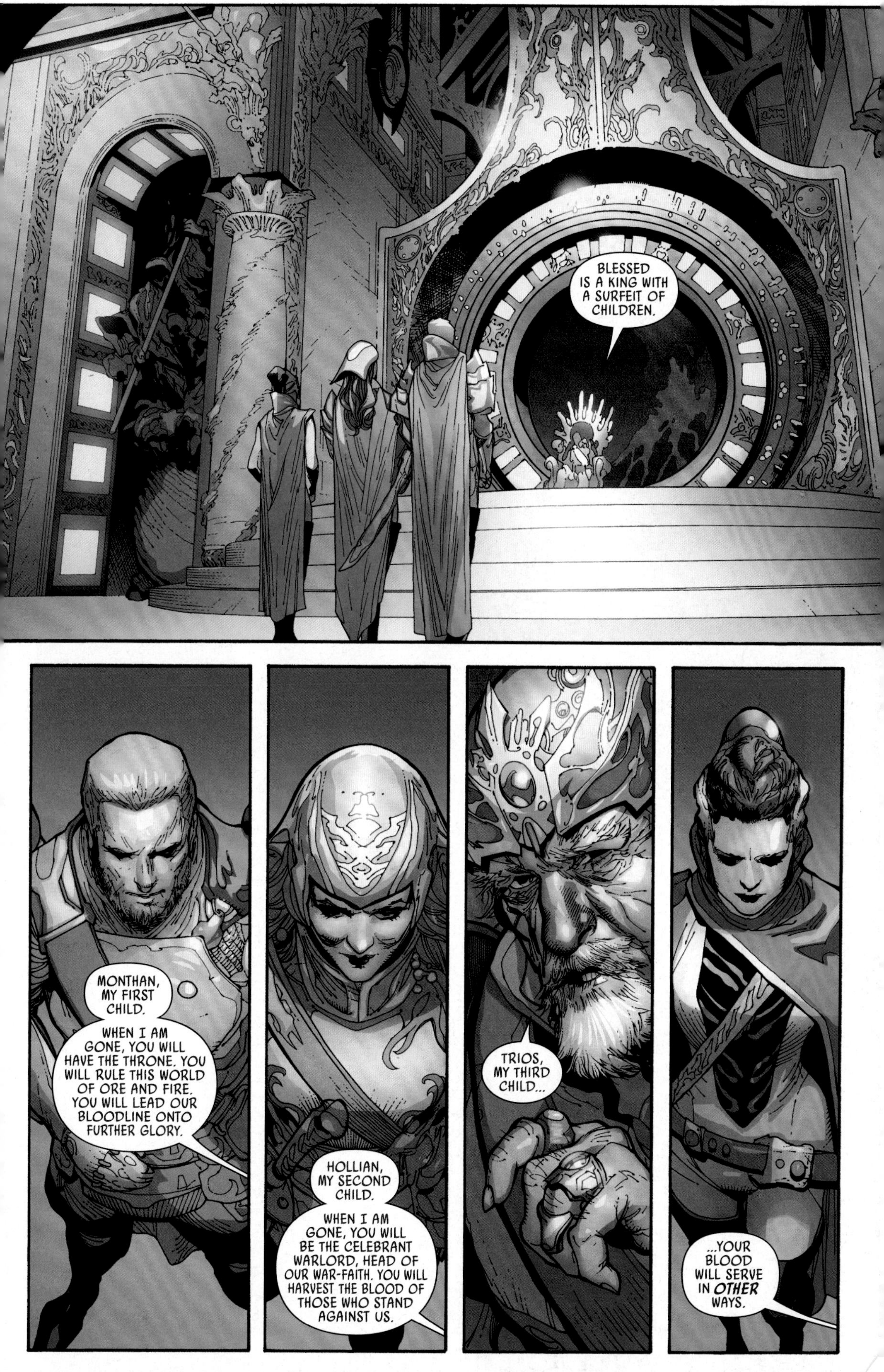
BLESSED IS A KING WITH A SURFEIT OF CHILDREN.
MONTHAN, MY FIRST CHILD.
WHEN I AM GONE, YOU WILL HAVE THE THRONE. YOU WILL RULE THIS WORLD OF ORE AND FIRE. YOU WILL LEAD OUR BLOODLINE ONTO FURTHER GLORY.
HOLLIAN, MY SECOND CHILD.
WHEN I AM GONE, YOU WILL BE THE CELEBRANT WARLORD, HEAD OF OUR WAR-FAITH. YOU WILL HARVEST THE BLOOD OF THOSE WHO STAND AGAINST US.
TRIOS, MY THIRD CHILD...
...YOUR BLOOD WILL SERVE IN OTHER WAYS.

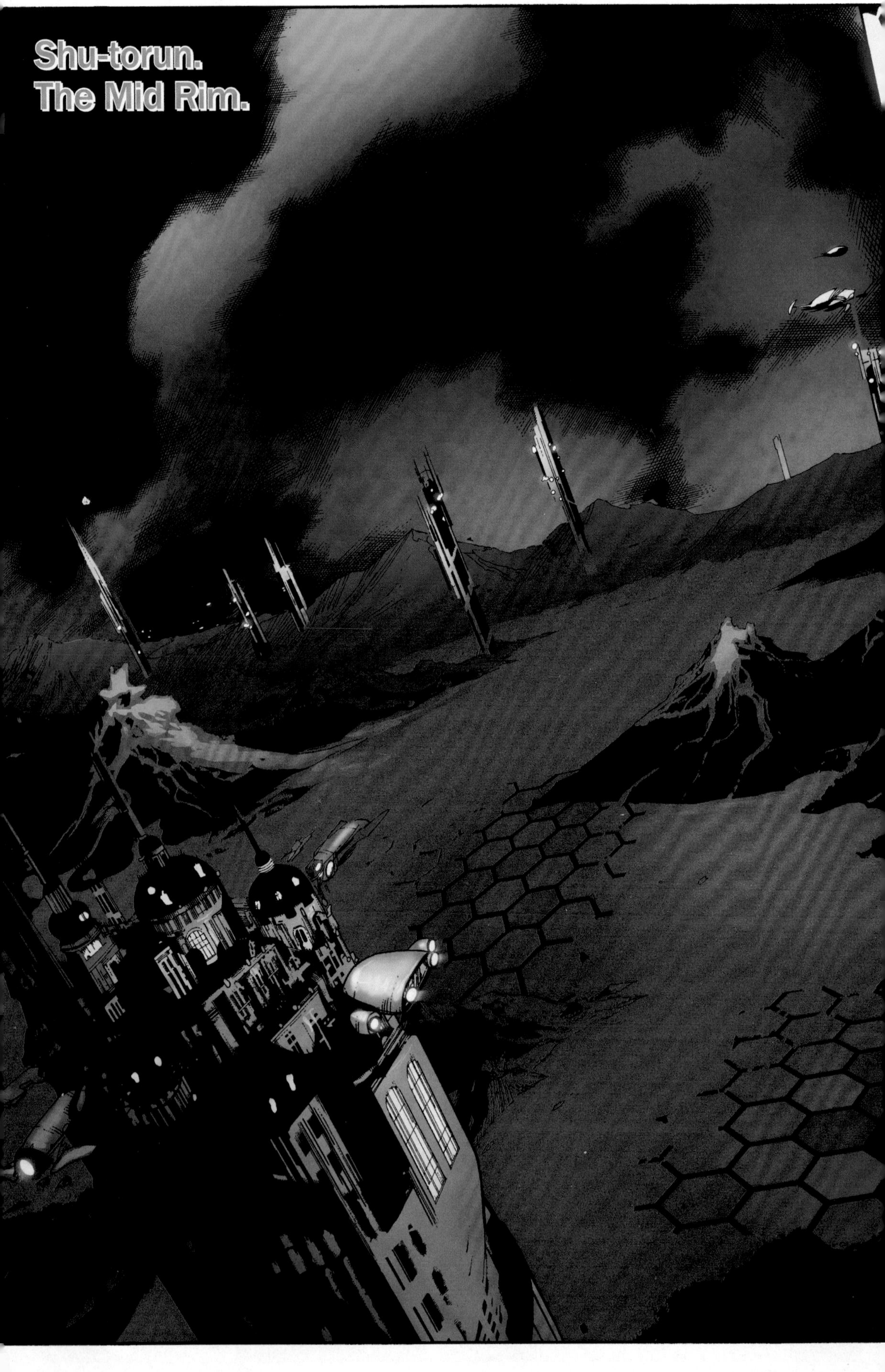
Shu-torun.
The Mid Rim.

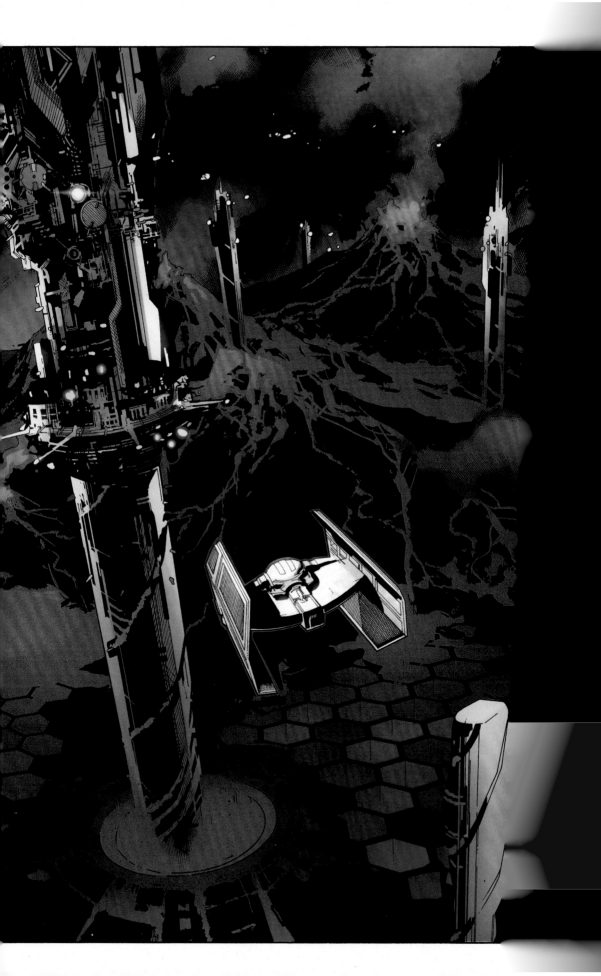

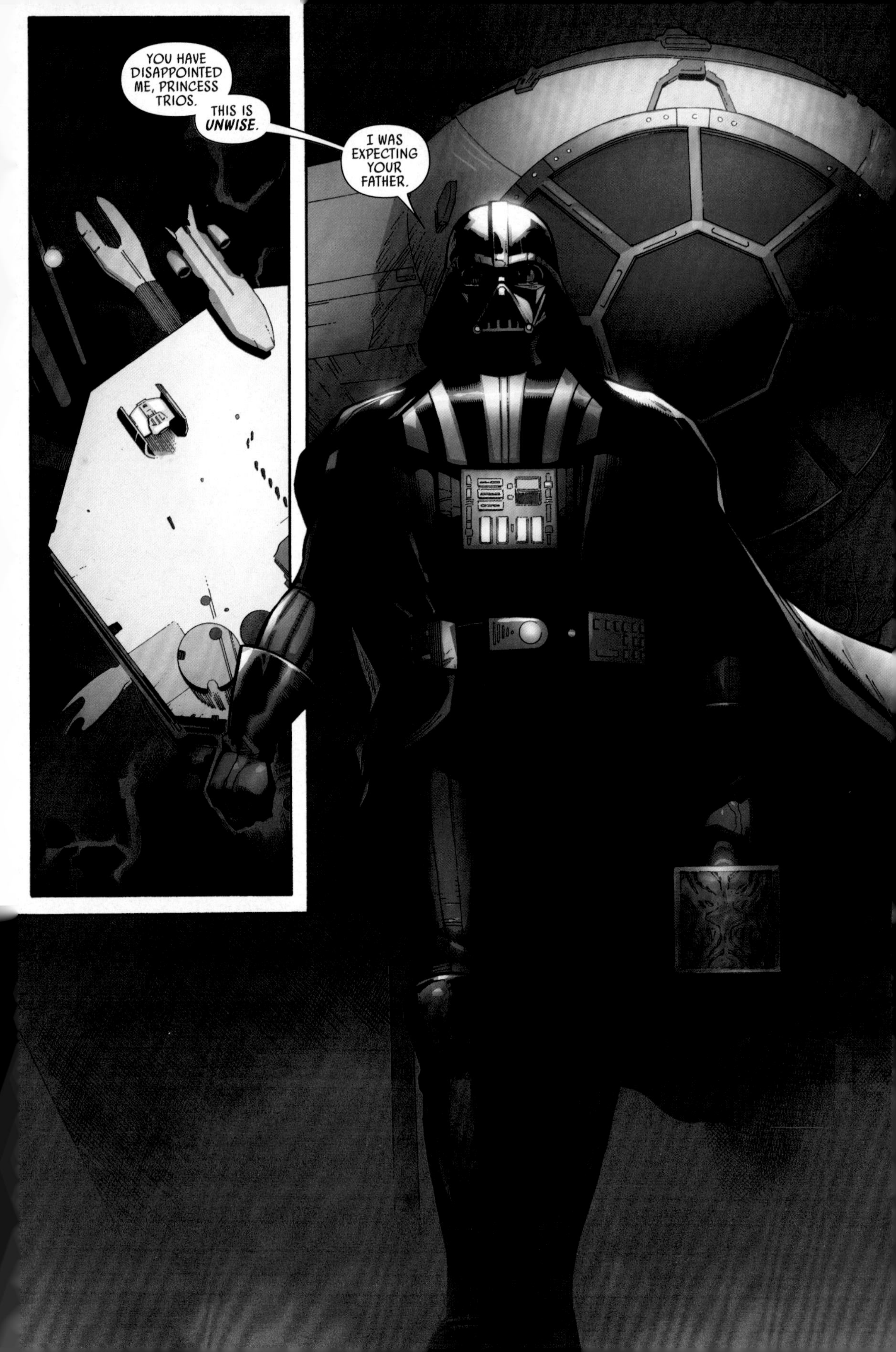

YOU HAVE DISAPPOINTED ME, PRINCESS TRIOS.
THIS IS UNWISE.
I WAS EXPECTING YOUR FATHER.

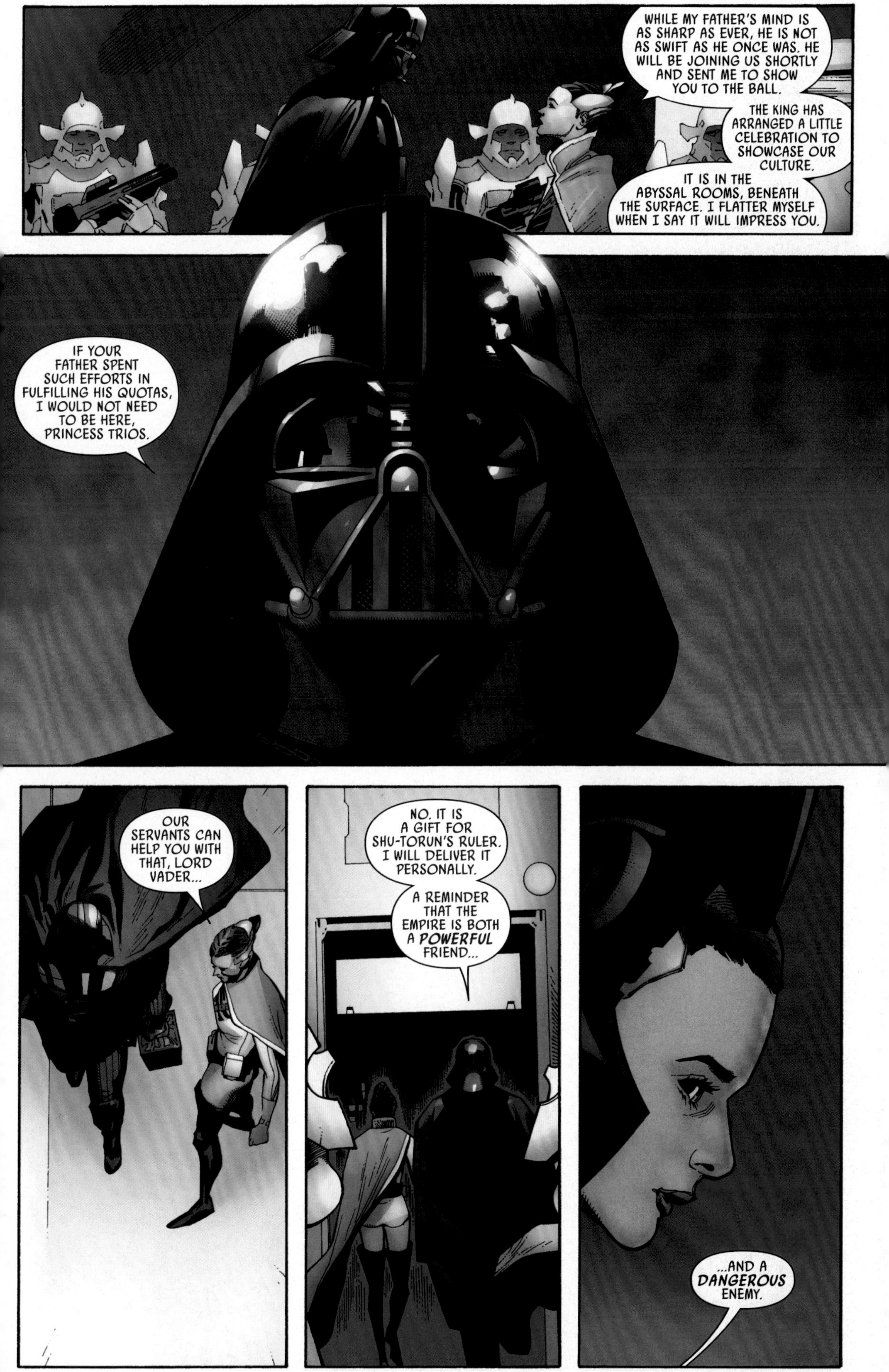
WHILE MY FATHER'S MIND IS AS SHARP AS EVER, HE IS NOT AS SWIFT AS HE ONCE WAS. HE WILL BE JOINING US SHORTLY AND SENT ME TO SHOW YOU TO THE BALL.
THE KING HAS ARRANGED A LITTLE CELEBRATION TO SHOWCASE OUR CULTURE.
IT IS IN THE ABYSSAL ROOMS, BENEATH THE SURFACE. I FLATTER MYSELF WHEN I SAY IT WILL IMPRESS YOU.
IF YOUR FATHER SPENT SUCH EFFORTS IN FULFILLING HIS QUOTAS, I WOULD NOT NEED TO BE HERE, PRINCESS TRIOS.
OUR SERVANTS CAN HELP YOU WITH THAT, LORD VADER...
NO. IT IS A GIFT FOR SHU-TORUN'S RULER. I WILL DELIVER IT PERSONALLY.
A REMINDER THAT THE EMPIRE IS BOTH A *POWERFUL* FRIEND...
...AND A *DANGEROUS* ENEMY.

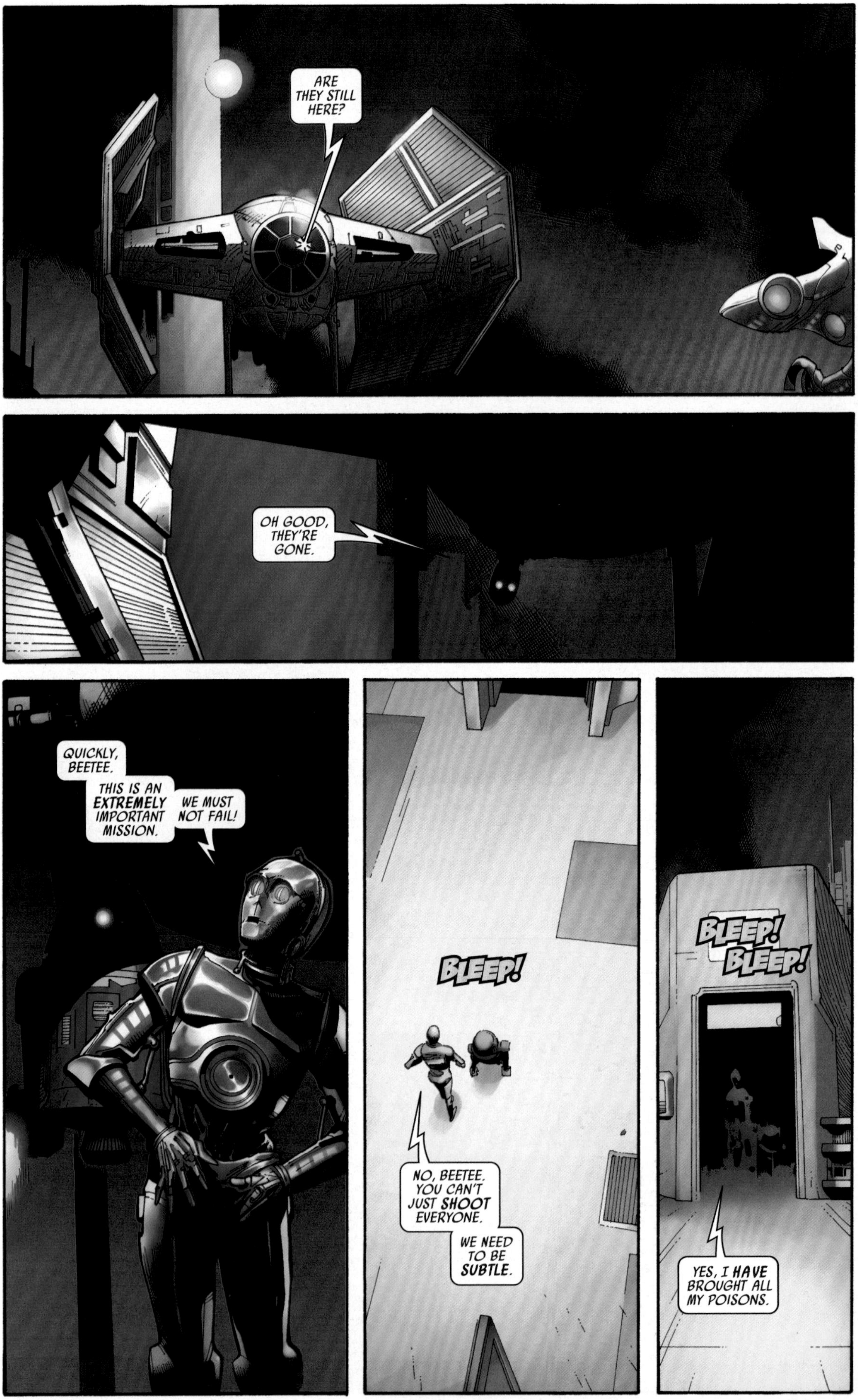
ARE THEY STILL HERE?
OH GOOD, THEY'RE GONE.
QUICKLY, BEETEE.
THIS IS AN EXTREMELY IMPORTANT MISSION.
WE MUST NOT FAIL!
BLEEP!
NO, BEETEE. YOU CAN'T JUST SHOOT EVERYONE.
WE NEED TO BE SUBTLE.
BLEEP! BLEEP!
YES, I HAVE BROUGHT ALL MY POISONS.

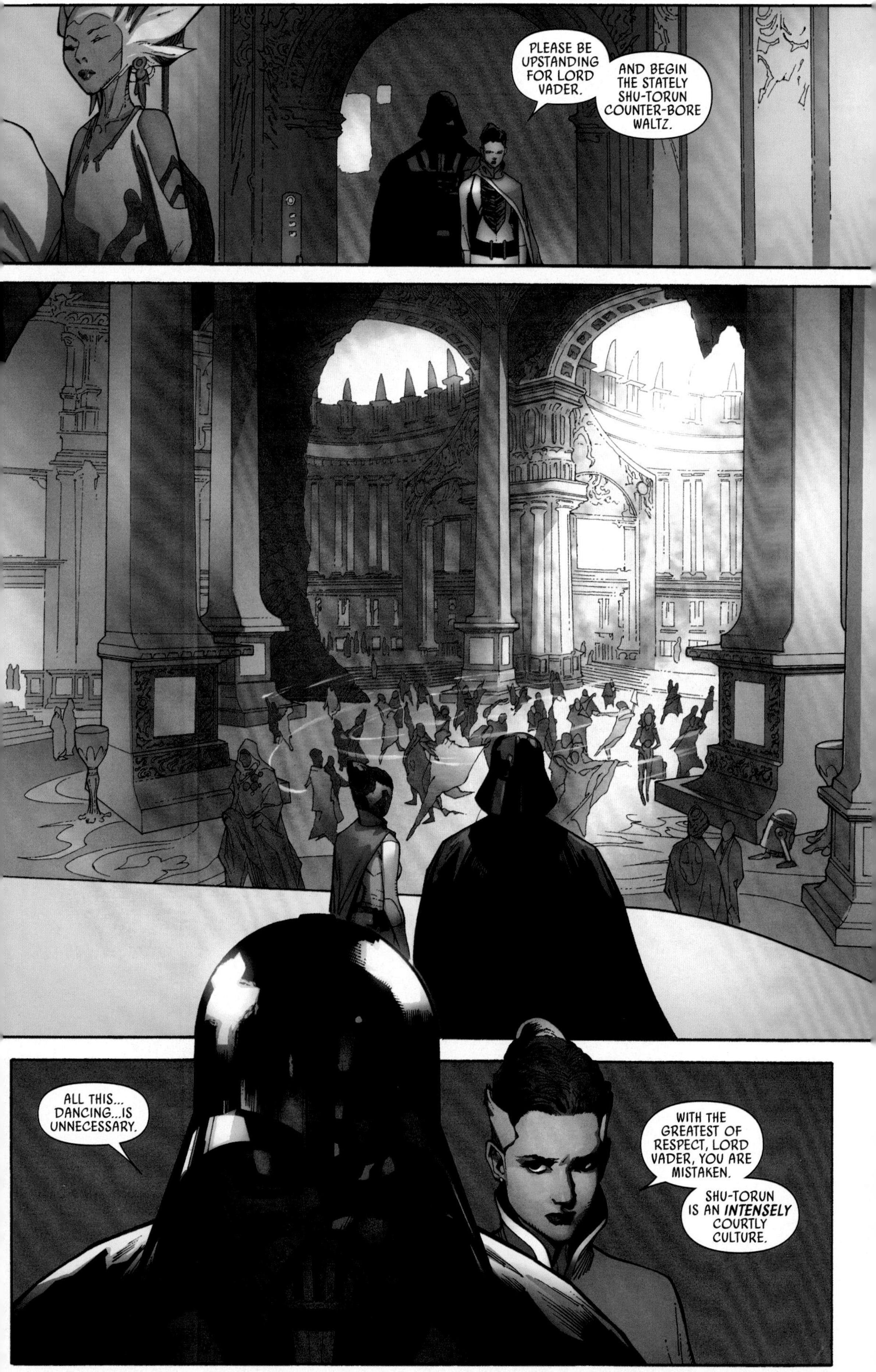
PLEASE BE UPSTANDING FOR LORD VADER.
AND BEGIN THE STATELY SHU-TORUN COUNTER-BORE WALTZ.
ALL THIS... DANCING...IS UNNECESSARY.
WITH THE GREATEST OF RESPECT, LORD VADER, YOU ARE MISTAKEN.
SHU-TORUN IS AN *INTENSELY* COURTLY CULTURE.

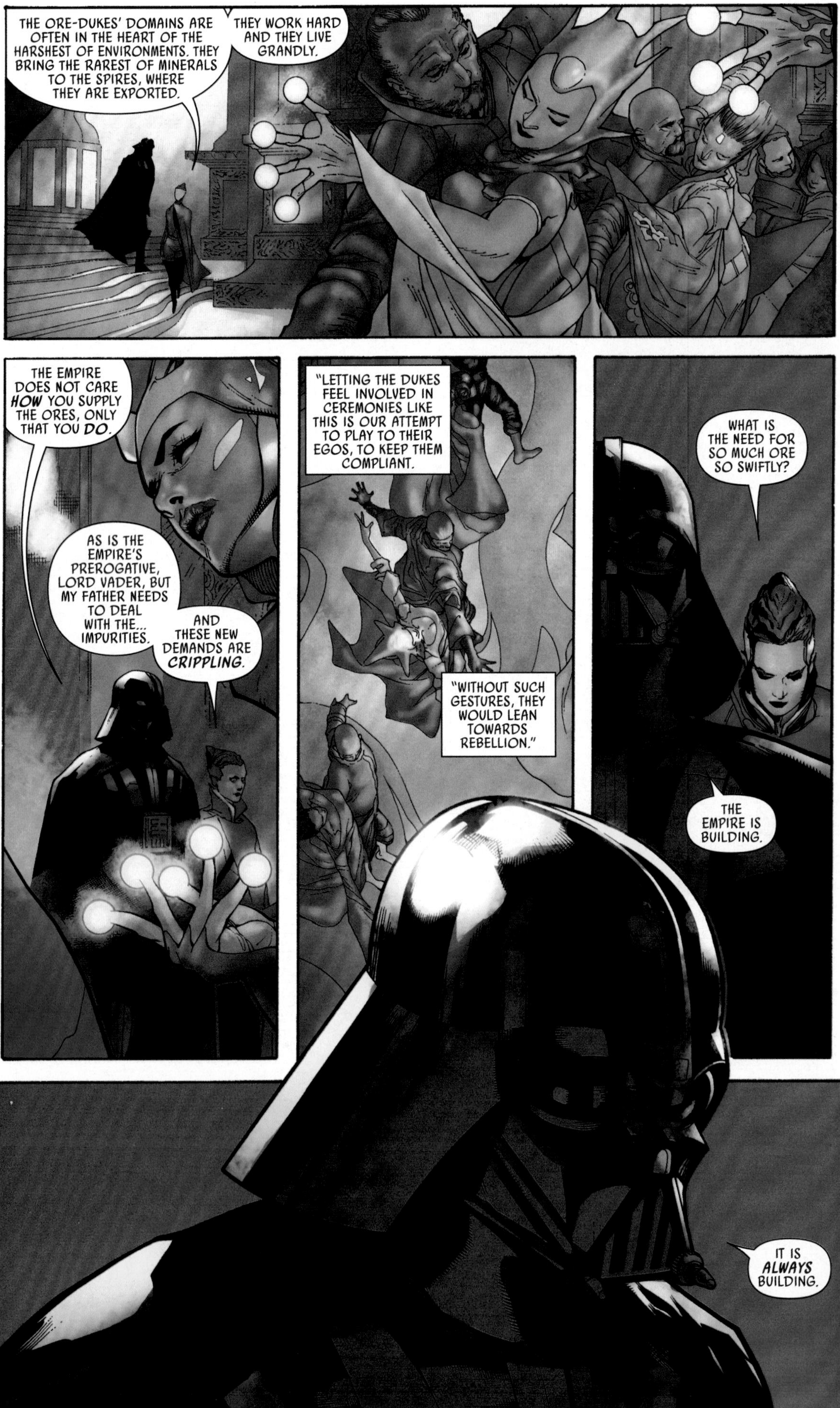
THE ORE-DUKES' DOMAINS ARE OFTEN IN THE HEART OF THE HARSHEST OF ENVIRONMENTS. THEY BRING THE RAREST OF MINERALS TO THE SPIRES, WHERE THEY ARE EXPORTED.
THEY WORK HARD AND THEY LIVE GRANDLY.
THE EMPIRE DOES NOT CARE HOW YOU SUPPLY THE ORES, ONLY THAT YOU DO.
AS IS THE EMPIRE'S PREROGATIVE, LORD VADER, BUT MY FATHER NEEDS TO DEAL WITH THE... IMPURITIES.
AND THESE NEW DEMANDS ARE CRIPPLING.
"LETTING THE DUKES FEEL INVOLVED IN CEREMONIES LIKE THIS IS OUR ATTEMPT TO PLAY TO THEIR EGOS, TO KEEP THEM COMPLIANT.
"WITHOUT SUCH GESTURES, THEY WOULD LEAN TOWARDS REBELLION."
WHAT IS THE NEED FOR SO MUCH ORE SO SWIFTLY?
THE EMPIRE IS BUILDING.
IT IS ALWAYS BUILDING.

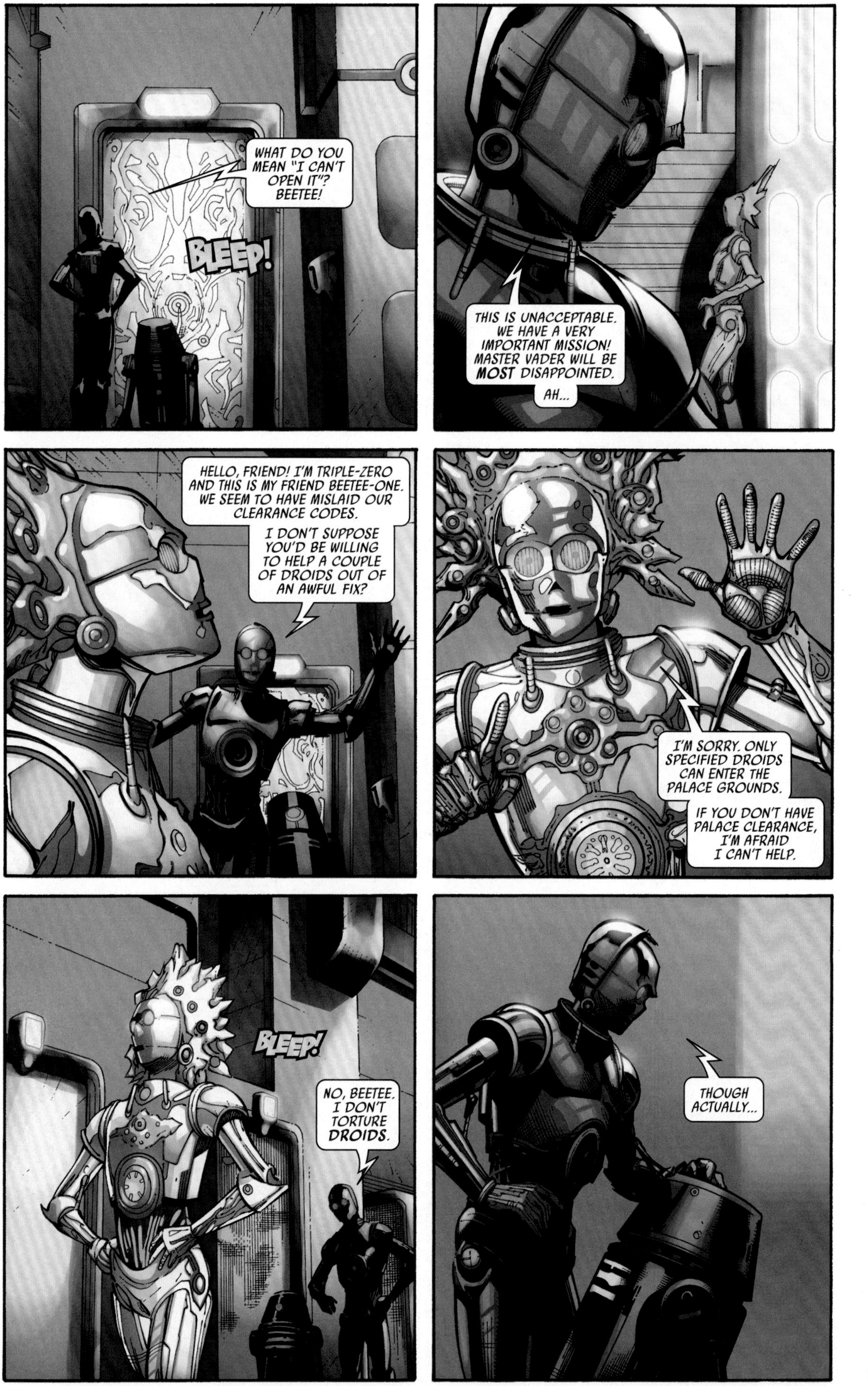
WHAT DO YOU MEAN "I CAN'T OPEN IT"? BEETEE!
BLEEP!
THIS IS UNACCEPTABLE. WE HAVE A VERY IMPORTANT MISSION! MASTER VADER WILL BE MOST DISAPPOINTED.
AH...
HELLO, FRIEND! I'M TRIPLE-ZERO AND THIS IS MY FRIEND BEETEE-ONE. WE SEEM TO HAVE MISLAID OUR CLEARANCE CODES.
I DON'T SUPPOSE YOU'D BE WILLING TO HELP A COUPLE OF DROIDS OUT OF AN AWFUL FIX?
I'M SORRY. ONLY SPECIFIED DROIDS CAN ENTER THE PALACE GROUNDS.
IF YOU DON'T HAVE PALACE CLEARANCE, I'M AFRAID I CAN'T HELP.
BLEEP!
NO, BEETEE. I DON'T TORTURE DROIDS.
THOUGH ACTUALLY...

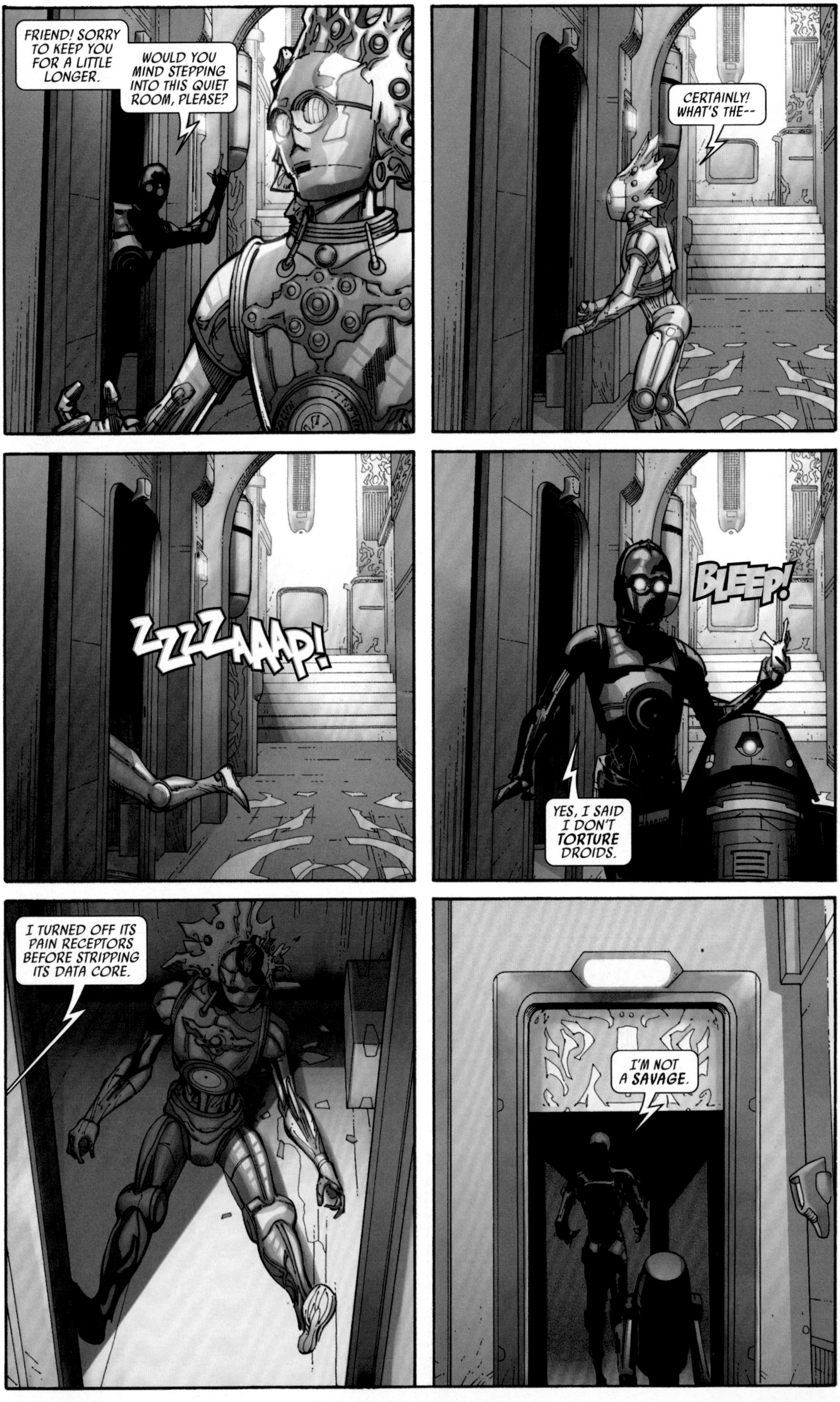
FRIEND! SORRY TO KEEP YOU FOR A LITTLE LONGER.
WOULD YOU MIND STEPPING INTO THIS QUIET ROOM, PLEASE?
CERTAINLY! WHAT'S THE--
ZZZZAAAP!
BLEEP!
YES, I SAID I DON'T TORTURE DROIDS.
I TURNED OFF ITS PAIN RECEPTORS BEFORE STRIPPING ITS DATA CORE.
I'M NOT A SAVAGE.

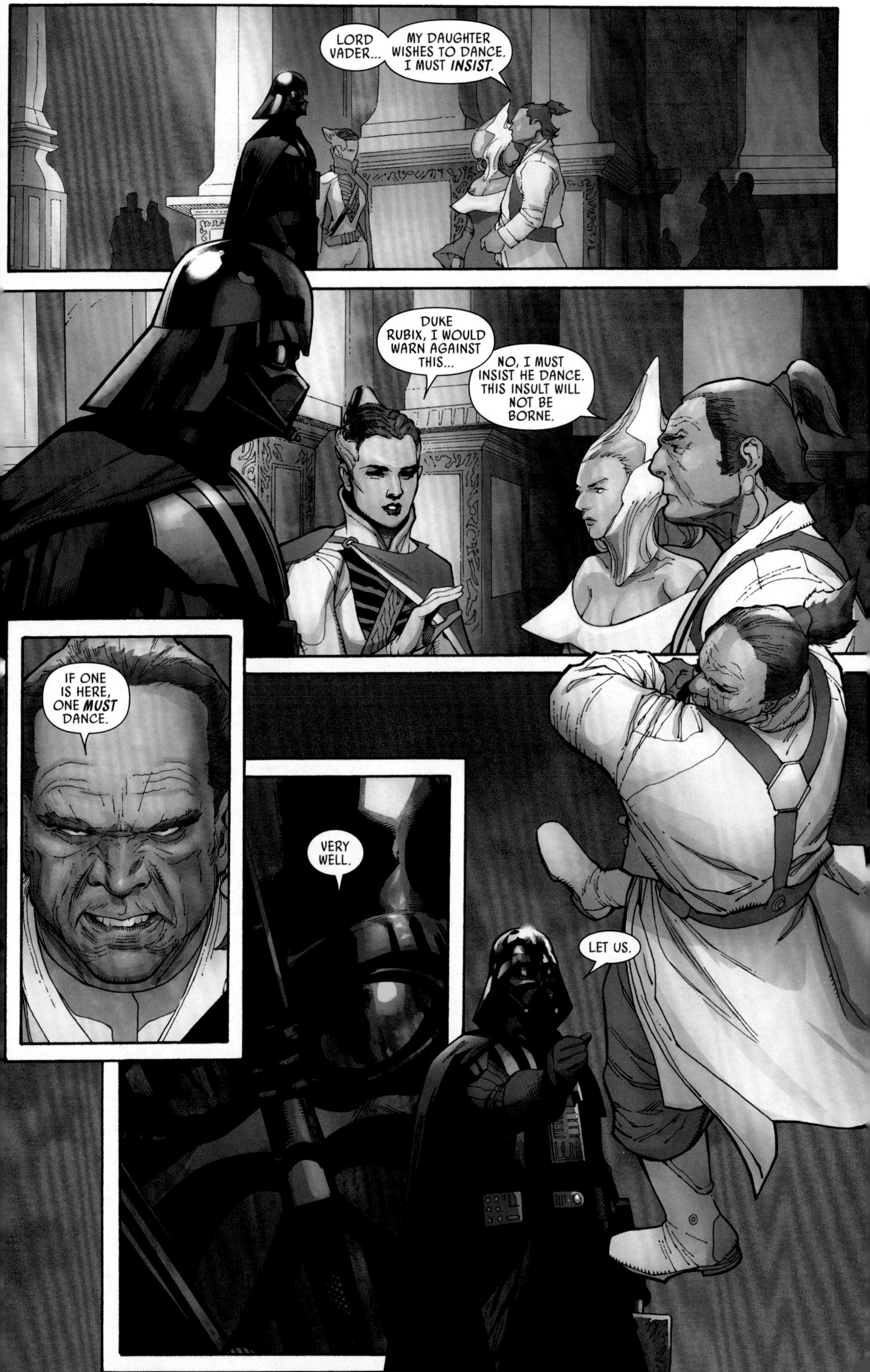
LORD VADER...
MY DAUGHTER WISHES TO DANCE. I MUST INSIST.
DUKE RUBIX, I WOULD WARN AGAINST THIS...
NO, I MUST INSIST HE DANCE. THIS INSULT WILL NOT BE BORNE.
IF ONE IS HERE, ONE MUST DANCE.
VERY WELL.
LET US.

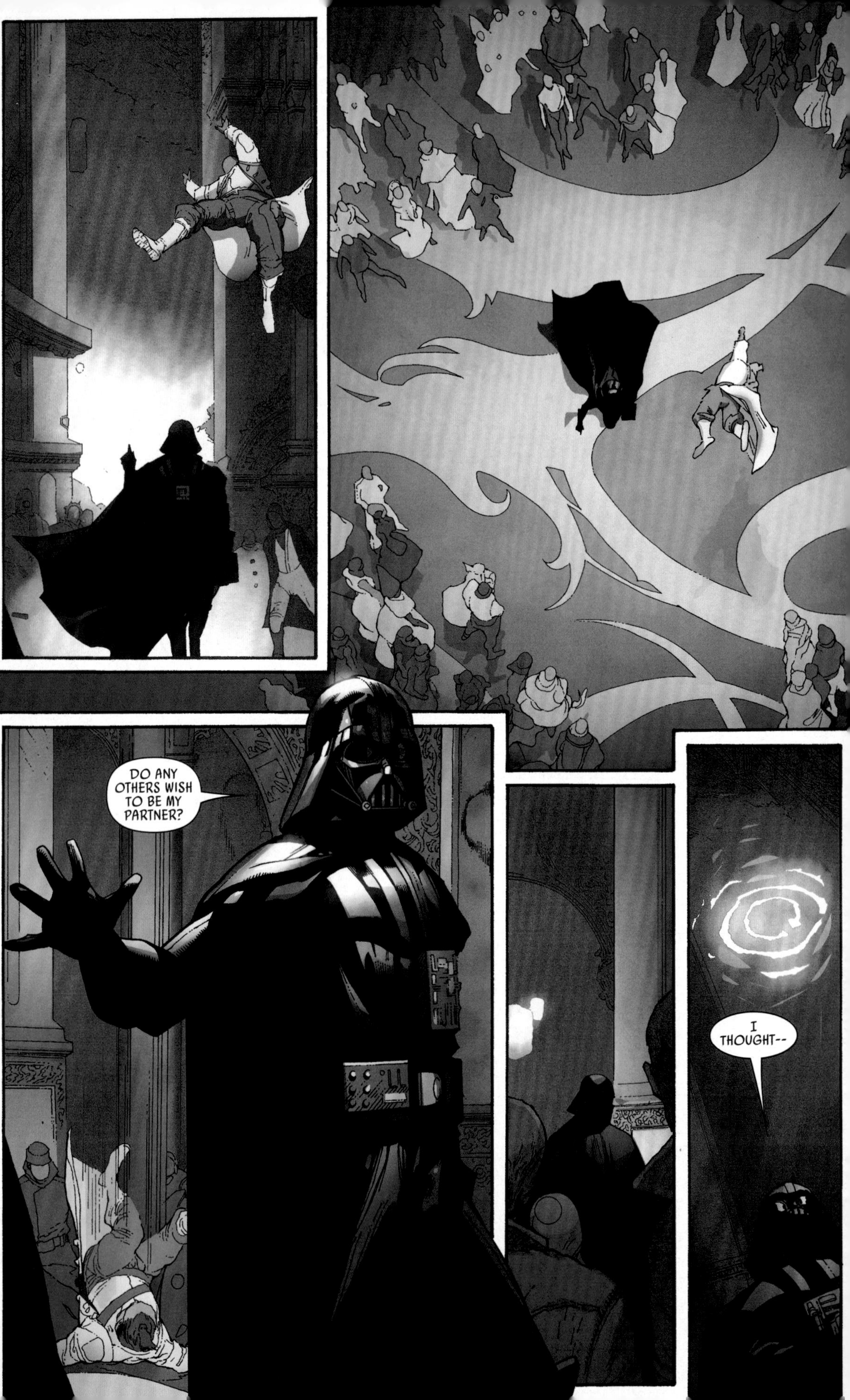
DO ANY OTHERS WISH TO BE MY PARTNER?
I THOUGHT--

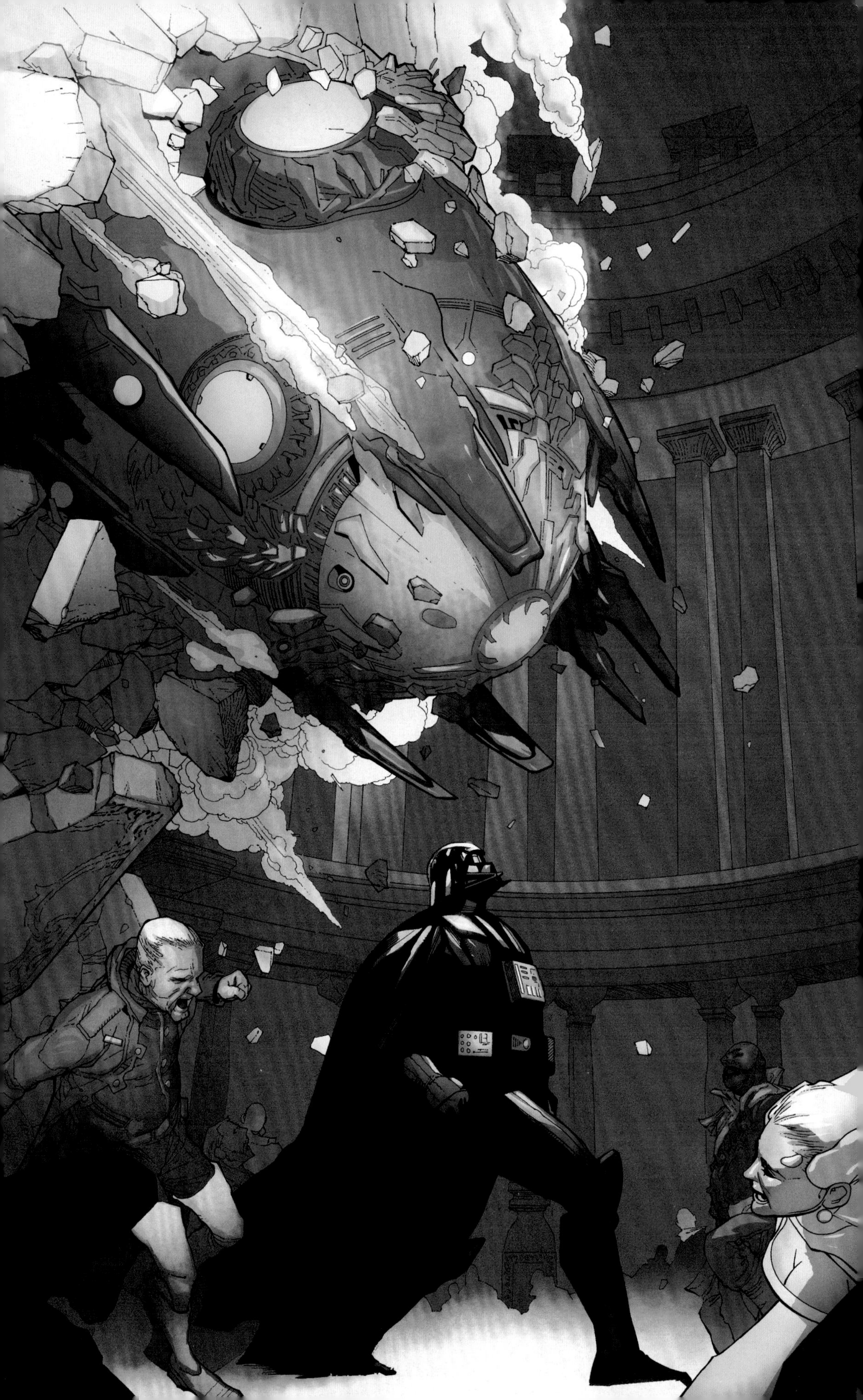

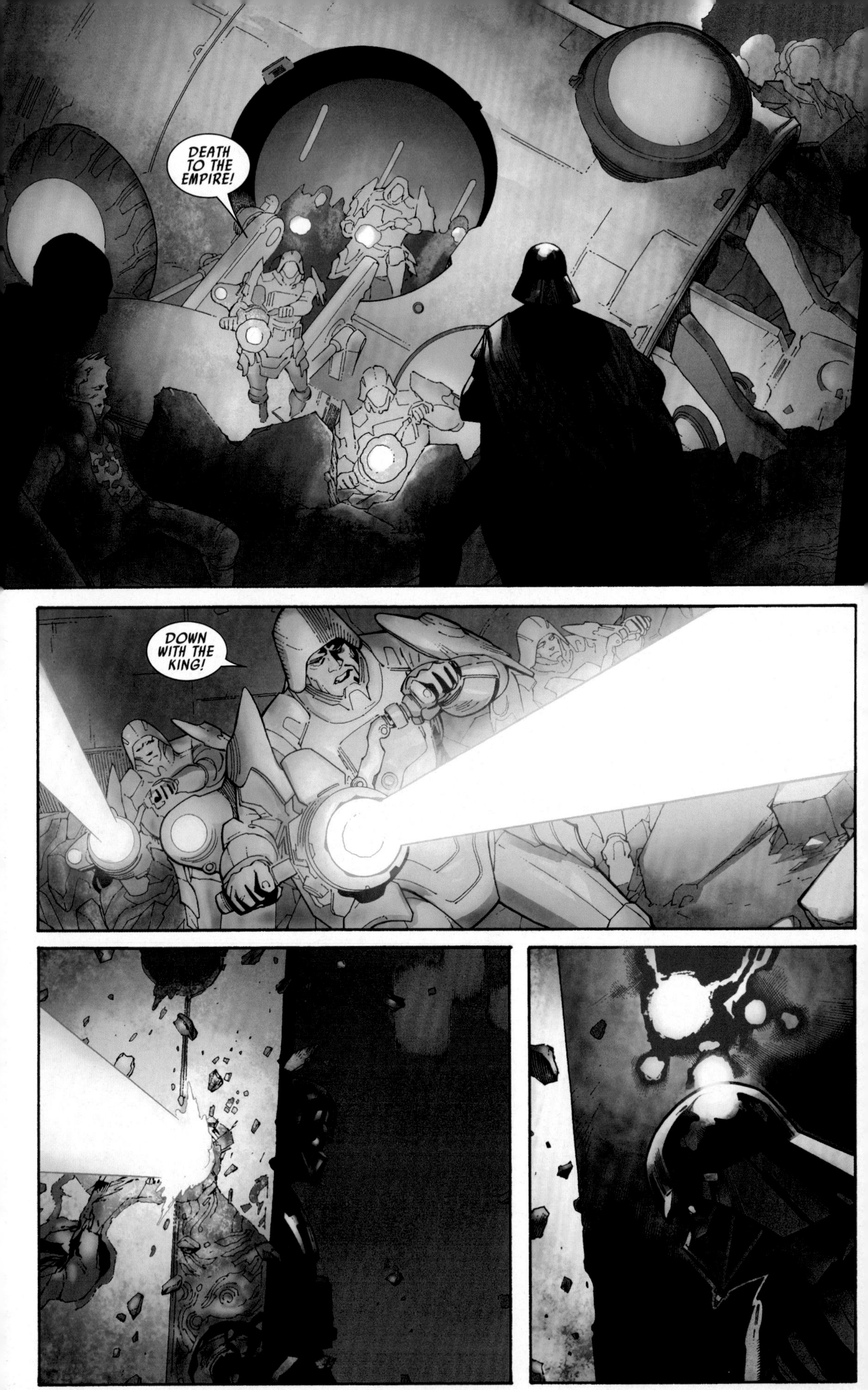
DEATH TO THE EMPIRE!
DOWN WITH THE KING!

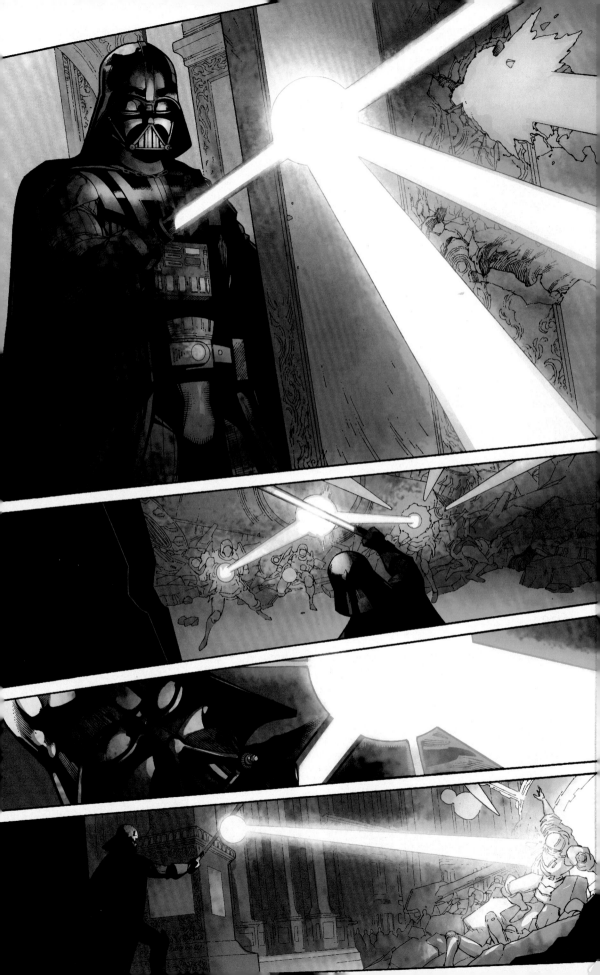

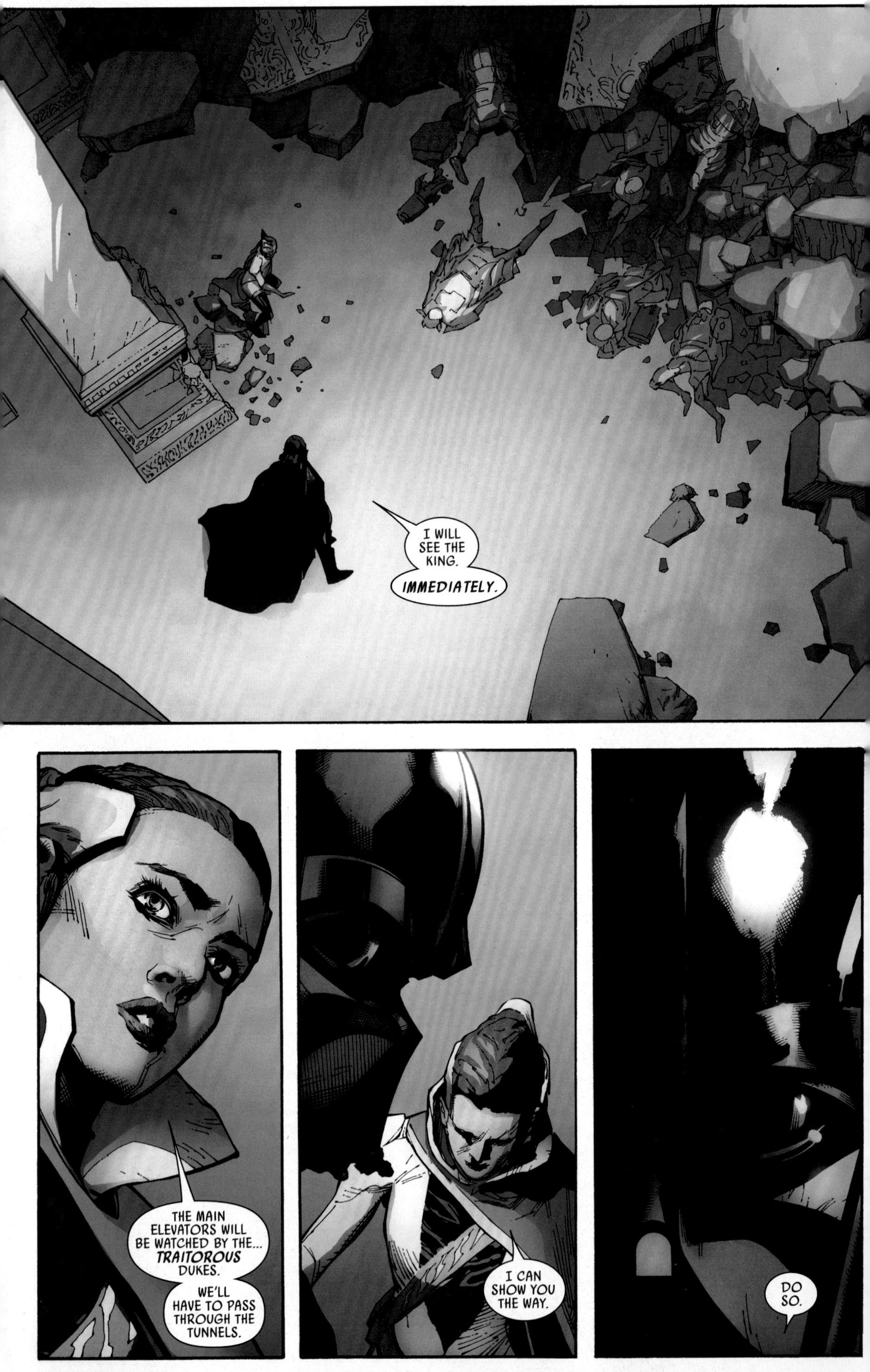
I WILL SEE THE KING.
IMMEDIATELY.
THE MAIN ELEVATORS WILL BE WATCHED BY THE... TRAITOROUS DUKES.
WE'LL HAVE TO PASS THROUGH THE TUNNELS.
I CAN SHOW YOU THE WAY.
DO SO.

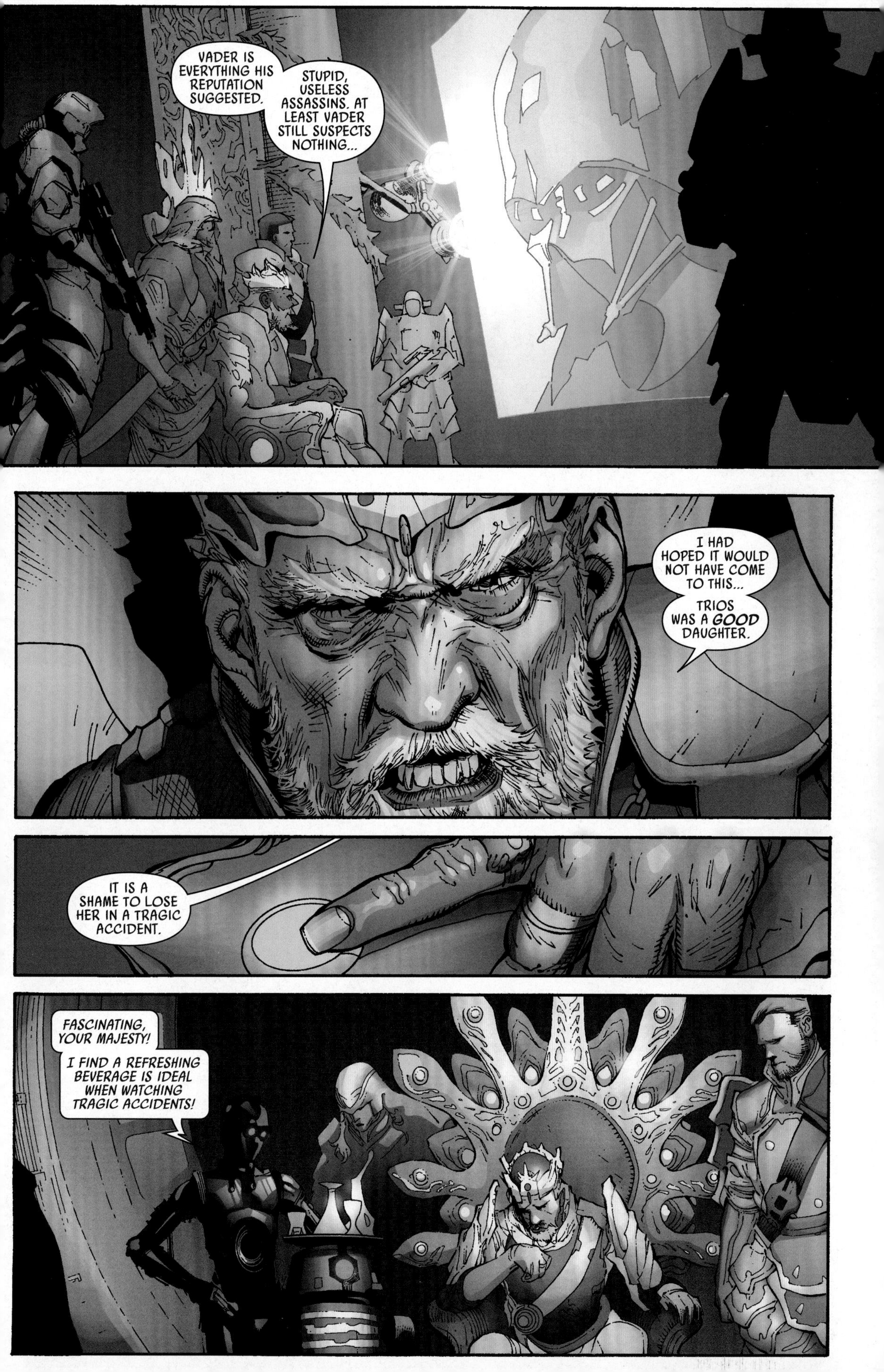
VADER IS EVERYTHING HIS REPUTATION SUGGESTED.
STUPID, USELESS ASSASSINS. AT LEAST VADER STILL SUSPECTS NOTHING...
I HAD HOPED IT WOULD NOT HAVE COME TO THIS...
TRIOS WAS A GOOD DAUGHTER.
IT IS A SHAME TO LOSE HER IN A TRAGIC ACCIDENT.
FASCINATING, YOUR MAJESTY!
I FIND A REFRESHING BEVERAGE IS IDEAL WHEN WATCHING TRAGIC ACCIDENTS!

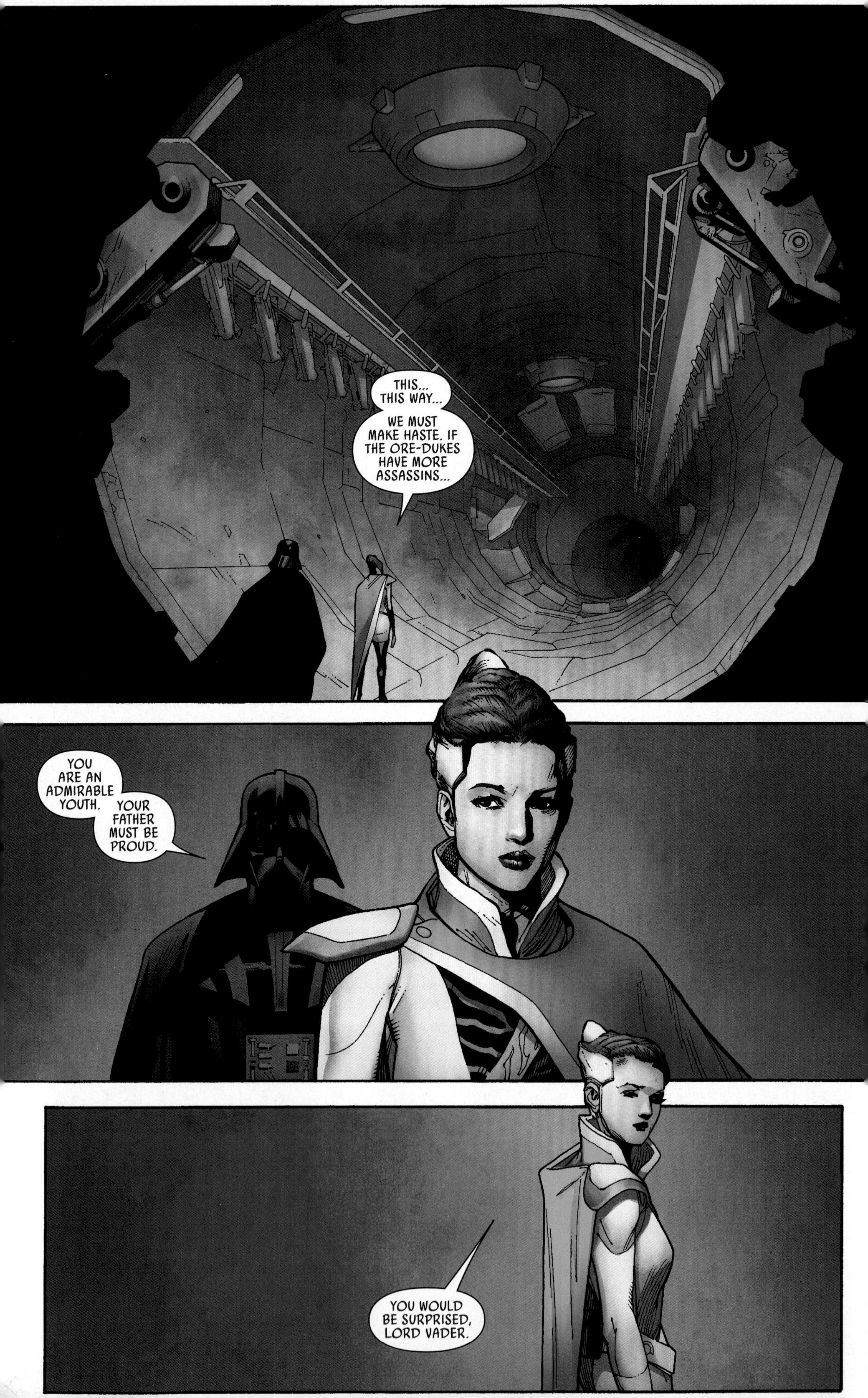
THIS... THIS WAY...
WE MUST MAKE HASTE. IF THE ORE-DUKES HAVE MORE ASSASSINS...
YOU ARE AN ADMIRABLE YOUTH.
YOUR FATHER MUST BE PROUD.
YOU WOULD BE SURPRISED, LORD VADER.

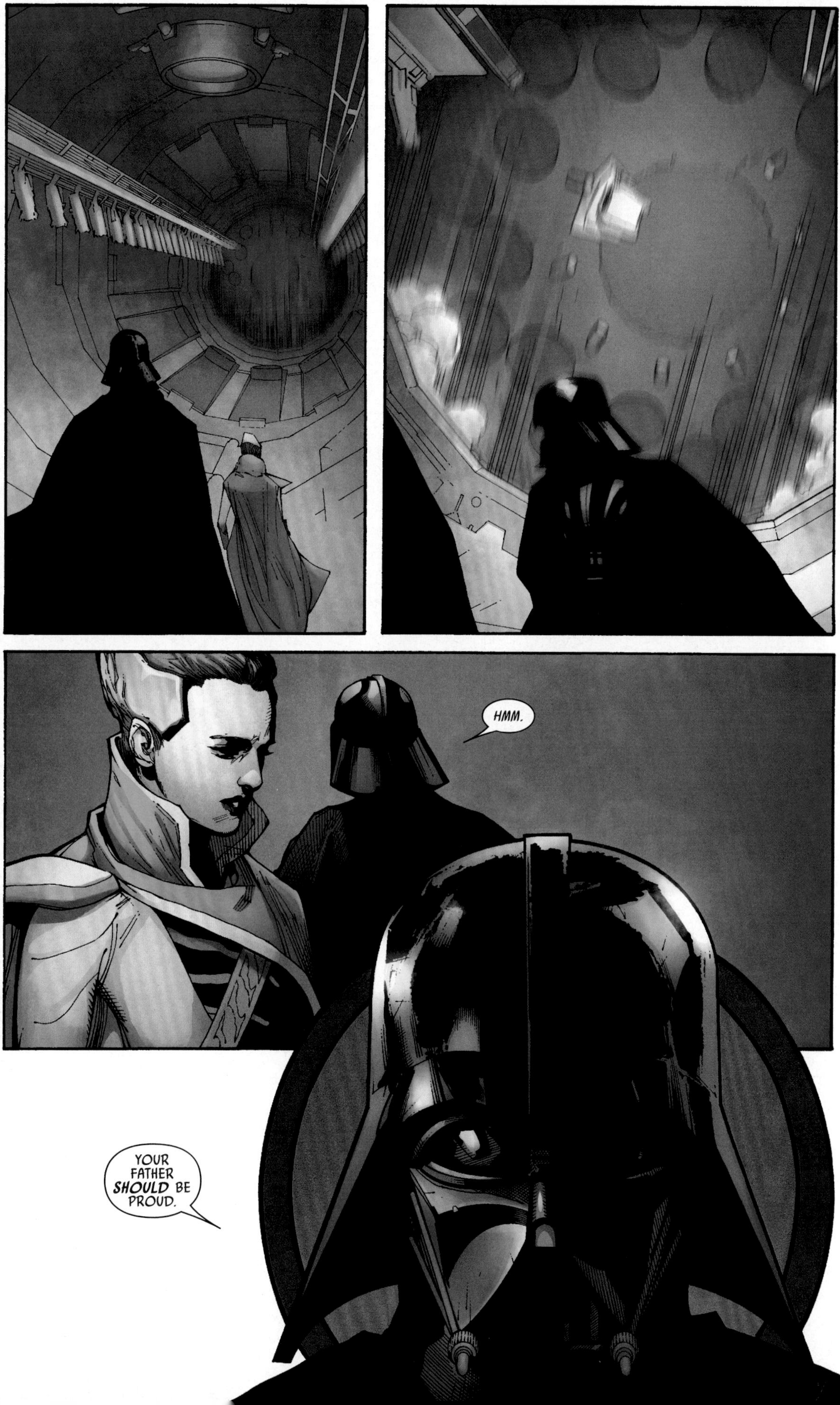
HMM.
YOUR FATHER SHOULD BE PROUD.

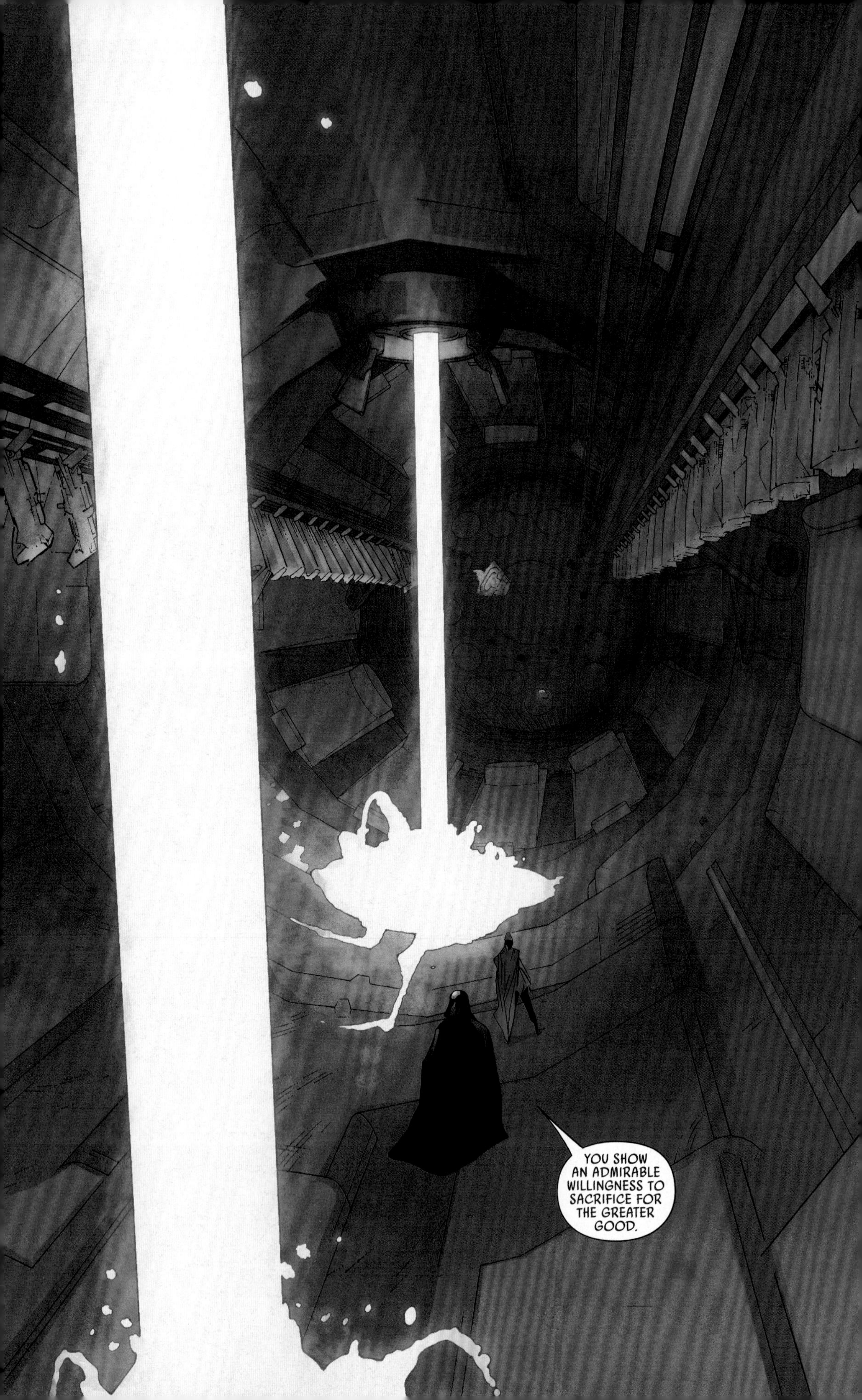
YOU SHOW AN ADMIRABLE WILLINGNESS TO SACRIFICE FOR THE GREATER GOOD.

THERE'S NO PASSAGES THERE. THERE IS NO ESCAPE, LORD VADER!

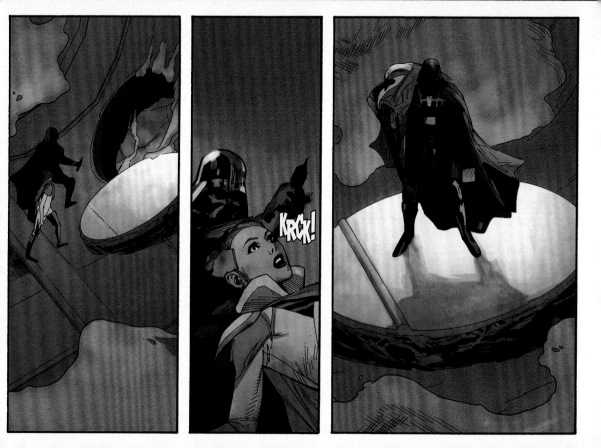

KRCK!

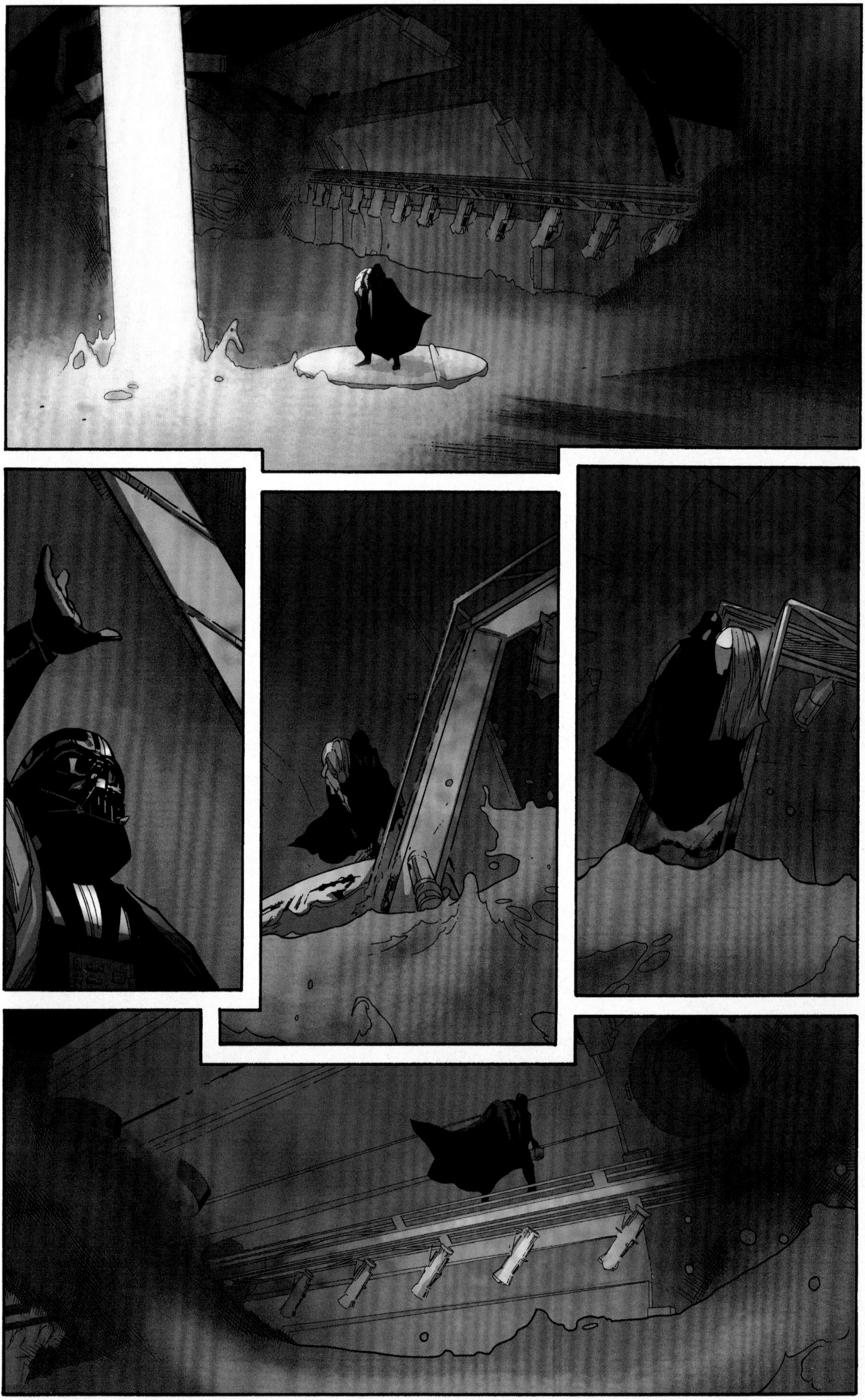

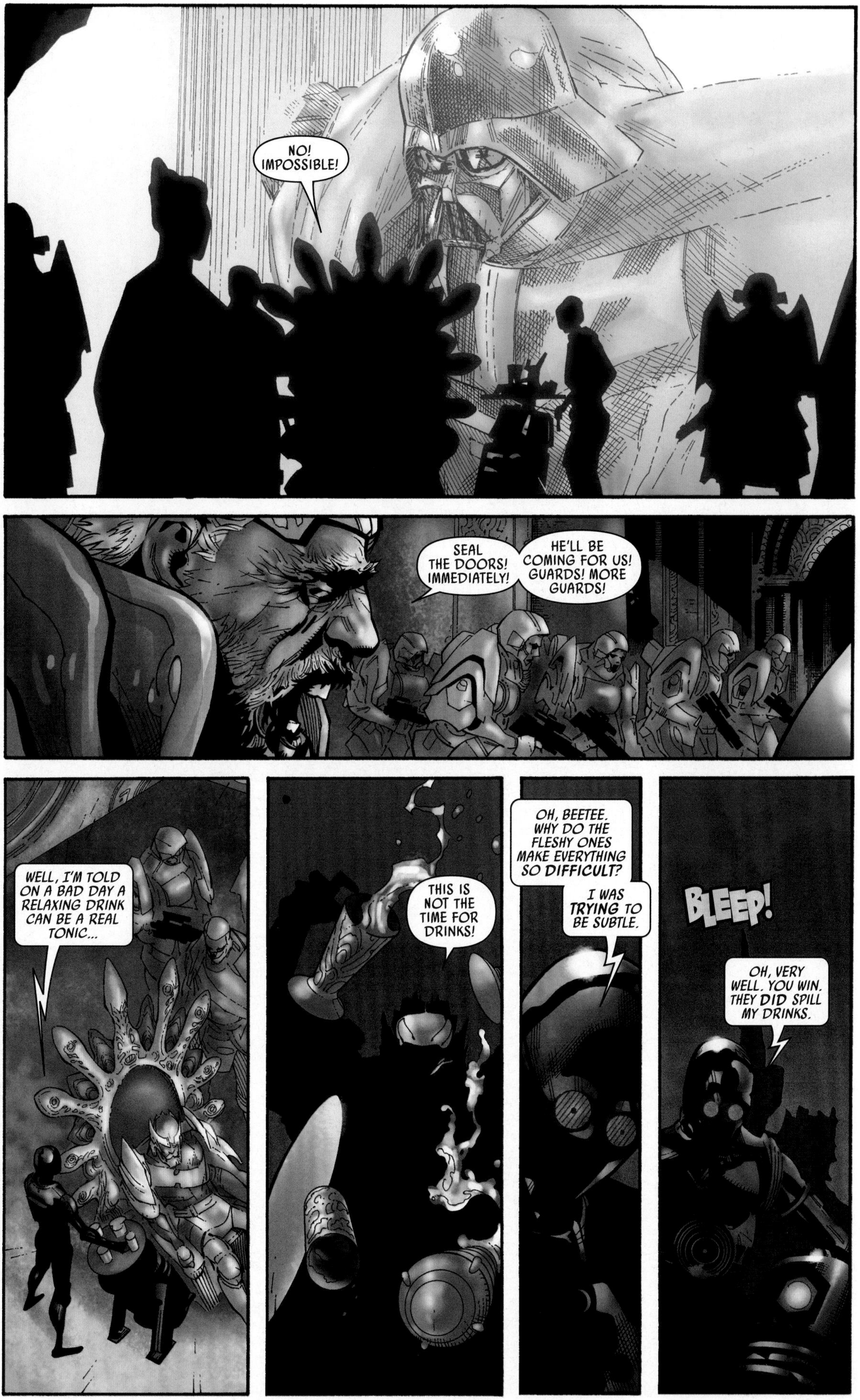
NO! IMPOSSIBLE!
SEAL THE DOORS! IMMEDIATELY!
HE'LL BE COMING FOR US! GUARDS! MORE GUARDS!
WELL, I'M TOLD ON A BAD DAY A RELAXING DRINK CAN BE A REAL TONIC...
THIS IS NOT THE TIME FOR DRINKS!
OH, BEETEE. WHY DO THE FLESHY ONES MAKE EVERYTHING SO DIFFICULT?
I WAS TRYING TO BE SUBTLE.
BLEEP!
OH, VERY WELL. YOU WIN. THEY DID SPILL MY DRINKS.

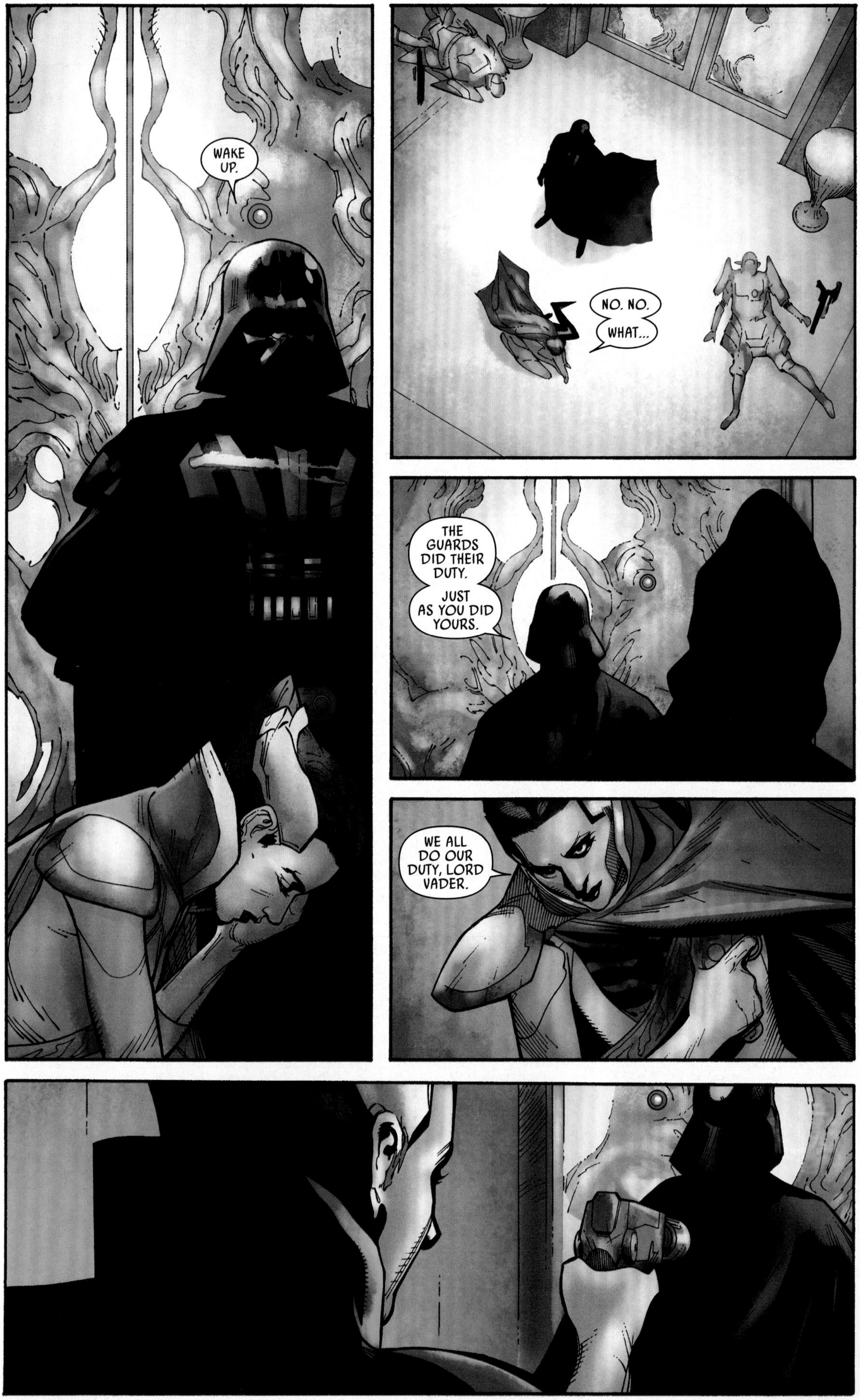
WAKE UP.
NO. NO.
WHAT...
THE GUARDS DID THEIR DUTY.
JUST AS YOU DID YOURS.
WE ALL DO OUR DUTY, LORD VADER.

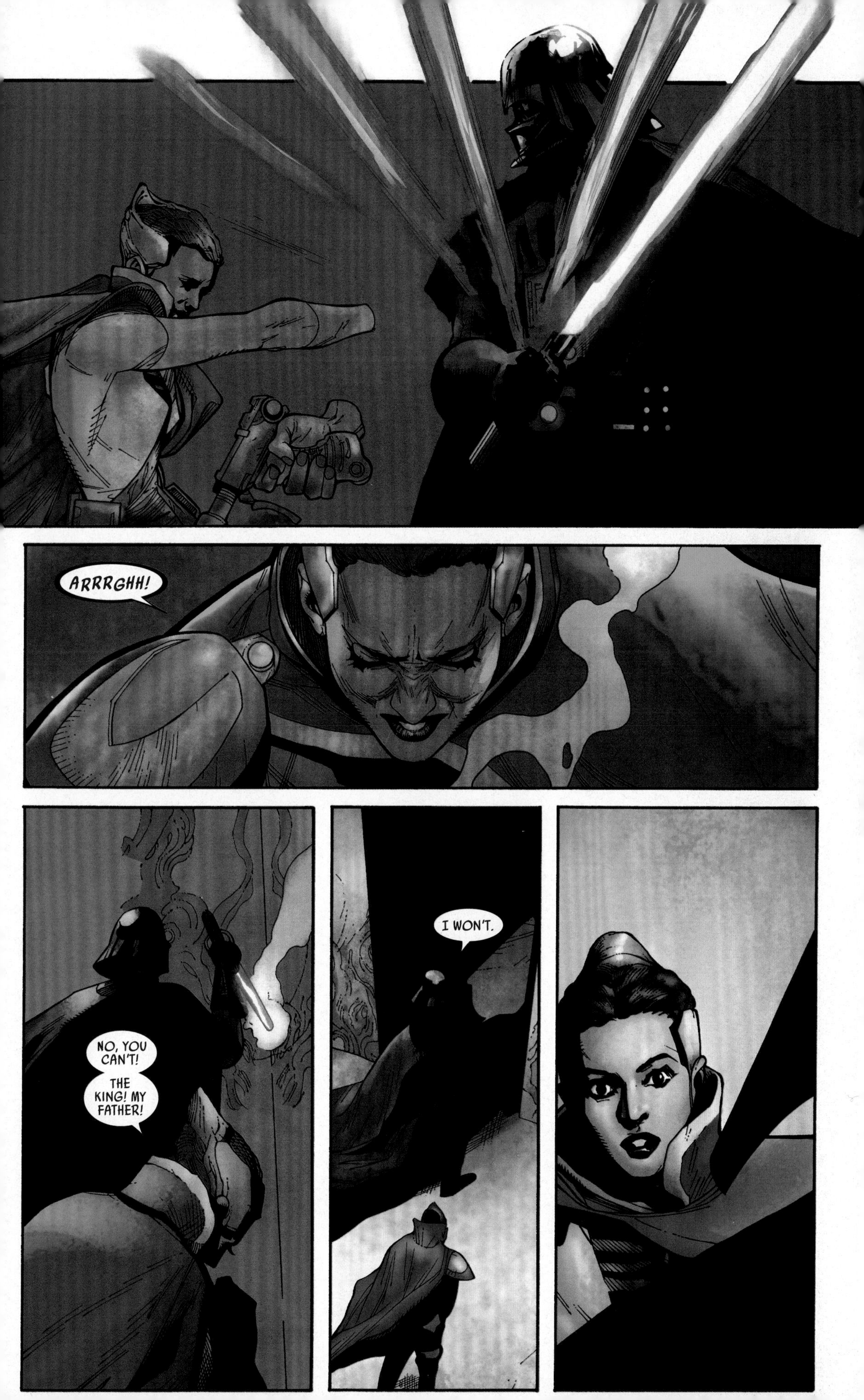
ARRRGHH!
NO, YOU CAN'T!
THE KING! MY FATHER!
I WON'T.

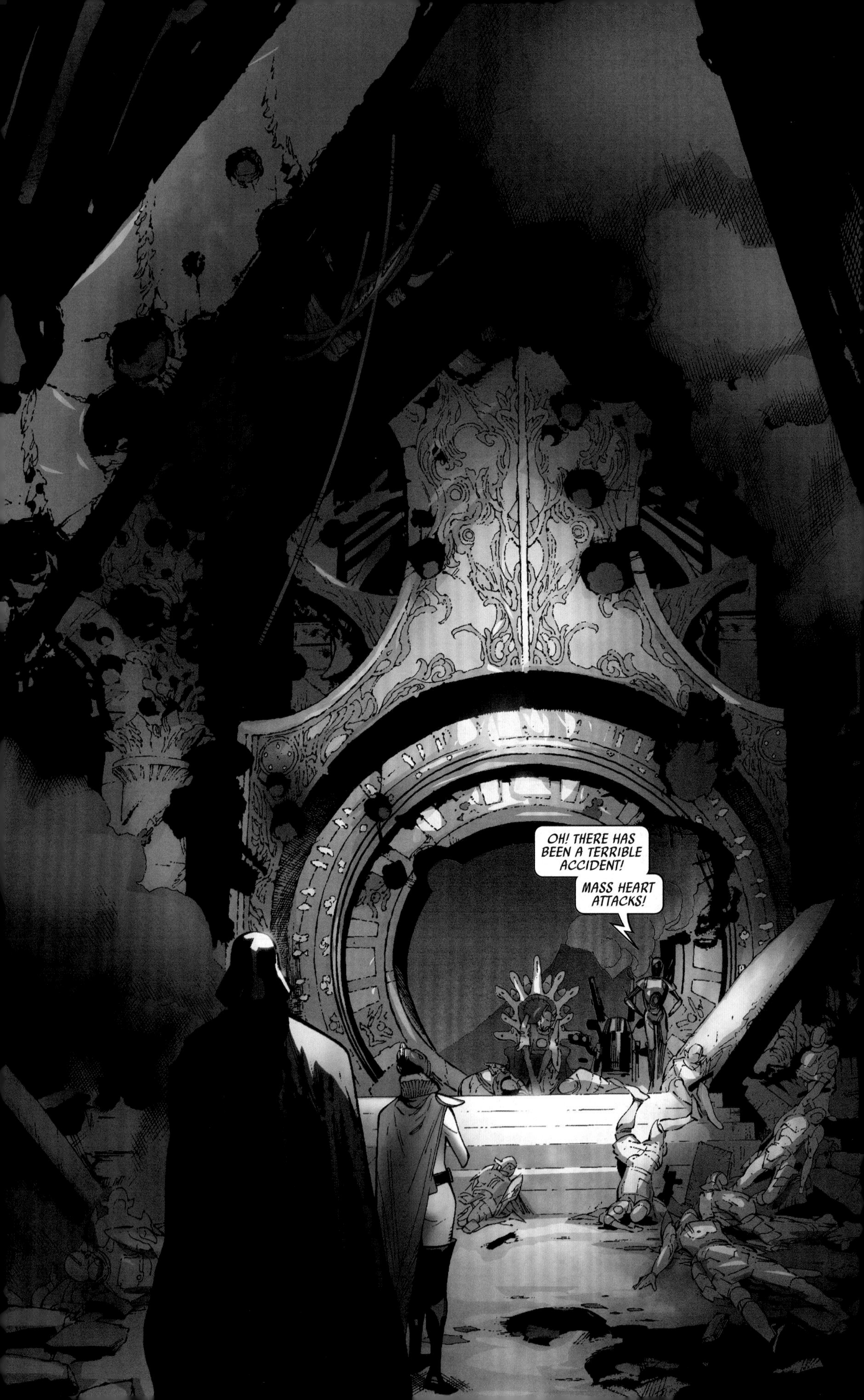
OH! THERE HAS BEEN A TERRIBLE ACCIDENT!
MASS HEART ATTACKS!

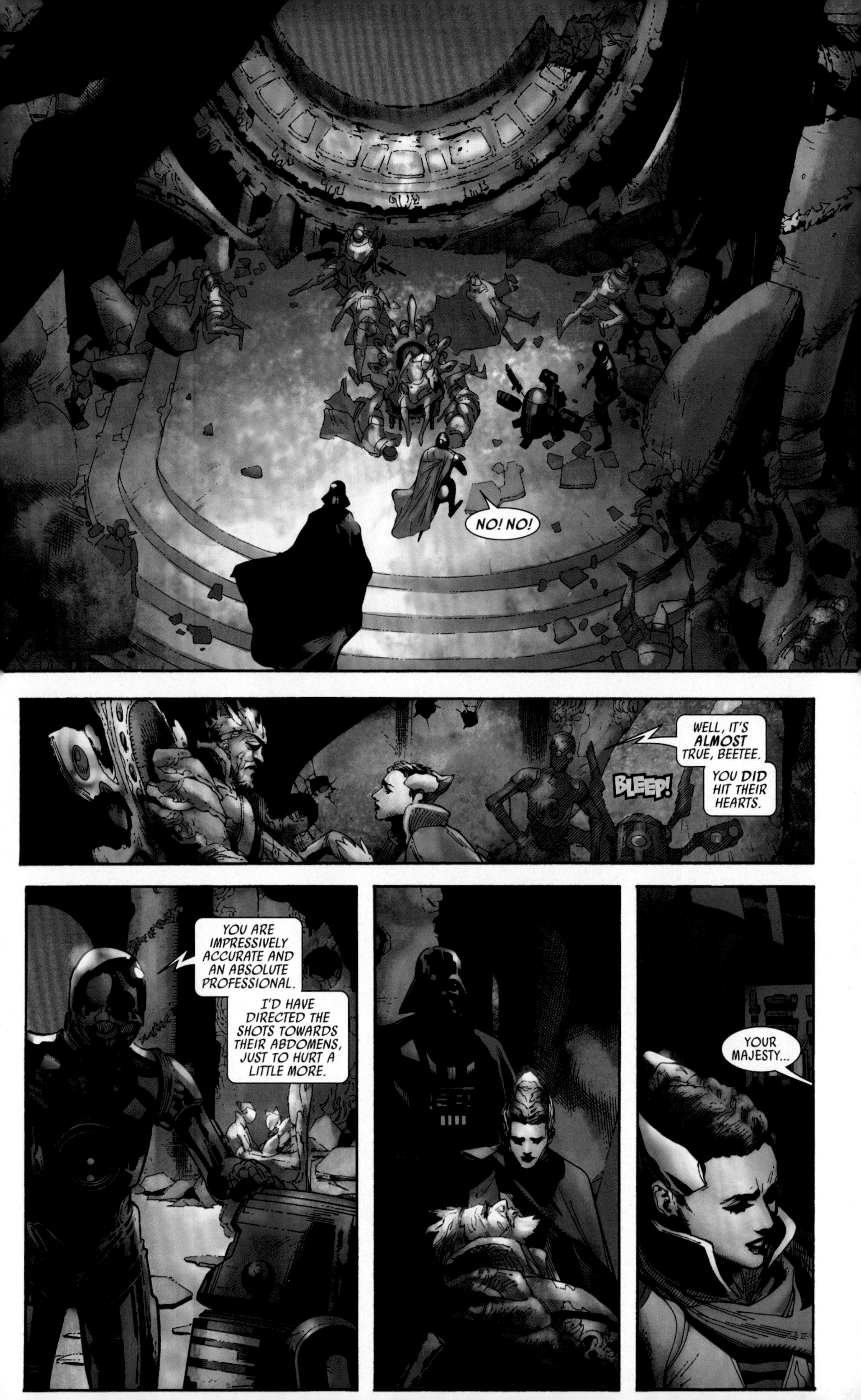
NO! NO!
WELL, IT'S ALMOST TRUE, BEETEE.
YOU DID HIT THEIR HEARTS.
BLEEP!
YOU ARE IMPRESSIVELY ACCURATE AND AN ABSOLUTE PROFESSIONAL.
I'D HAVE DIRECTED THE SHOTS TOWARDS THEIR ABDOMENS, JUST TO HURT A LITTLE MORE.
YOUR MAJESTY...

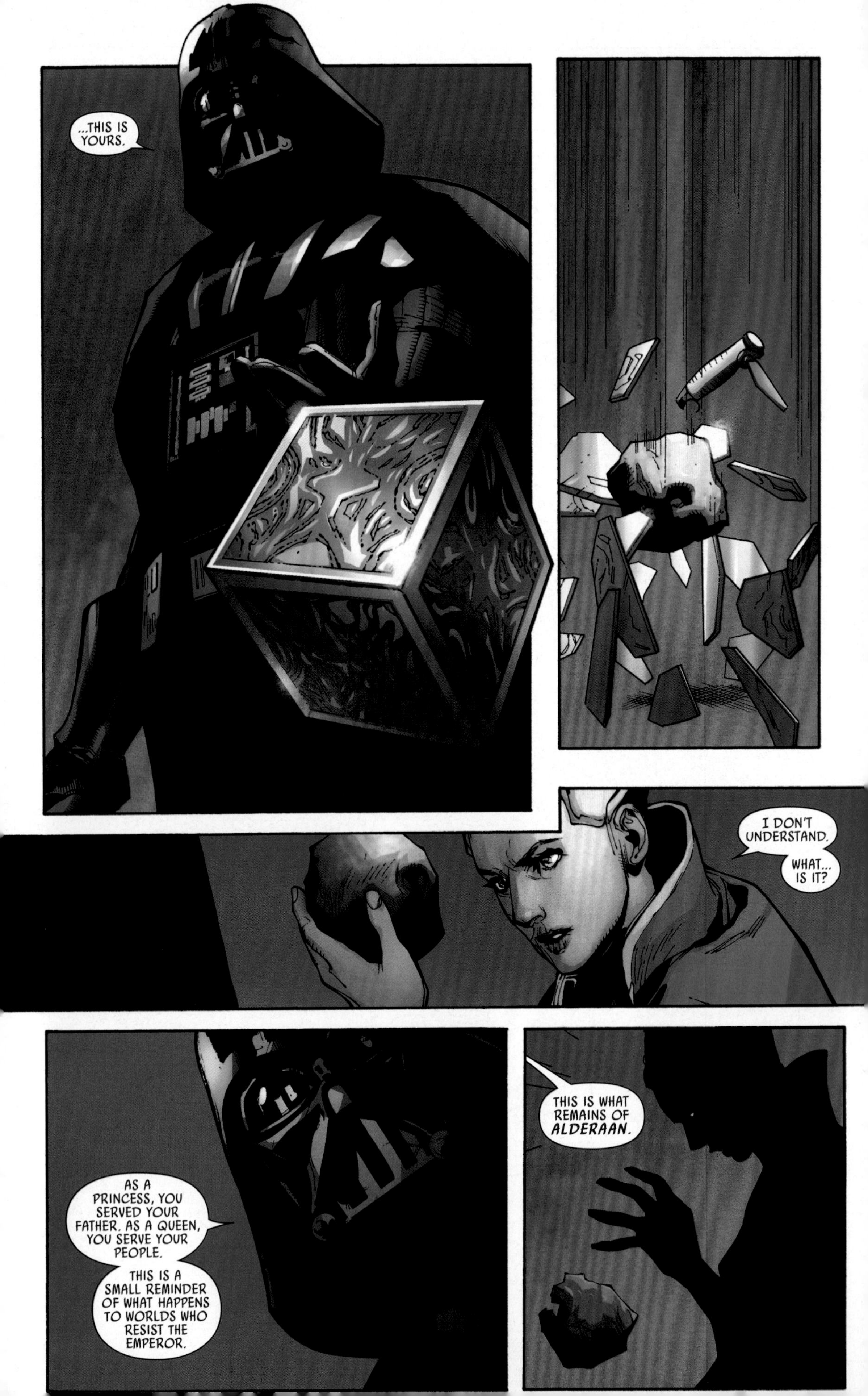
...THIS IS YOURS.
I DON'T UNDERSTAND.
WHAT... IS IT?
AS A PRINCESS, YOU SERVED YOUR FATHER. AS A QUEEN, YOU SERVE YOUR PEOPLE.
THIS IS A SMALL REMINDER OF WHAT HAPPENS TO WORLDS WHO RESIST THE EMPEROR.
THIS IS WHAT REMAINS OF ALDERAAN.

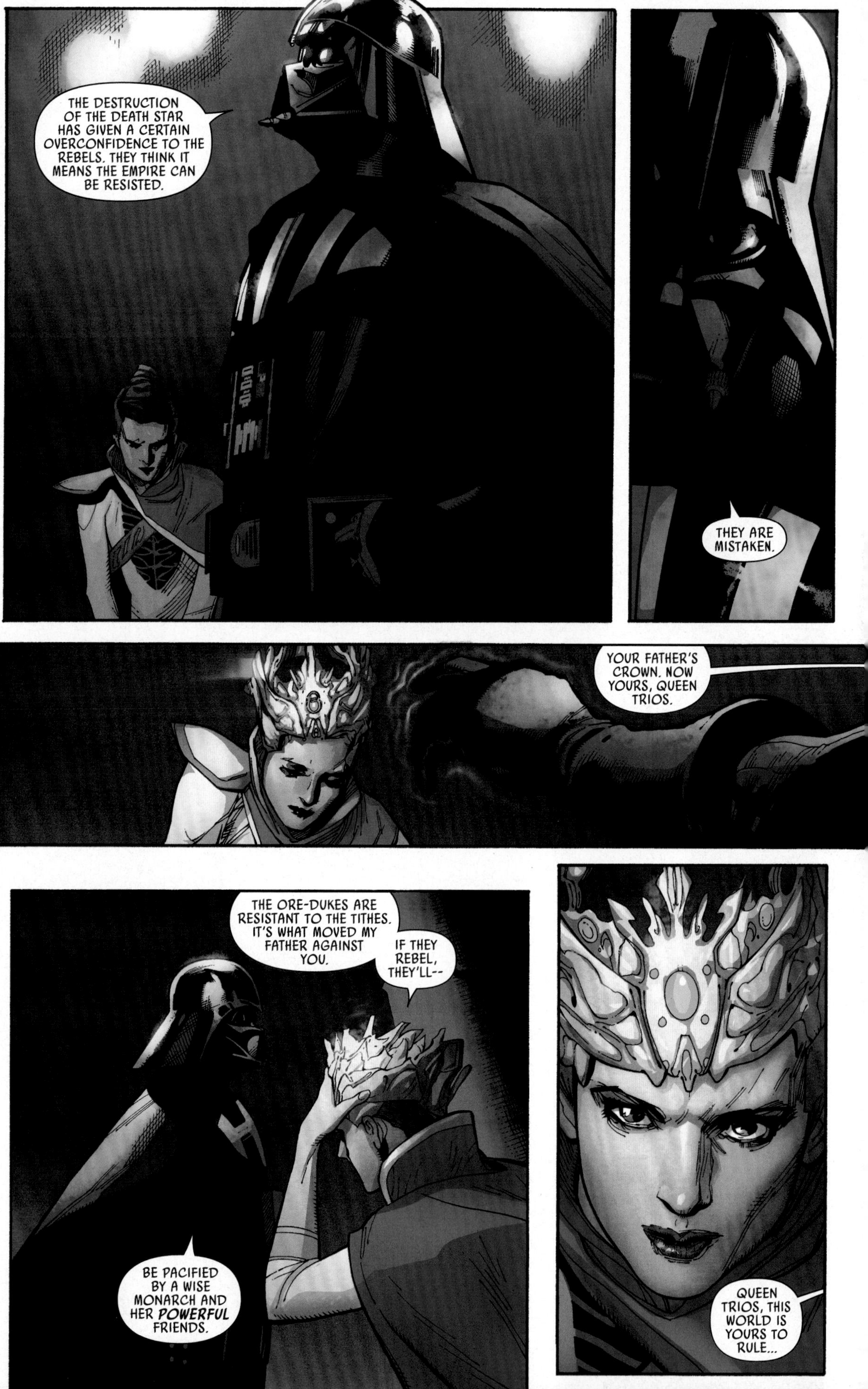
THE DESTRUCTION OF THE DEATH STAR HAS GIVEN A CERTAIN OVERCONFIDENCE TO THE REBELS. THEY THINK IT MEANS THE EMPIRE CAN BE RESISTED.
THEY ARE MISTAKEN.
YOUR FATHER'S CROWN. NOW YOURS, QUEEN TRIOS.
THE ORE-DUKES ARE RESISTANT TO THE TITHES. IT'S WHAT MOVED MY FATHER AGAINST YOU.
IF THEY REBEL, THEY'LL--
BE PACIFIED BY A WISE MONARCH AND HER *POWERFUL* FRIENDS.
QUEEN TRIOS, THIS WORLD IS YOURS TO RULE...

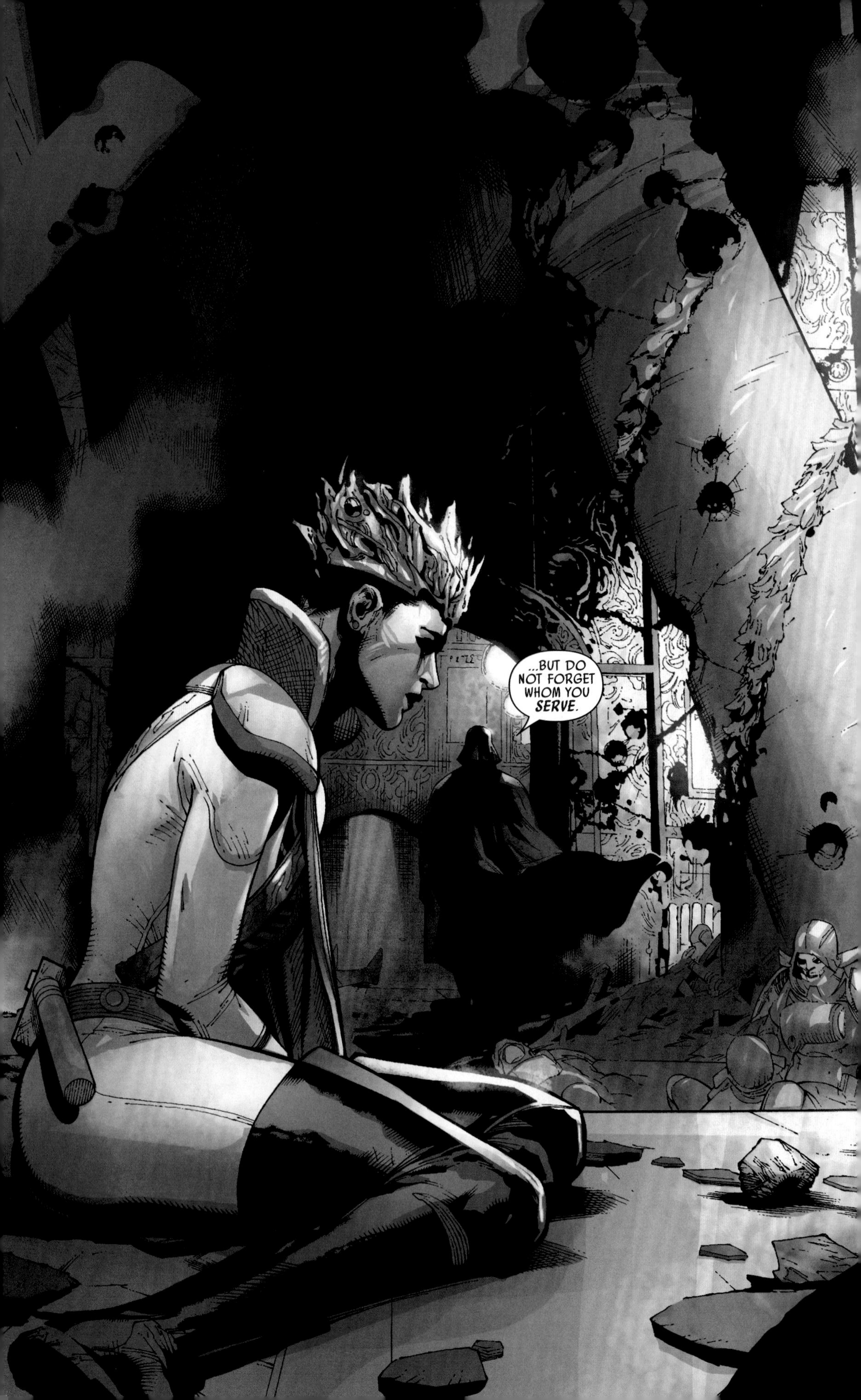
...BUT DO NOT FORGET WHOM YOU SERVE.

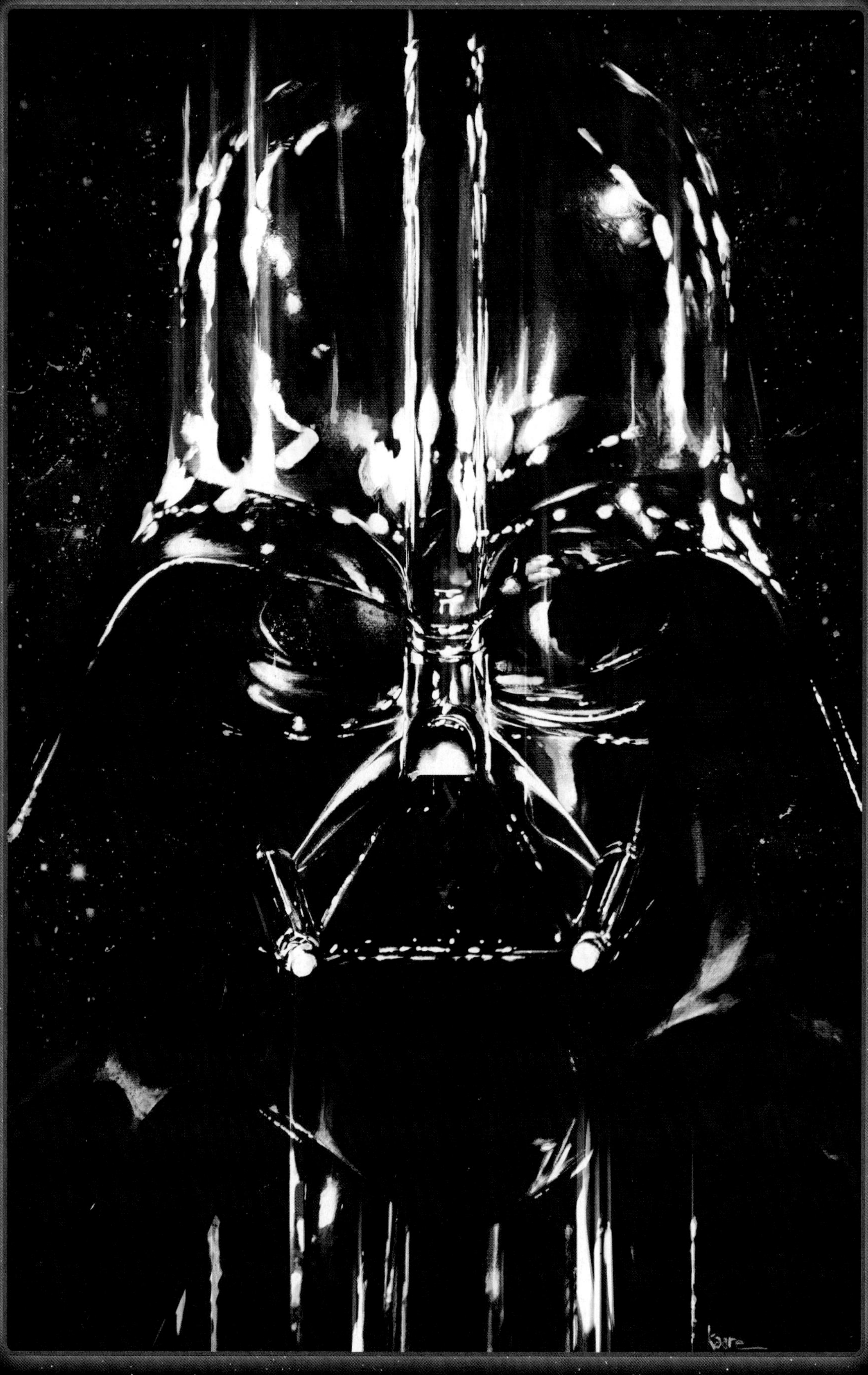

**Book III**
# THE SHU-TORUN WAR

*It is a time of rebuilding for the Empire. After the Death Star's destruction, Darth Vader, the Emperor's chief enforcer, struggled to keep his place after he was seemingly put in a rivalry with the cybernetically-enchanced operatives of a cyborg specialist named Cylo.*

*Vader was sent to the ore-rich planet Shu-Torun to bring its leadership in line. After assassinating the ruling family and installing its youngest daughter as Queen, Vader promised worse for their planet should it not fall in line.*

*Soon after, one of Cylo's agents, a cyborg Mon Calamari named General Karbin, laid a trap for Vader, setting the Dark Lord against a Rebel Fleet with no backup. Vader survived and made Karbin pay for his deception, but in doing so, his secret ally Doctor Aphra, was captured by rebels....*

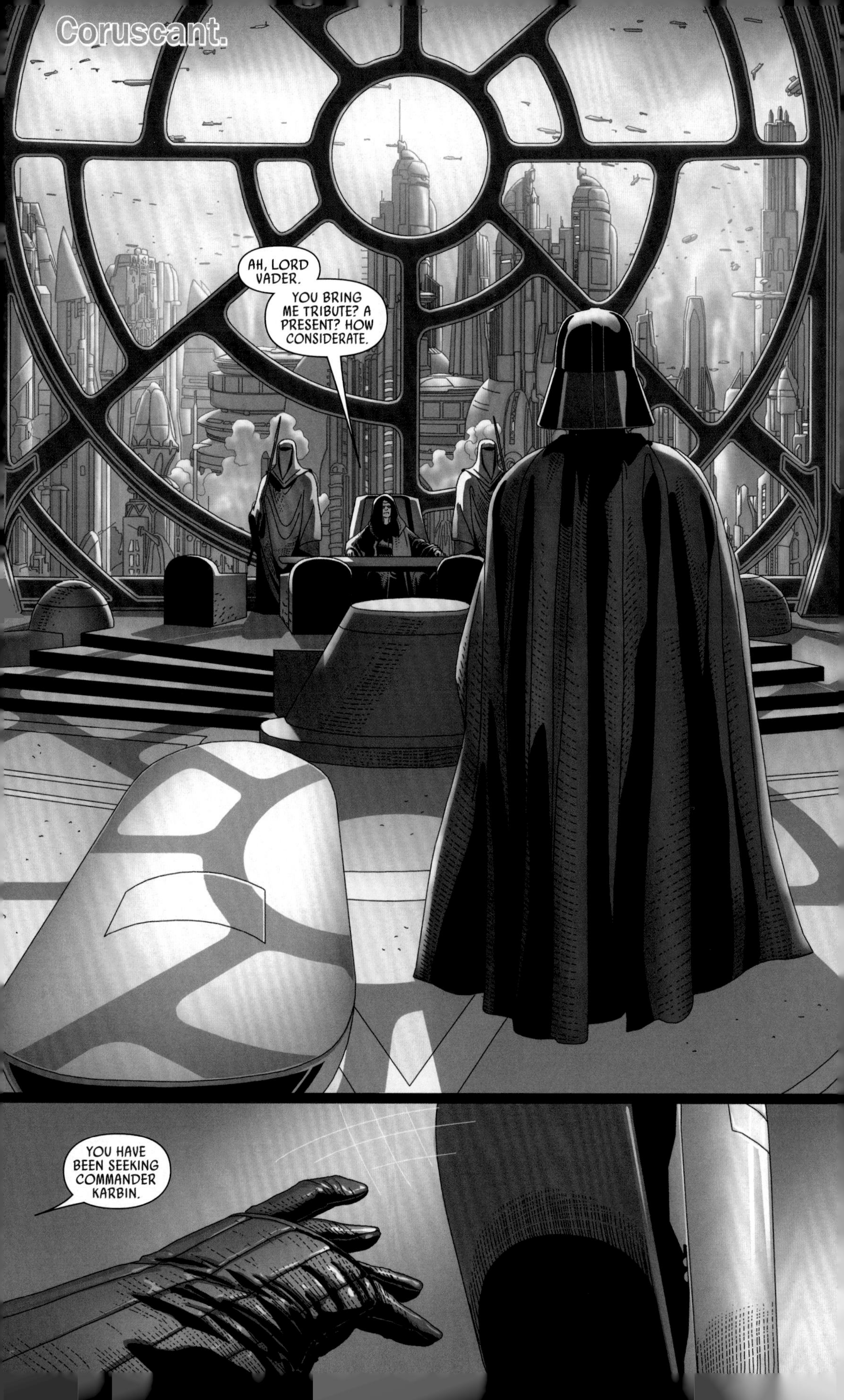
Coruscant.
AH, LORD VADER.
YOU BRING ME TRIBUTE? A PRESENT? HOW CONSIDERATE.
YOU HAVE BEEN SEEKING COMMANDER KARBIN.

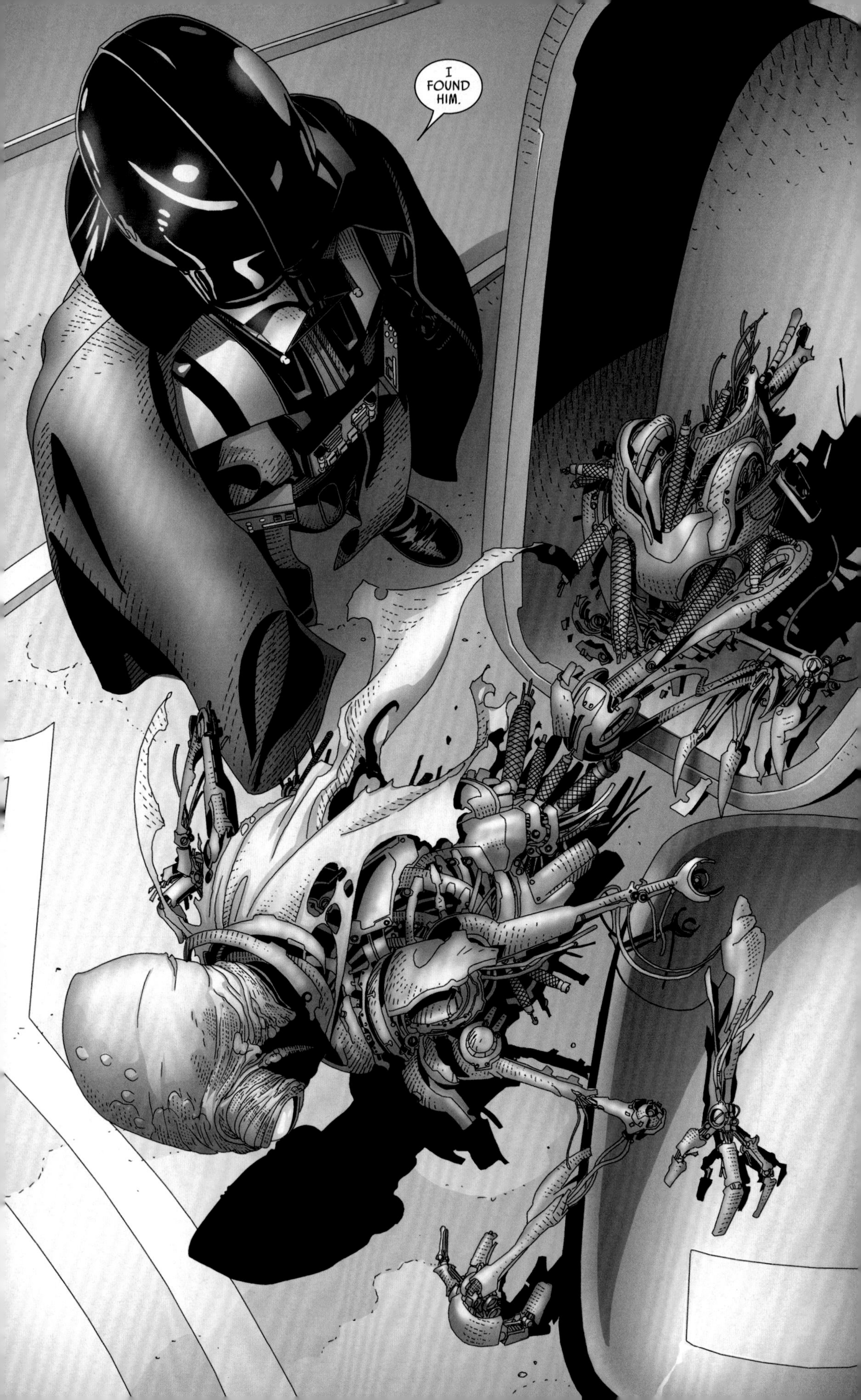
I FOUND HIM.

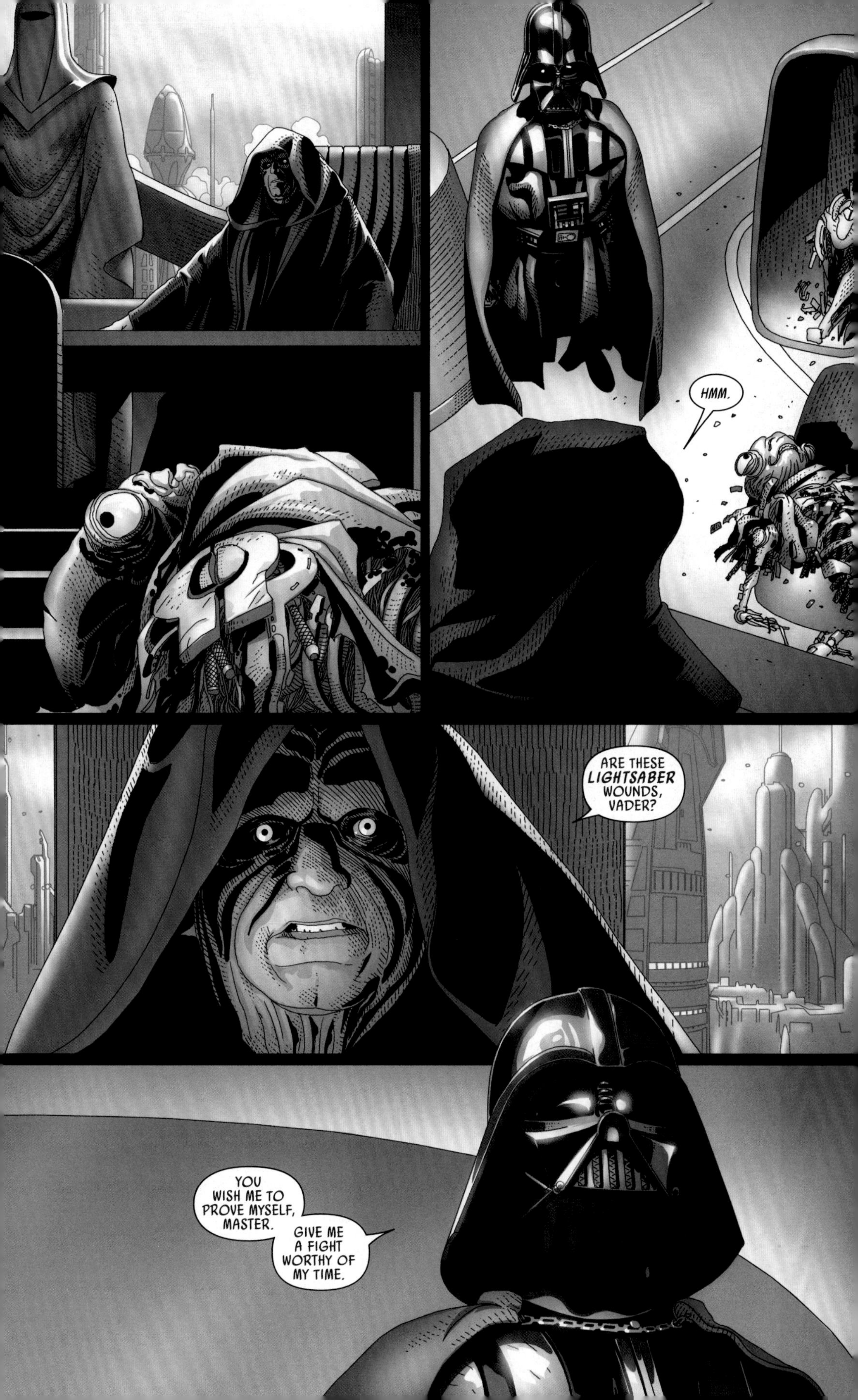
HMM.
ARE THESE LIGHTSABER WOUNDS, VADER?
YOU WISH ME TO PROVE MYSELF, MASTER.
GIVE ME A FIGHT WORTHY OF MY TIME.

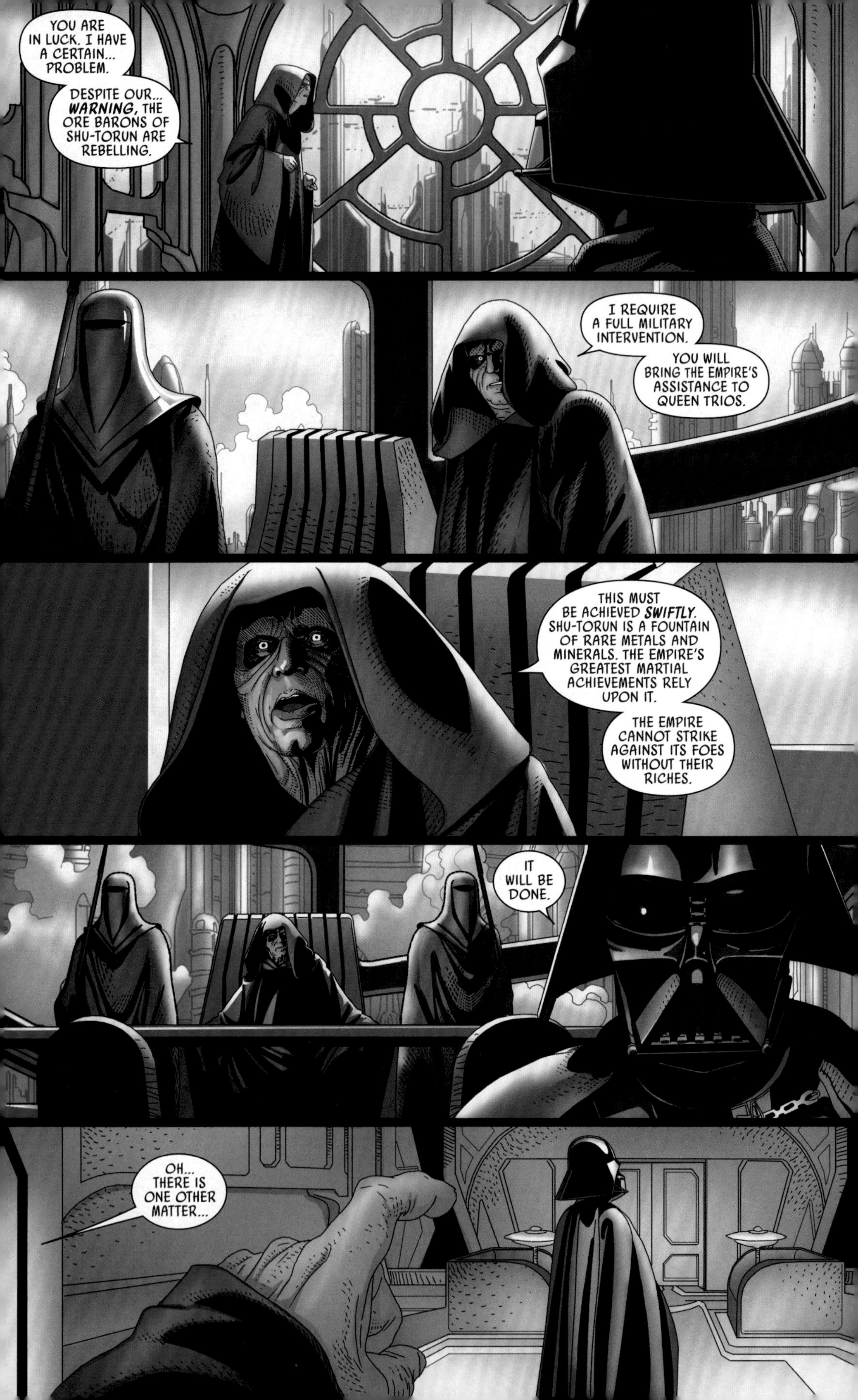
YOU ARE IN LUCK. I HAVE A CERTAIN... PROBLEM.
DESPITE OUR... **WARNING,** THE ORE BARONS OF SHU-TORUN ARE REBELLING.
I REQUIRE A FULL MILITARY INTERVENTION.
YOU WILL BRING THE EMPIRE'S ASSISTANCE TO QUEEN TRIOS.
THIS MUST BE ACHIEVED **SWIFTLY.** SHU-TORUN IS A FOUNTAIN OF RARE METALS AND MINERALS. THE EMPIRE'S GREATEST MARTIAL ACHIEVEMENTS RELY UPON IT.
THE EMPIRE CANNOT STRIKE AGAINST ITS FOES WITHOUT THEIR RICHES.
IT WILL BE DONE.
OH... THERE IS ONE OTHER MATTER...

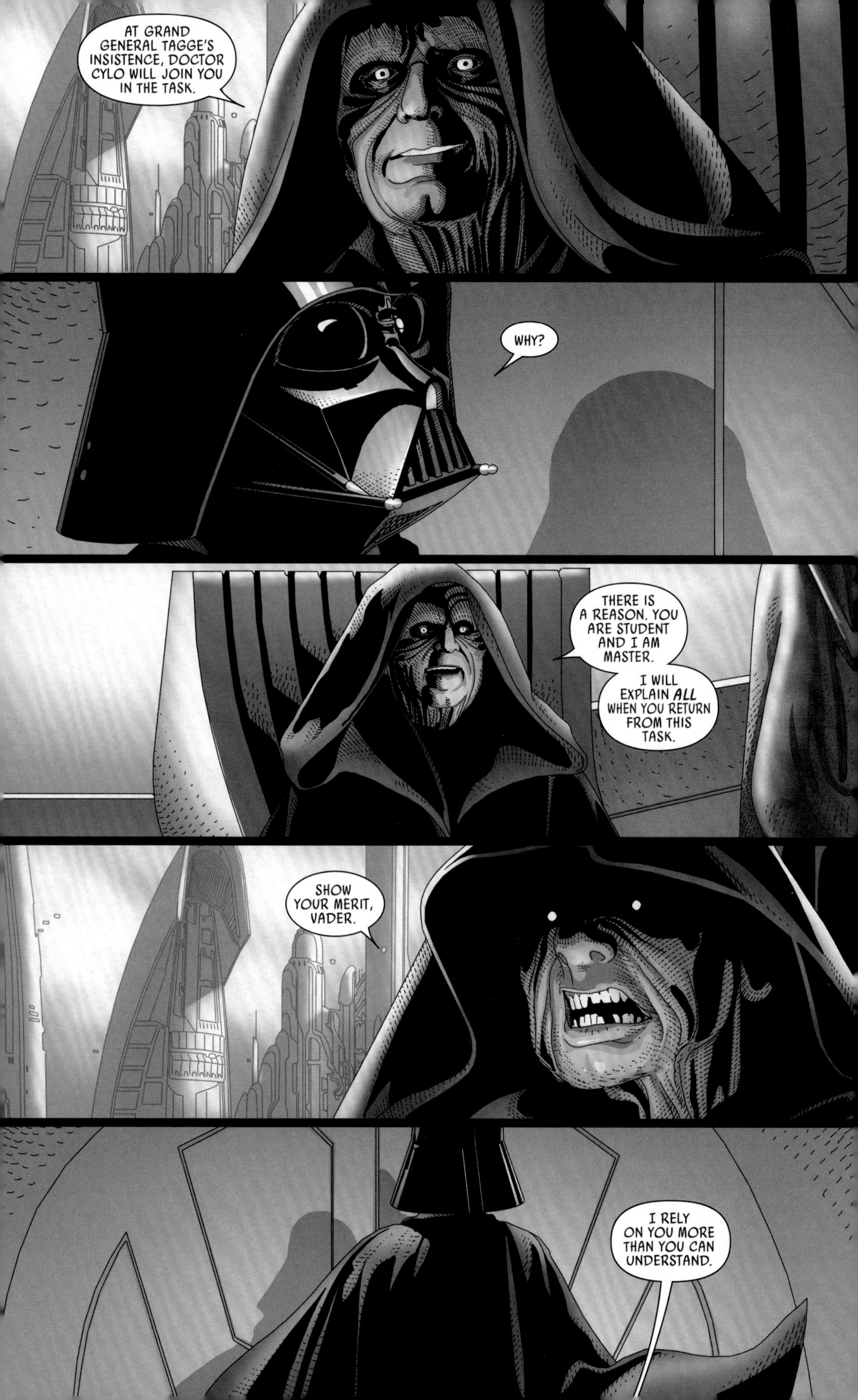
AT GRAND GENERAL TAGGE'S INSISTENCE, DOCTOR CYLO WILL JOIN YOU IN THE TASK.
WHY?
THERE IS A REASON. YOU ARE STUDENT AND I AM MASTER.
I WILL EXPLAIN ALL WHEN YOU RETURN FROM THIS TASK.
SHOW YOUR MERIT, VADER.
I RELY ON YOU MORE THAN YOU CAN UNDERSTAND.

# STAR

# DARTH

## THE SHU-T

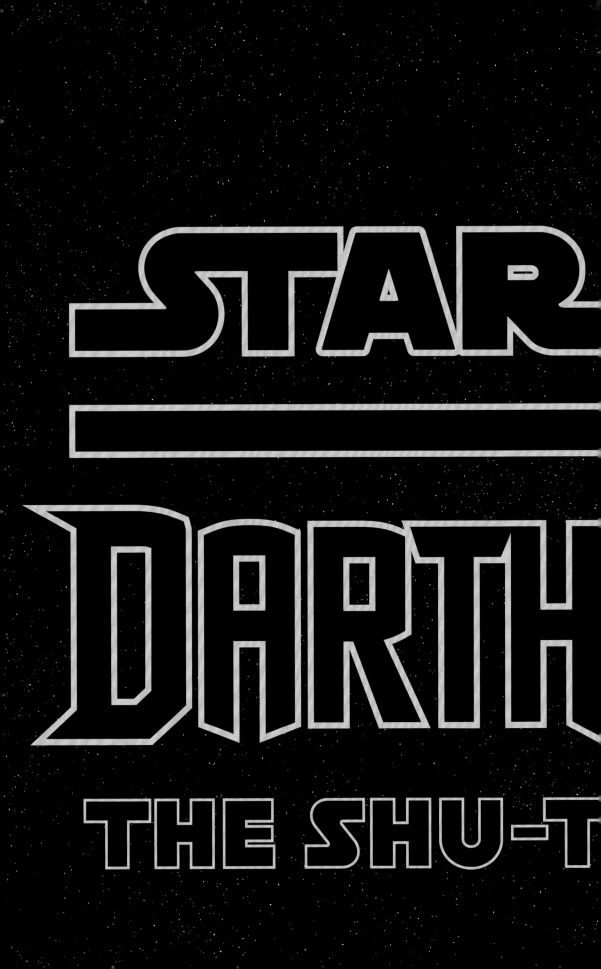

# WARS

# VADER

## ORUN WAR

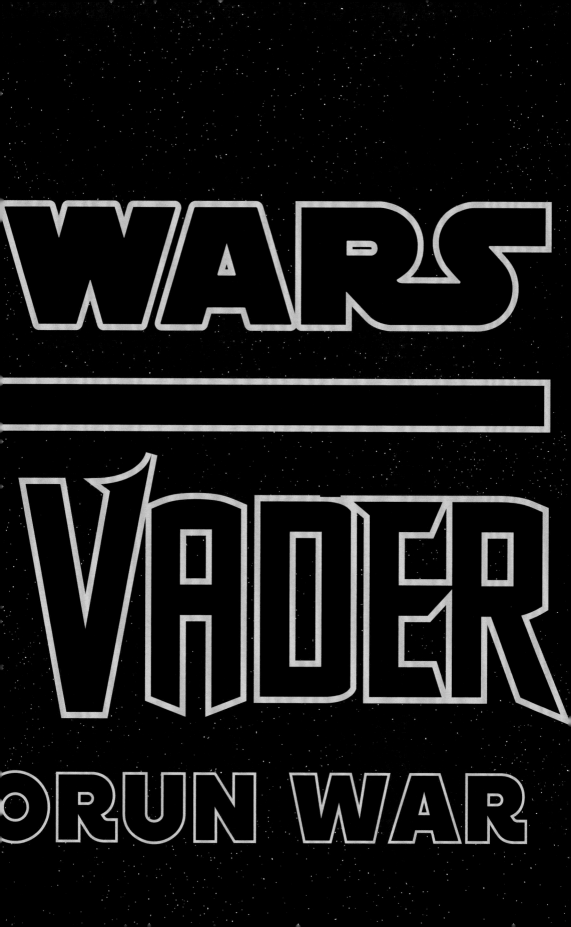

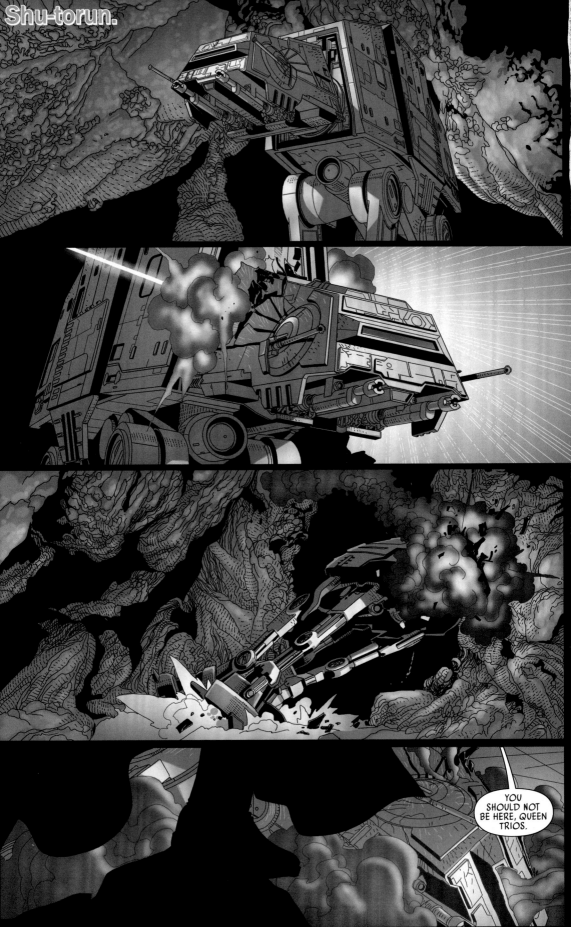

YOU SHOULD NOT BE HERE, QUEEN TRIOS.

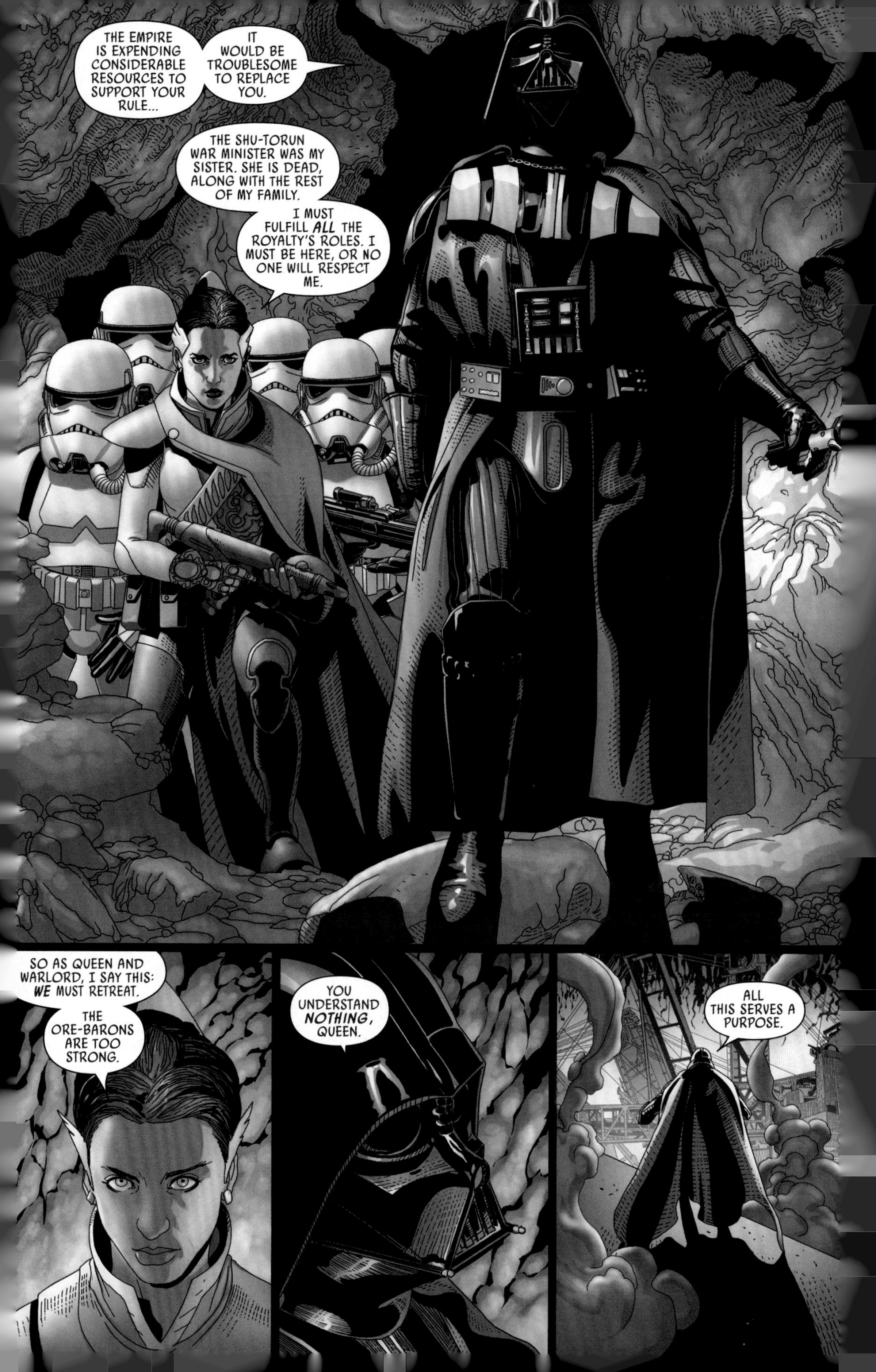
THE EMPIRE IS EXPENDING CONSIDERABLE RESOURCES TO SUPPORT YOUR RULE...
IT WOULD BE TROUBLESOME TO REPLACE YOU.
THE SHU-TORUN WAR MINISTER WAS MY SISTER. SHE IS DEAD, ALONG WITH THE REST OF MY FAMILY.
I MUST FULFILL *ALL* THE ROYALTY'S ROLES. I MUST BE HERE, OR NO ONE WILL RESPECT ME.
SO AS QUEEN AND WARLORD, I SAY THIS: *WE* MUST RETREAT.
THE ORE-BARONS ARE TOO STRONG.
YOU UNDERSTAND *NOTHING*, QUEEN.
ALL THIS SERVES A PURPOSE.

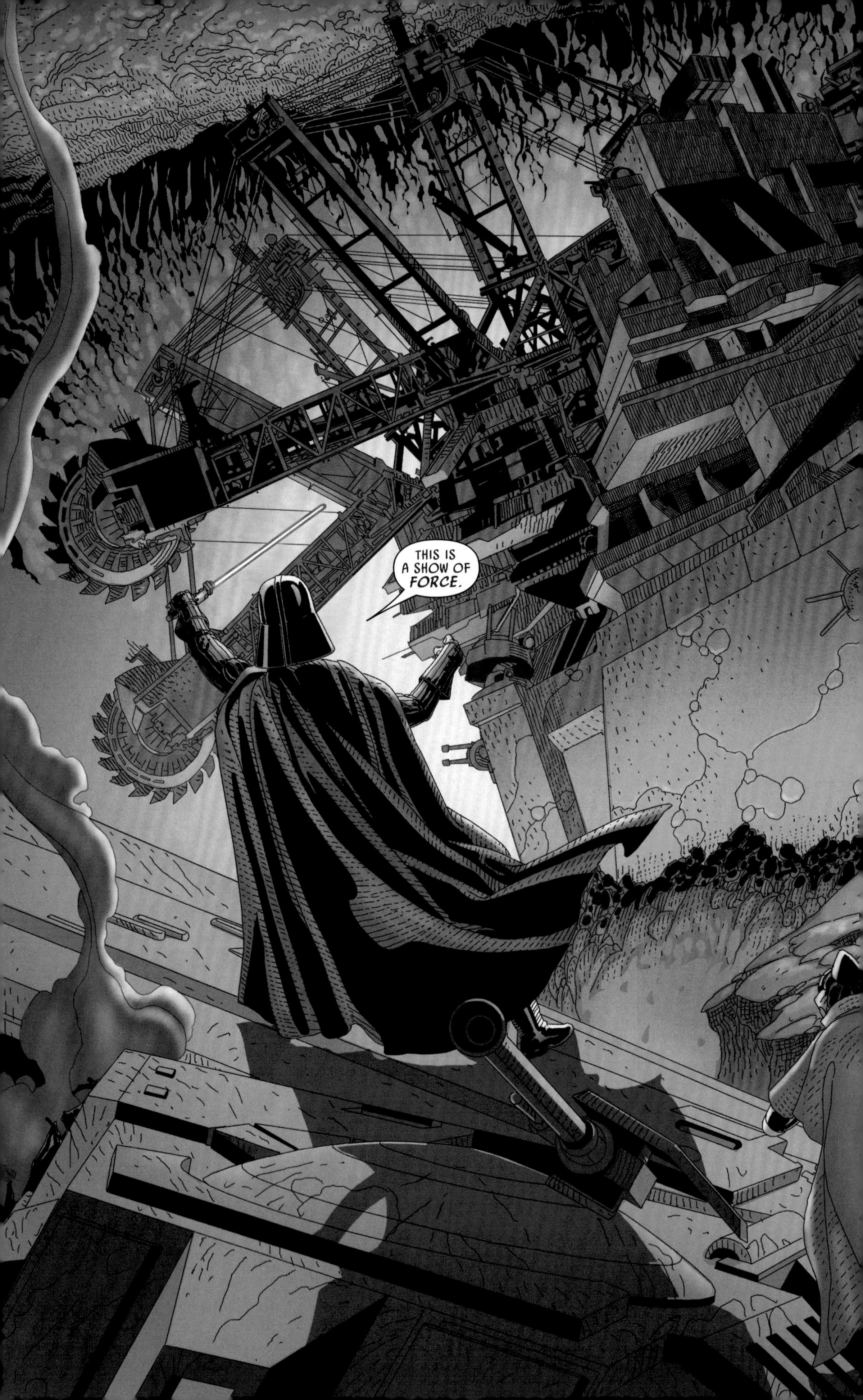
THIS IS A SHOW OF FORCE.

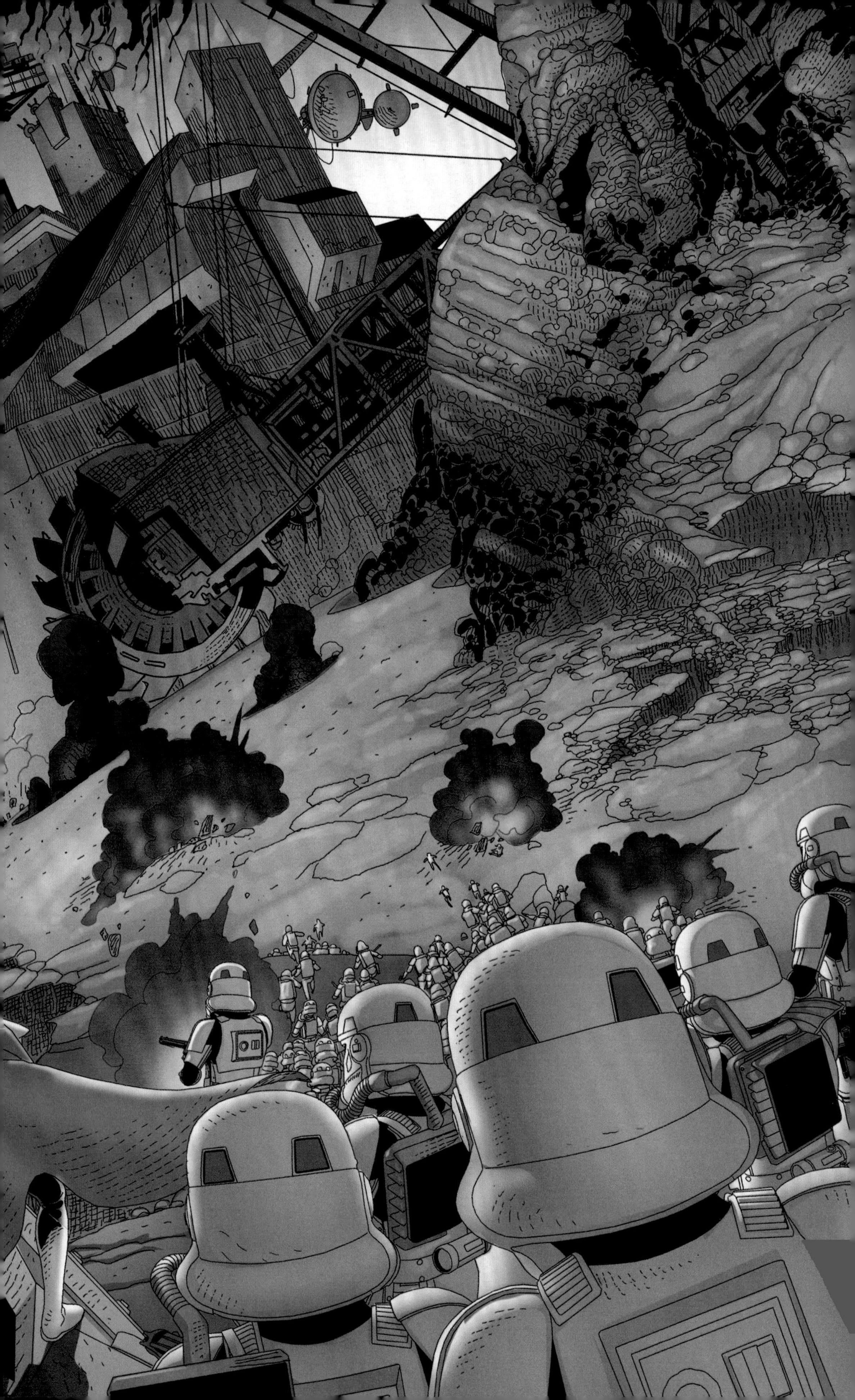

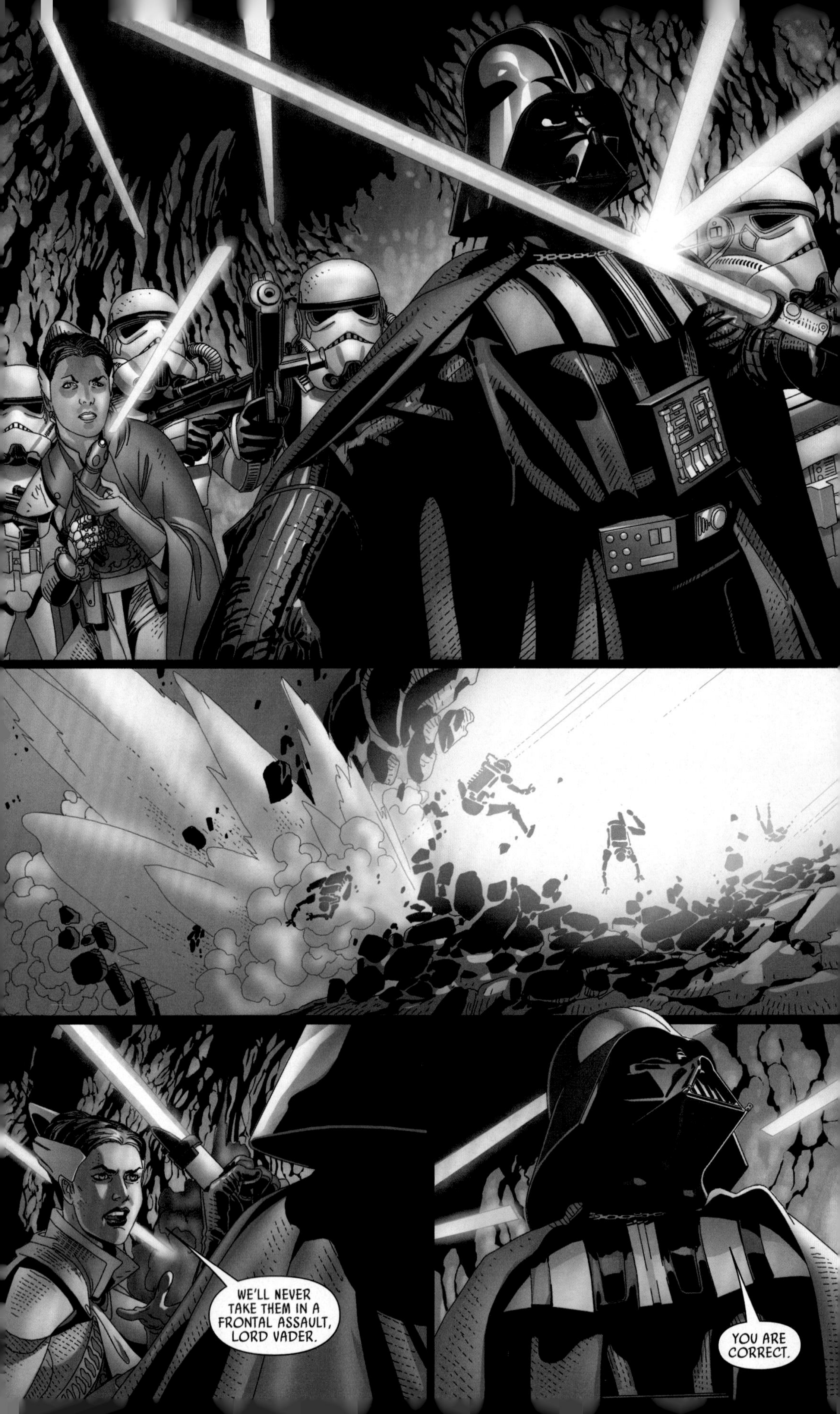
WE'LL NEVER TAKE THEM IN A FRONTAL ASSAULT, LORD VADER.
YOU ARE CORRECT.

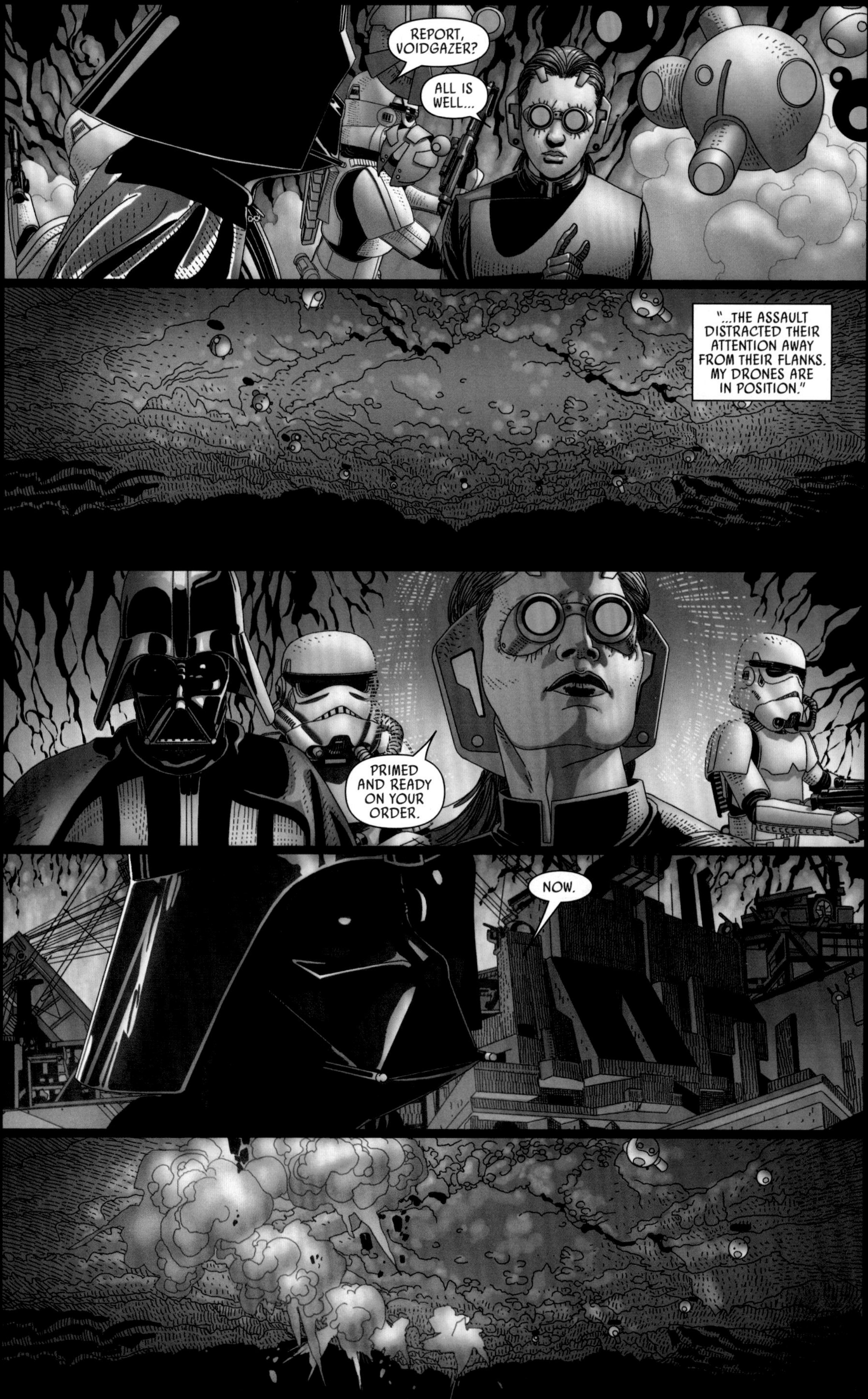
REPORT, VOIDGAZER?
ALL IS WELL...
"...THE ASSAULT DISTRACTED THEIR ATTENTION AWAY FROM THEIR FLANKS. MY DRONES ARE IN POSITION."
PRIMED AND READY ON YOUR ORDER.
NOW.

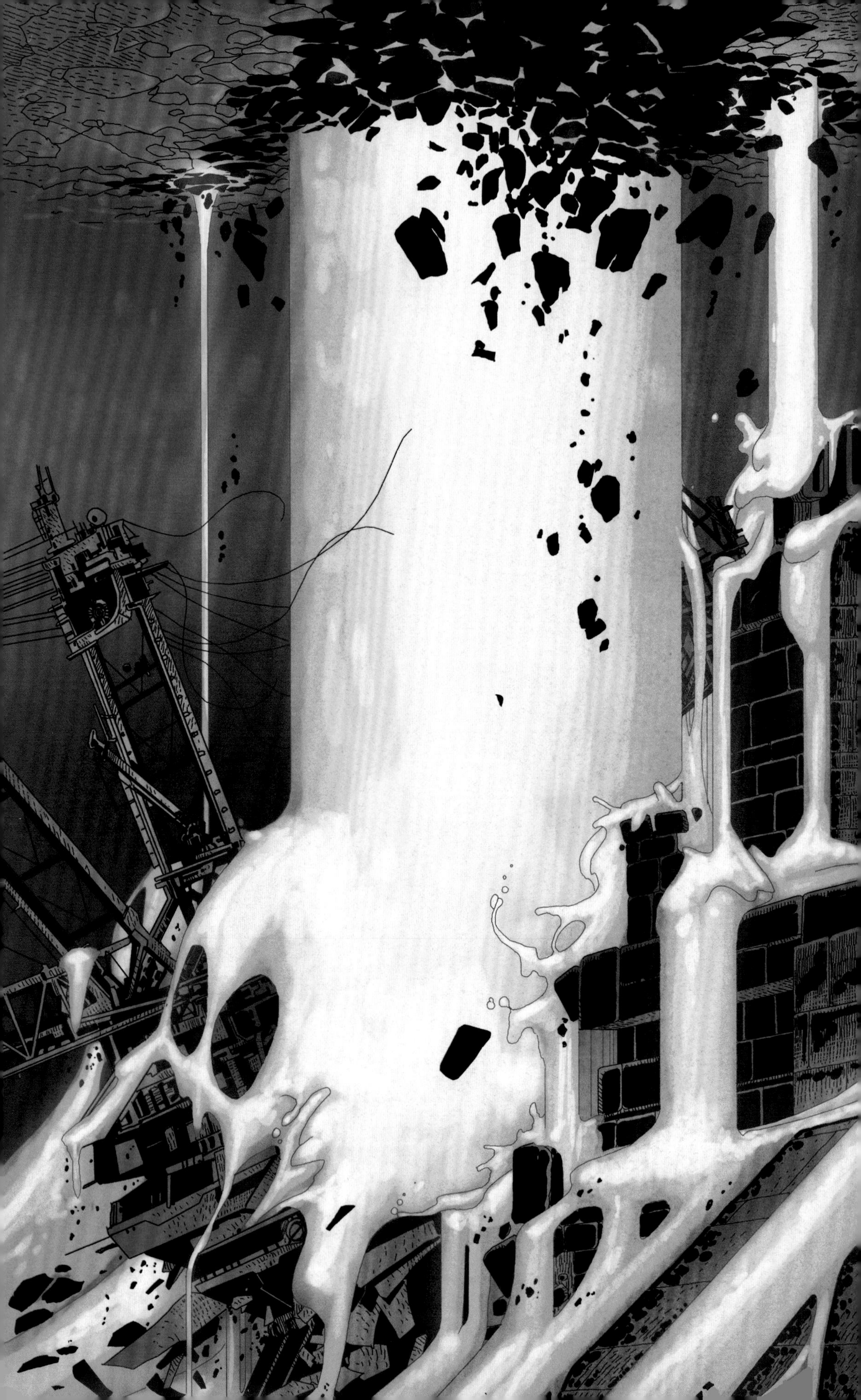

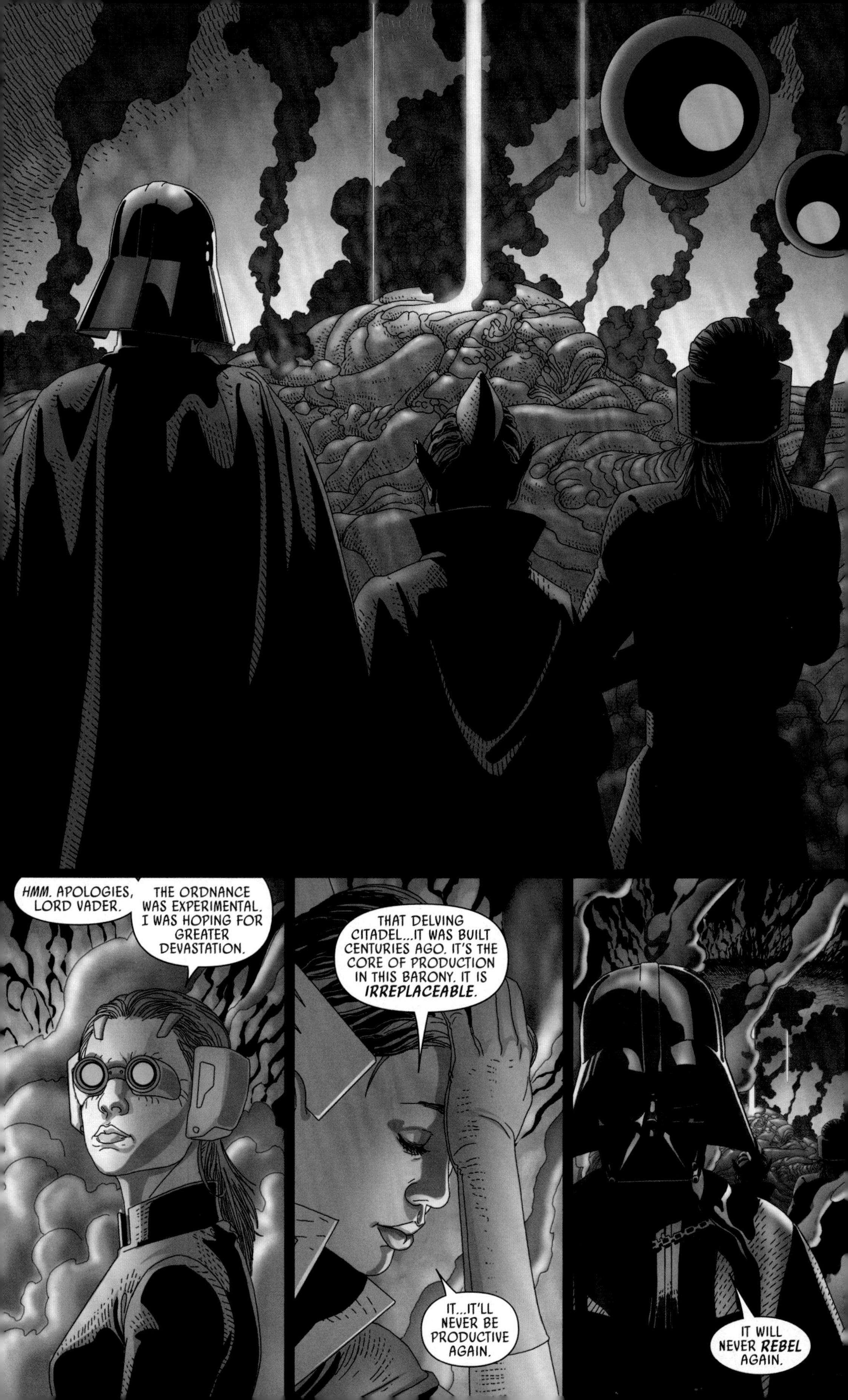

HMM. APOLOGIES, LORD VADER.
THE ORDNANCE WAS EXPERIMENTAL. I WAS HOPING FOR GREATER DEVASTATION.
THAT DELVING CITADEL...IT WAS BUILT CENTURIES AGO. IT'S THE CORE OF PRODUCTION IN THIS BARONY. IT IS IRREPLACEABLE.
IT...IT'LL NEVER BE PRODUCTIVE AGAIN.
IT WILL NEVER REBEL AGAIN.

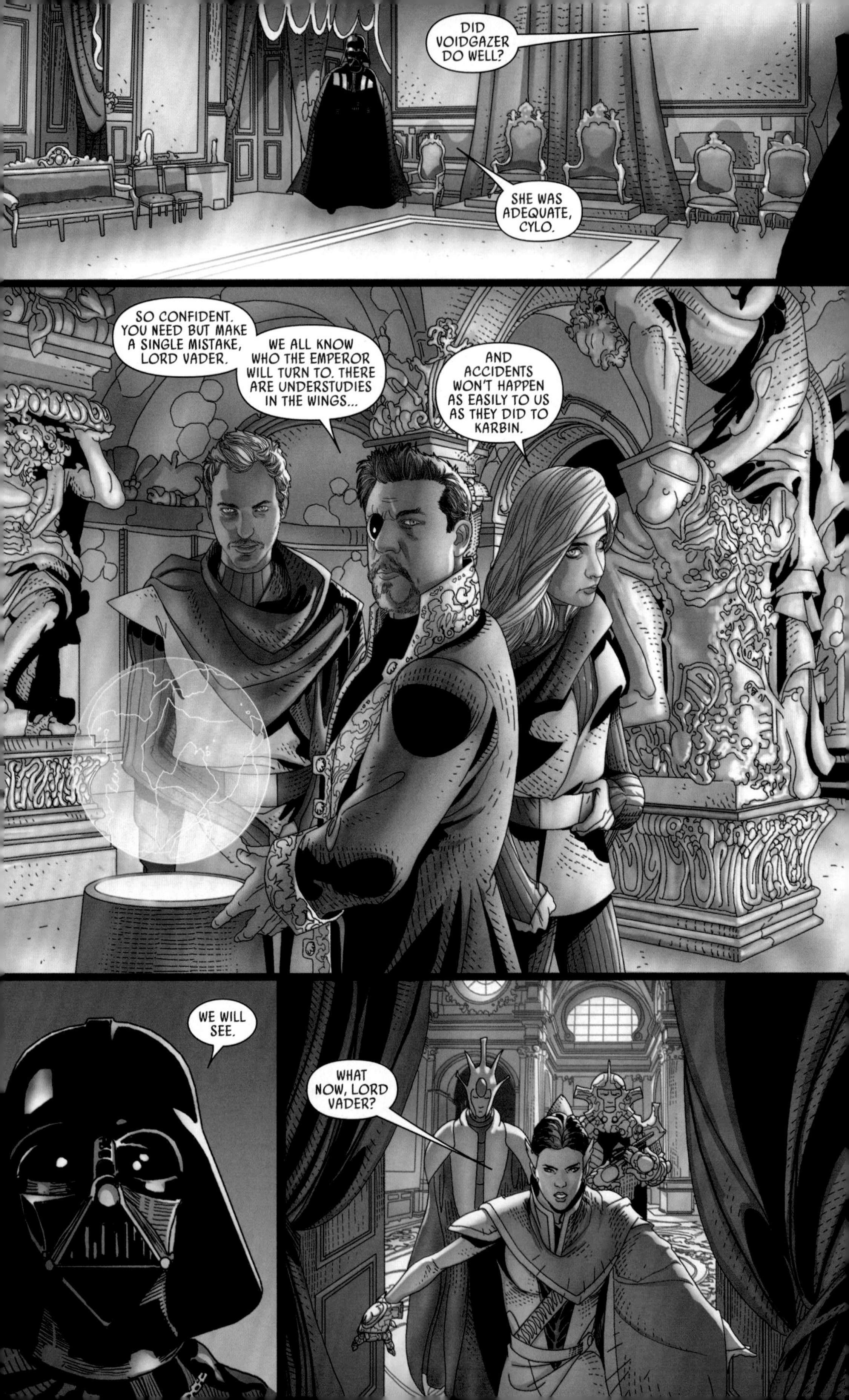
DID VOIDGAZER DO WELL?
SHE WAS ADEQUATE, CYLO.
SO CONFIDENT. YOU NEED BUT MAKE A SINGLE MISTAKE, LORD VADER.
WE ALL KNOW WHO THE EMPEROR WILL TURN TO. THERE ARE UNDERSTUDIES IN THE WINGS...
AND ACCIDENTS WON'T HAPPEN AS EASILY TO US AS THEY DID TO KARBIN.
WE WILL SEE.
WHAT NOW, LORD VADER?

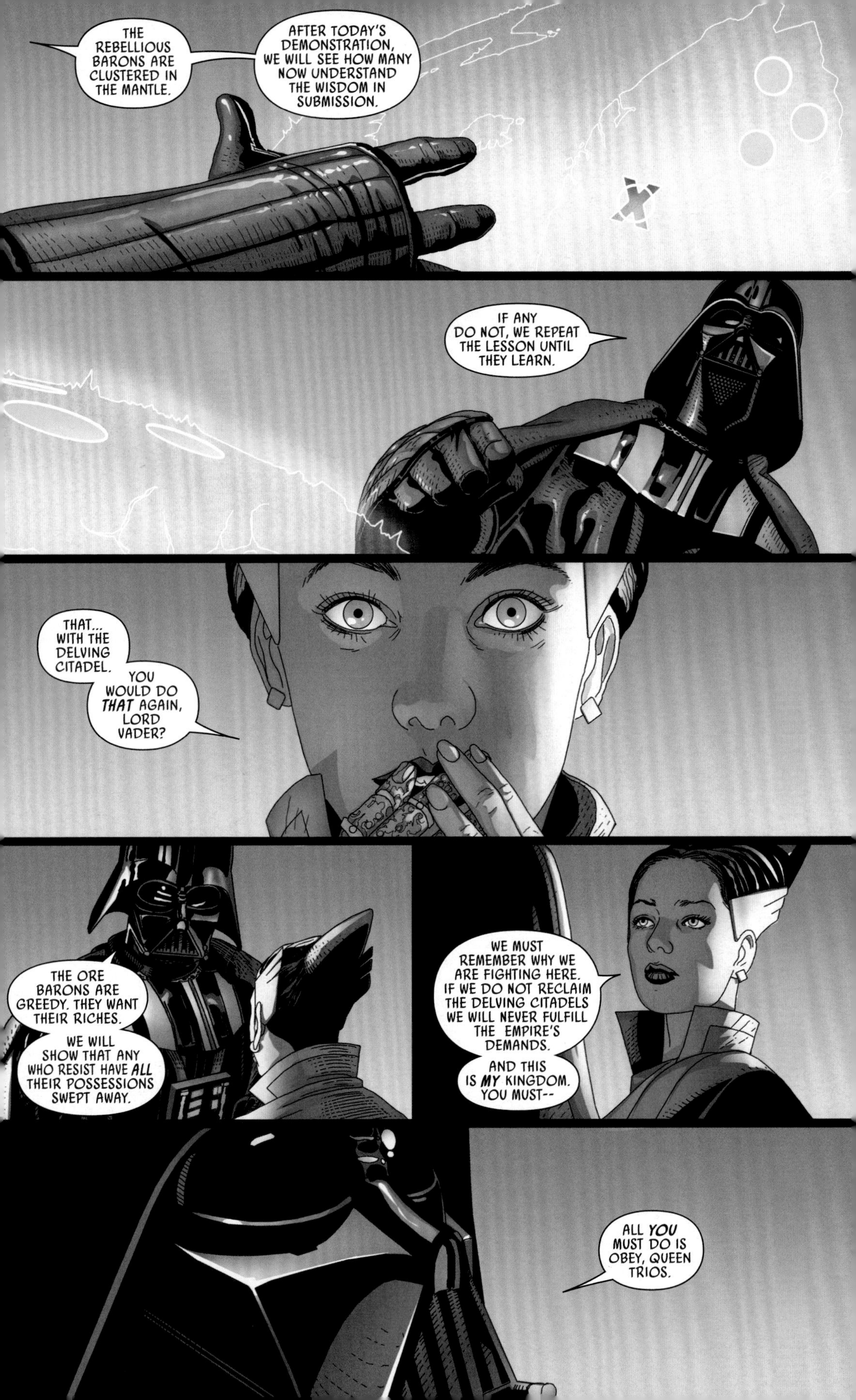
THE REBELLIOUS BARONS ARE CLUSTERED IN THE MANTLE.
AFTER TODAY'S DEMONSTRATION, WE WILL SEE HOW MANY NOW UNDERSTAND THE WISDOM IN SUBMISSION.
IF ANY DO NOT, WE REPEAT THE LESSON UNTIL THEY LEARN.
THAT... WITH THE DELVING CITADEL.
YOU WOULD DO *THAT* AGAIN, LORD VADER?
THE ORE BARONS ARE GREEDY. THEY WANT THEIR RICHES.
WE WILL SHOW THAT ANY WHO RESIST HAVE *ALL* THEIR POSSESSIONS SWEPT AWAY.
WE MUST REMEMBER WHY WE ARE FIGHTING HERE. IF WE DO NOT RECLAIM THE DELVING CITADELS WE WILL NEVER FULFILL THE EMPIRE'S DEMANDS.
AND THIS IS *MY* KINGDOM. YOU MUST--
ALL *YOU* MUST DO IS OBEY, QUEEN TRIOS.

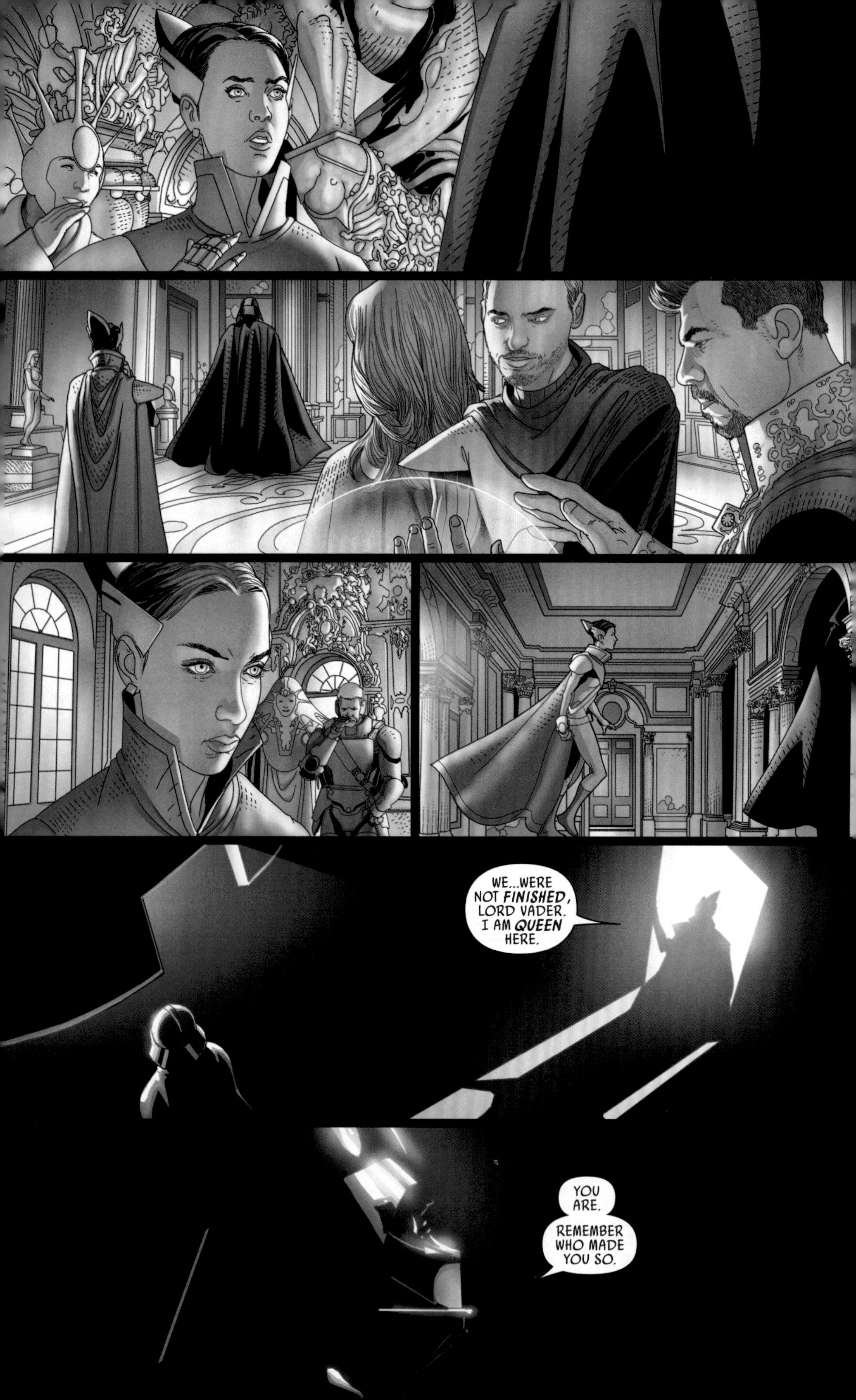
WE...WERE NOT FINISHED, LORD VADER. I AM QUEEN HERE.
YOU ARE.
REMEMBER WHO MADE YOU SO.

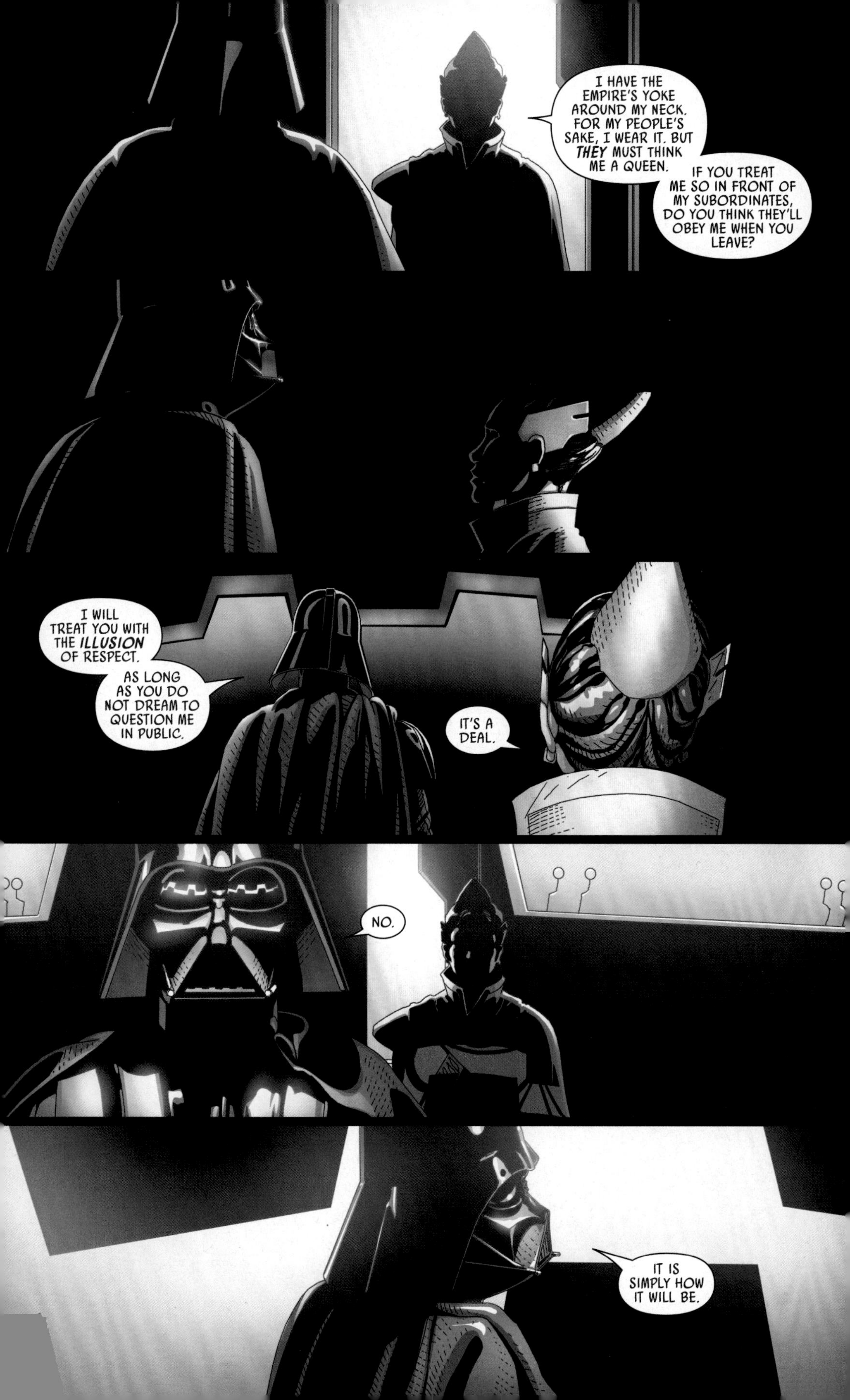
I HAVE THE EMPIRE'S YOKE AROUND MY NECK. FOR MY PEOPLE'S SAKE, I WEAR IT. BUT *THEY* MUST THINK ME A QUEEN.
IF YOU TREAT ME SO IN FRONT OF MY SUBORDINATES, DO YOU THINK THEY'LL OBEY ME WHEN YOU LEAVE?
I WILL TREAT YOU WITH THE *ILLUSION* OF RESPECT.
AS LONG AS YOU DO NOT DREAM TO QUESTION ME IN PUBLIC.
IT'S A DEAL.
NO.
IT IS SIMPLY HOW IT WILL BE.

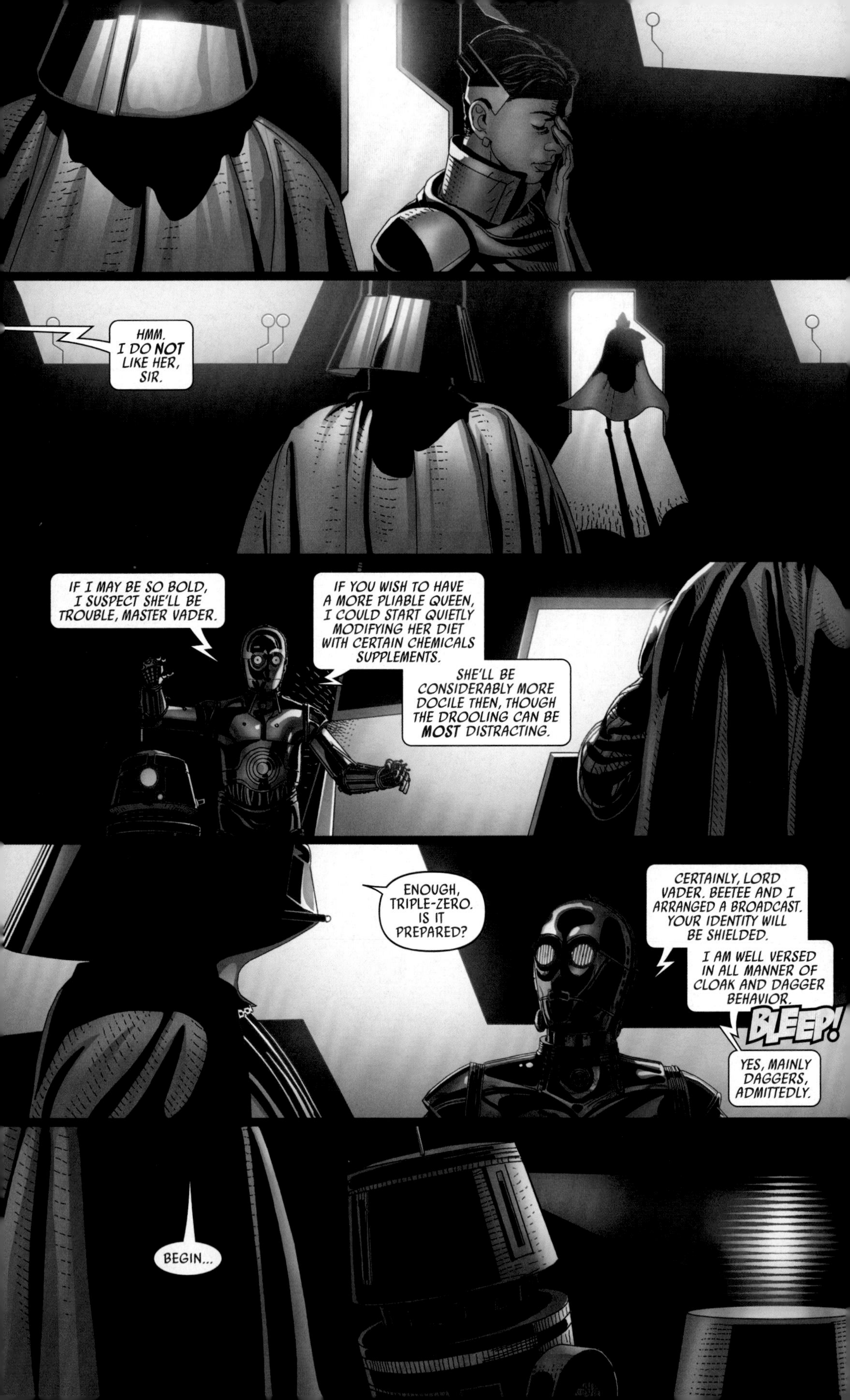
HMM. I DO NOT LIKE HER, SIR.
IF I MAY BE SO BOLD, I SUSPECT SHE'LL BE TROUBLE, MASTER VADER.
IF YOU WISH TO HAVE A MORE PLIABLE QUEEN, I COULD START QUIETLY MODIFYING HER DIET WITH CERTAIN CHEMICALS SUPPLEMENTS.
SHE'LL BE CONSIDERABLY MORE DOCILE THEN, THOUGH THE DROOLING CAN BE MOST DISTRACTING.
ENOUGH, TRIPLE-ZERO. IS IT PREPARED?
CERTAINLY, LORD VADER. BEETEE AND I ARRANGED A BROADCAST. YOUR IDENTITY WILL BE SHIELDED.
I AM WELL VERSED IN ALL MANNER OF CLOAK AND DAGGER BEHAVIOR.
BLEEP!
YES, MAINLY DAGGERS, ADMITTEDLY.
BEGIN...

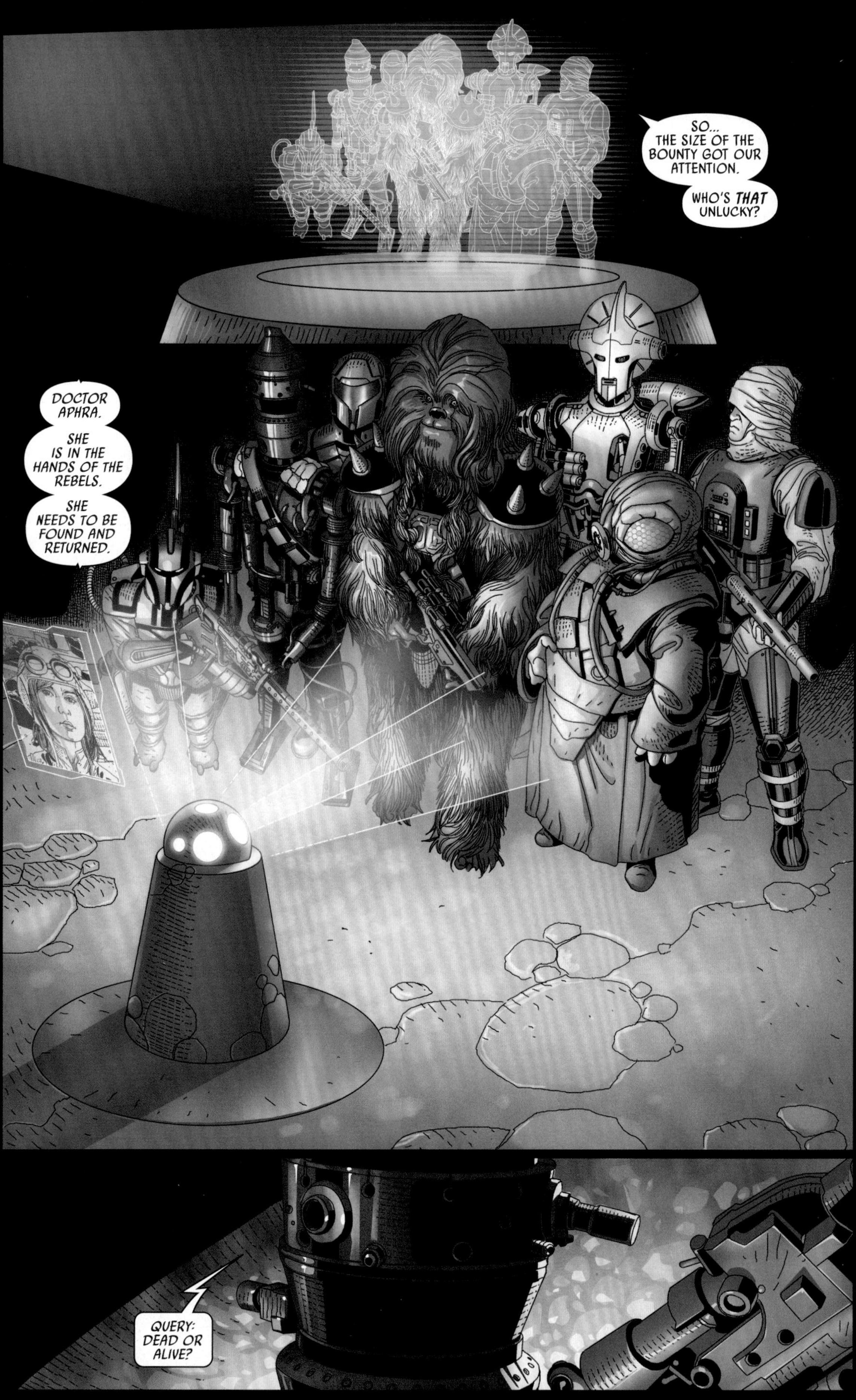
SO... THE SIZE OF THE BOUNTY GOT OUR ATTENTION.
WHO'S *THAT* UNLUCKY?
DOCTOR APHRA.
SHE IS IN THE HANDS OF THE REBELS.
SHE NEEDS TO BE FOUND AND RETURNED.
QUERY: DEAD OR ALIVE?

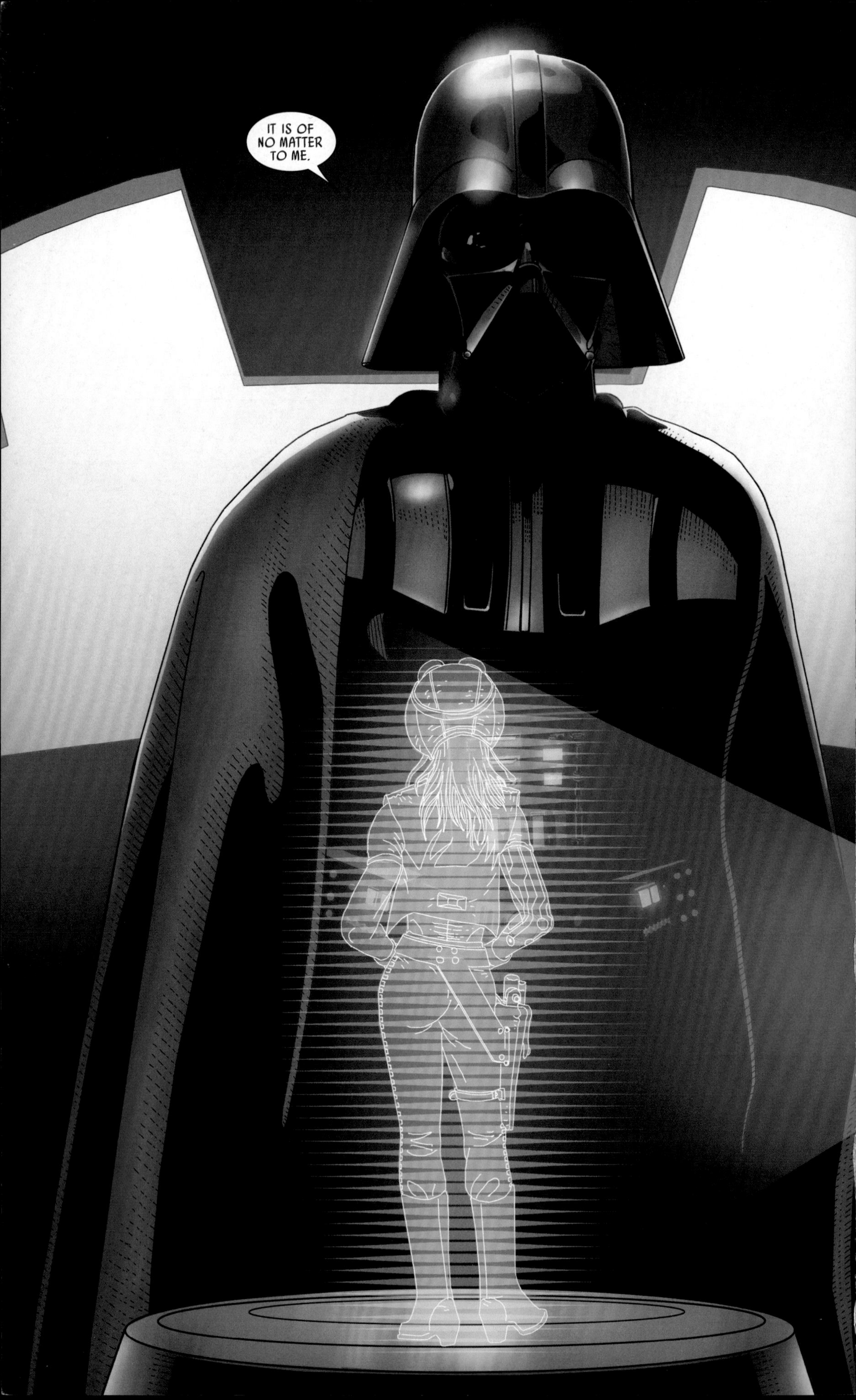
IT IS OF NO MATTER TO ME.

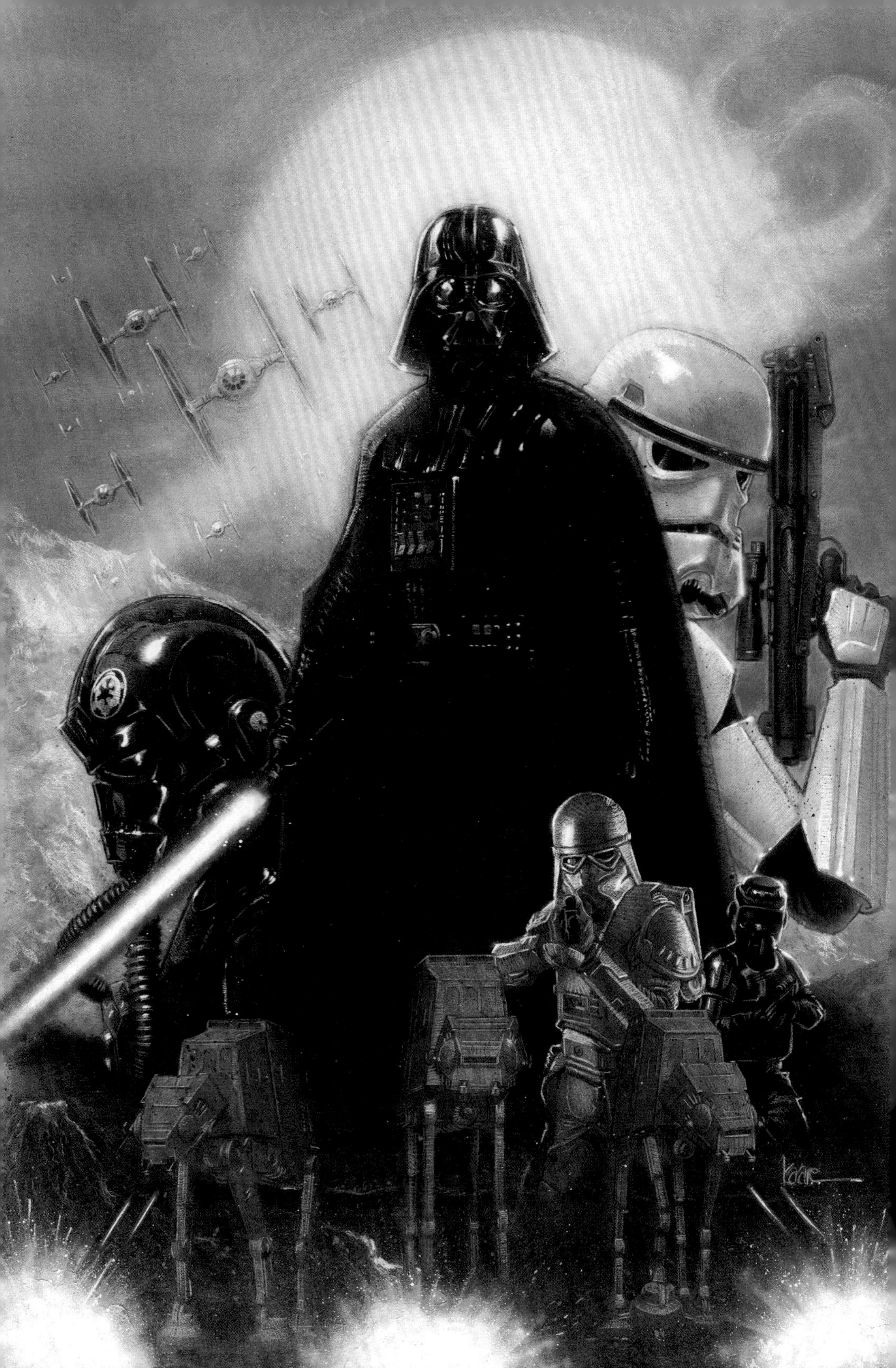

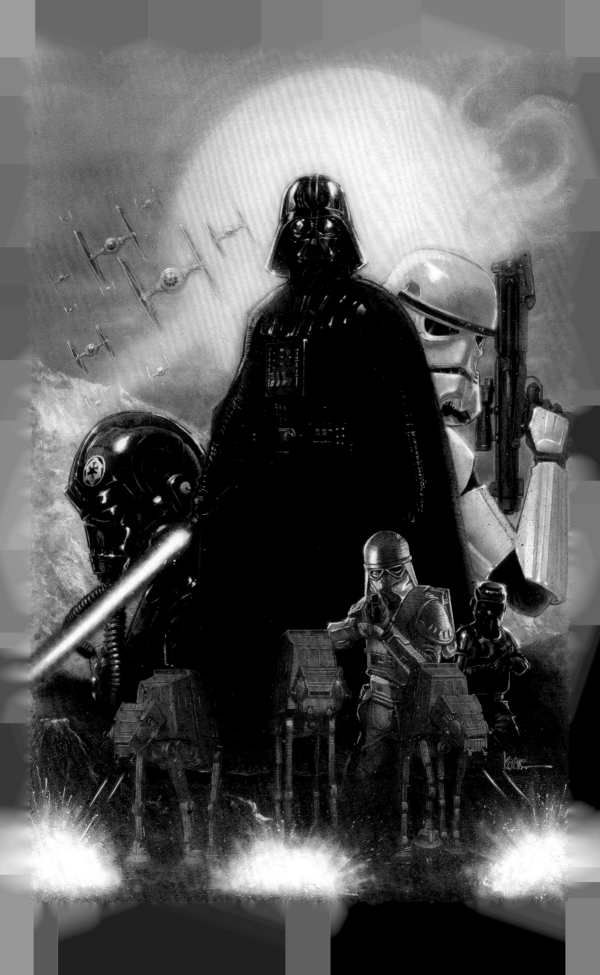

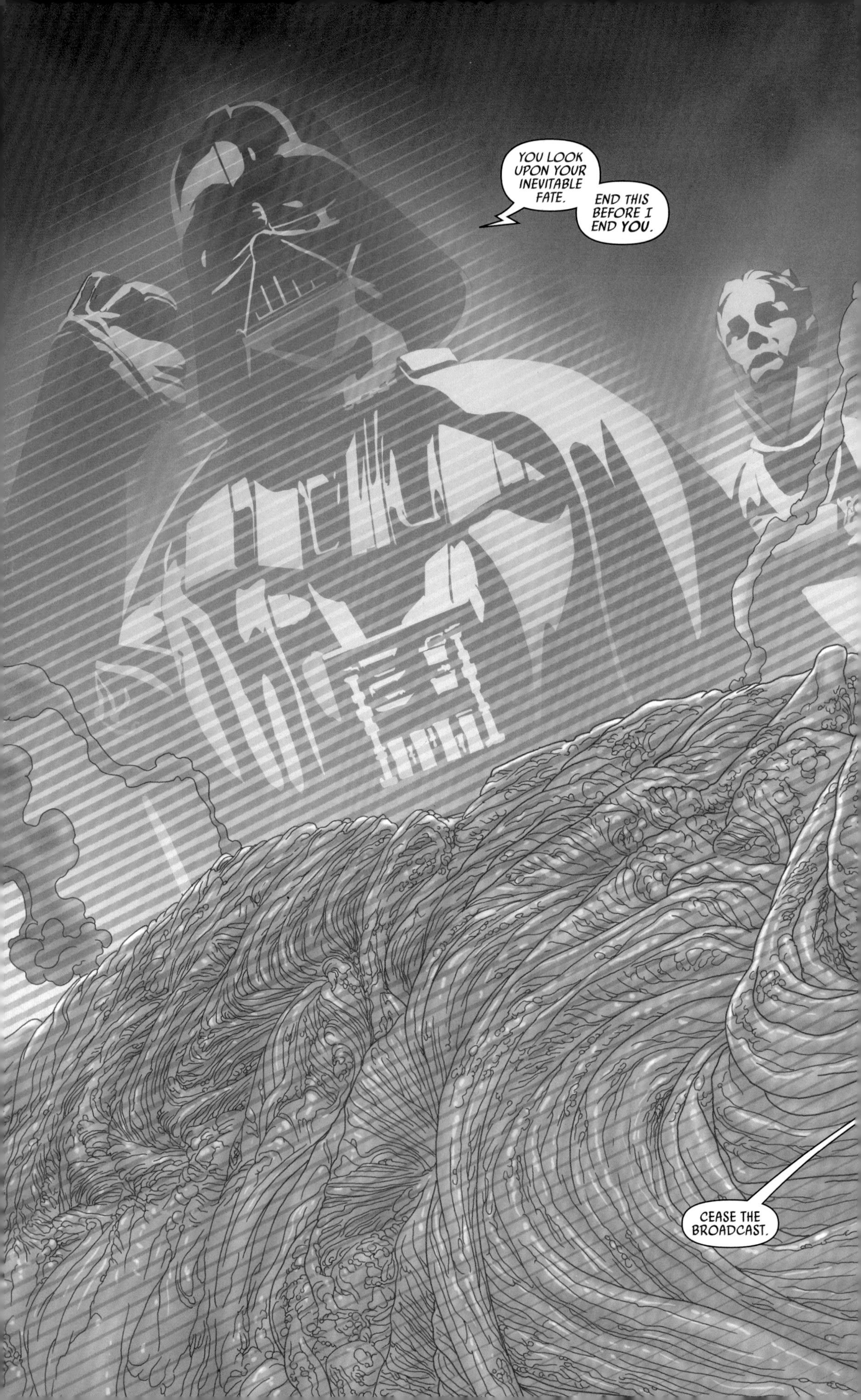
YOU LOOK UPON YOUR INEVITABLE FATE.
END THIS BEFORE I END YOU.
CEASE THE BROADCAST.

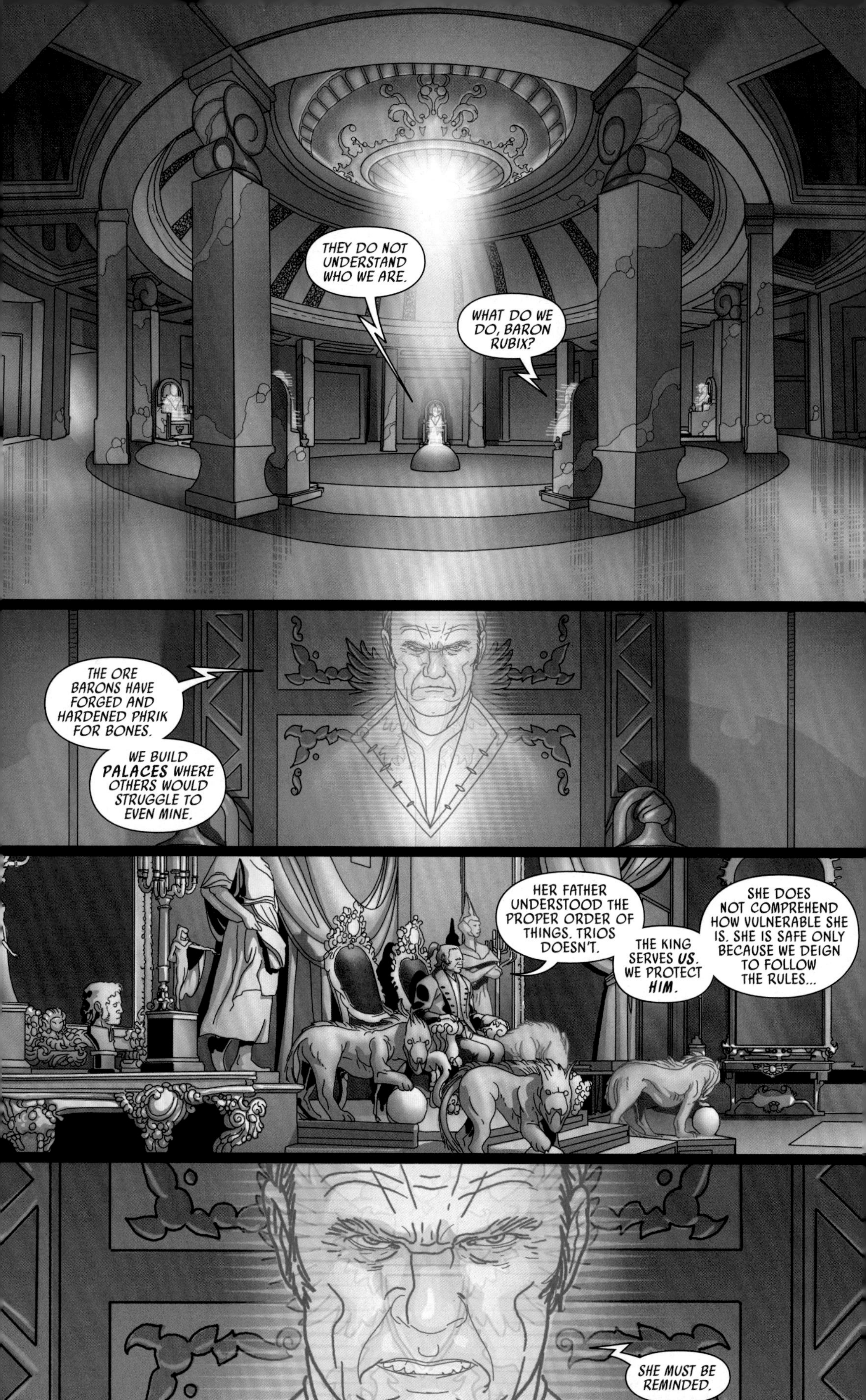
THEY DO NOT UNDERSTAND WHO WE ARE.
WHAT DO WE DO, BARON RUBIX?
THE ORE BARONS HAVE FORGED AND HARDENED PHRIK FOR BONES.
WE BUILD PALACES WHERE OTHERS WOULD STRUGGLE TO EVEN MINE.
HER FATHER UNDERSTOOD THE PROPER ORDER OF THINGS. TRIOS DOESN'T.
THE KING SERVES US. WE PROTECT HIM.
SHE DOES NOT COMPREHEND HOW VULNERABLE SHE IS. SHE IS SAFE ONLY BECAUSE WE DEIGN TO FOLLOW THE RULES...
SHE MUST BE REMINDED.

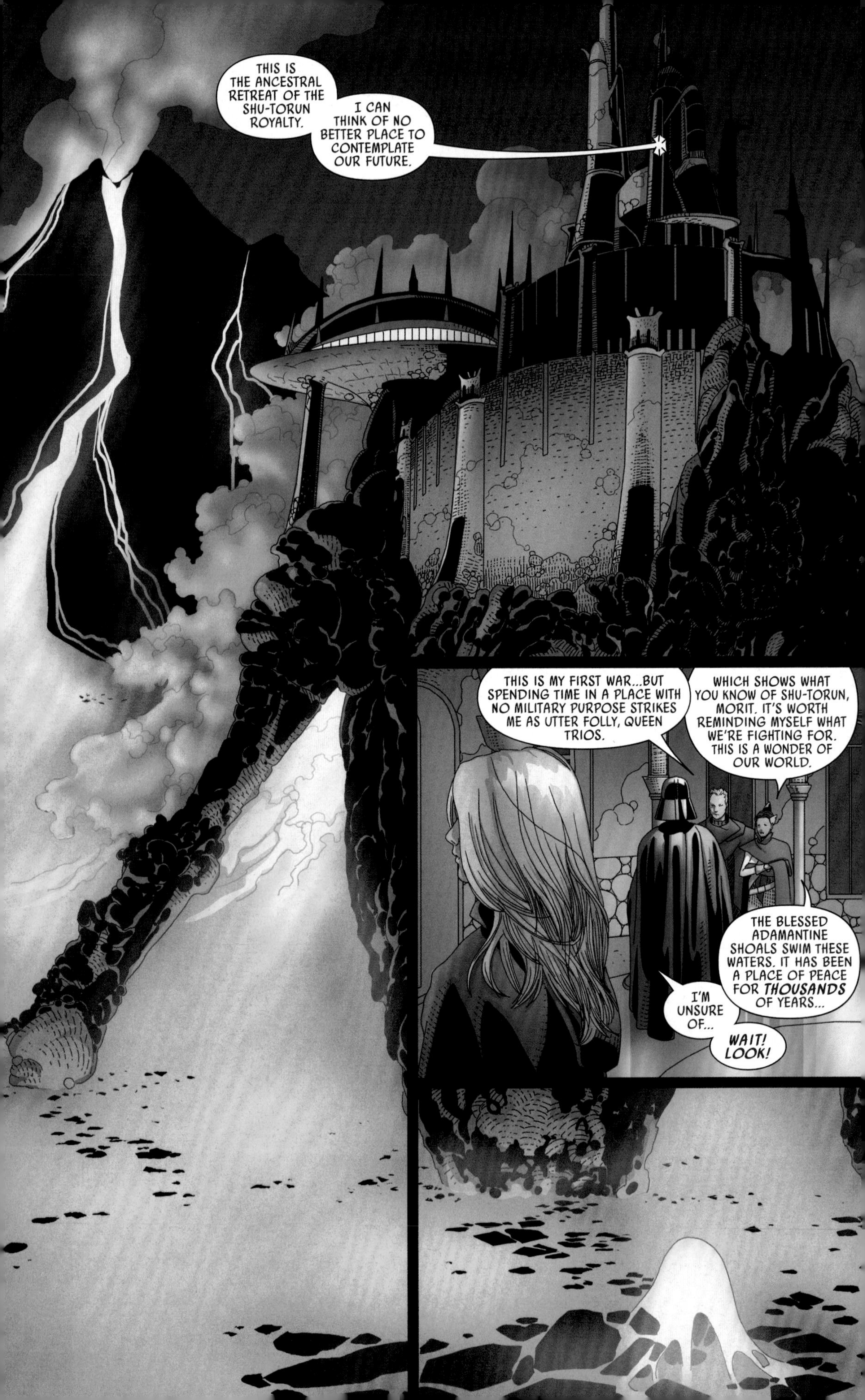
THIS IS THE ANCESTRAL RETREAT OF THE SHU-TORUN ROYALTY.
I CAN THINK OF NO BETTER PLACE TO CONTEMPLATE OUR FUTURE.
THIS IS MY FIRST WAR...BUT SPENDING TIME IN A PLACE WITH NO MILITARY PURPOSE STRIKES ME AS UTTER FOLLY, QUEEN TRIOS.
WHICH SHOWS WHAT YOU KNOW OF SHU-TORUN, MORIT. IT'S WORTH REMINDING MYSELF WHAT WE'RE FIGHTING FOR. THIS IS A WONDER OF OUR WORLD.
THE BLESSED ADAMANTINE SHOALS SWIM THESE WATERS. IT HAS BEEN A PLACE OF PEACE FOR THOUSANDS OF YEARS...
I'M UNSURE OF...
WAIT! LOOK!

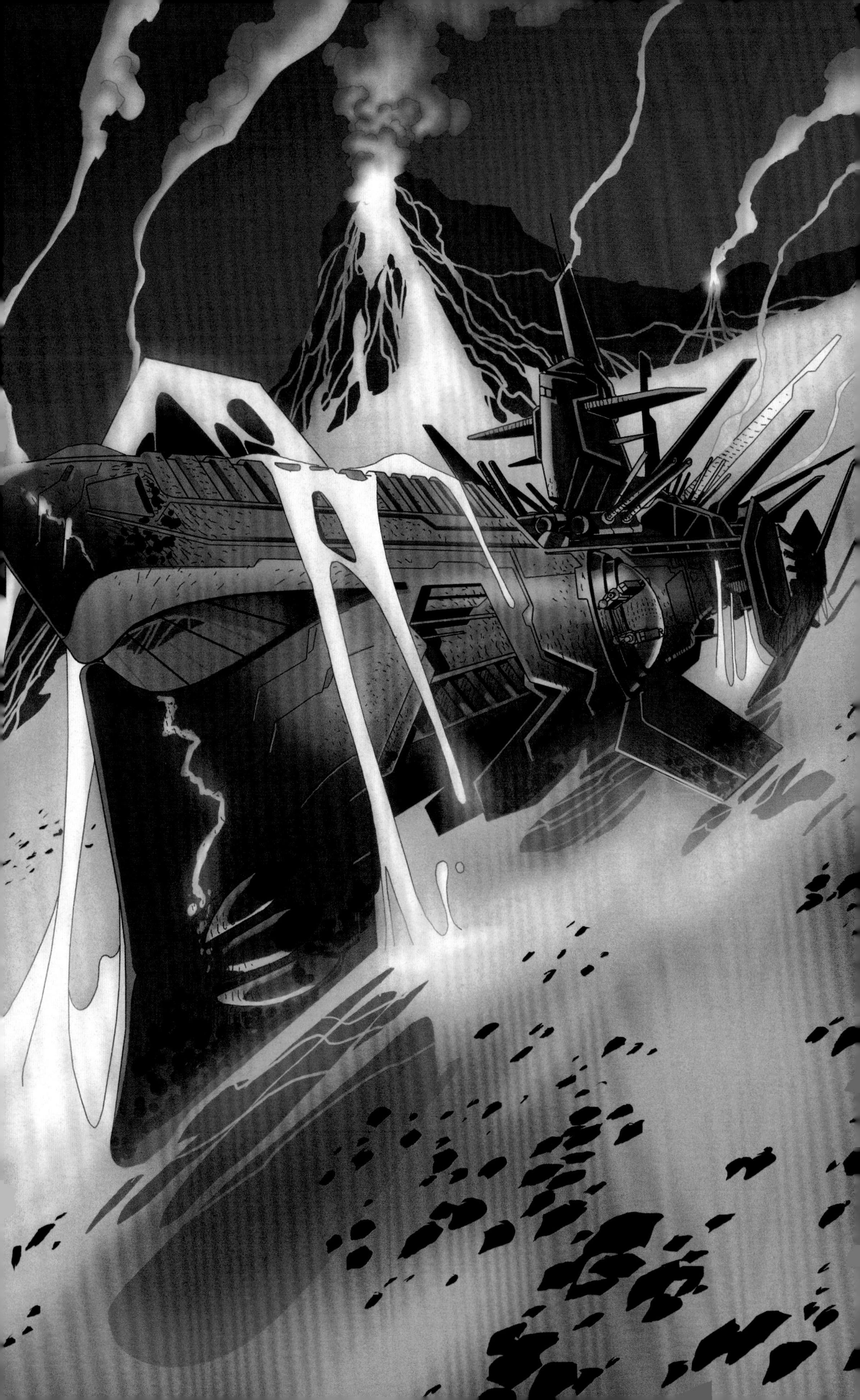

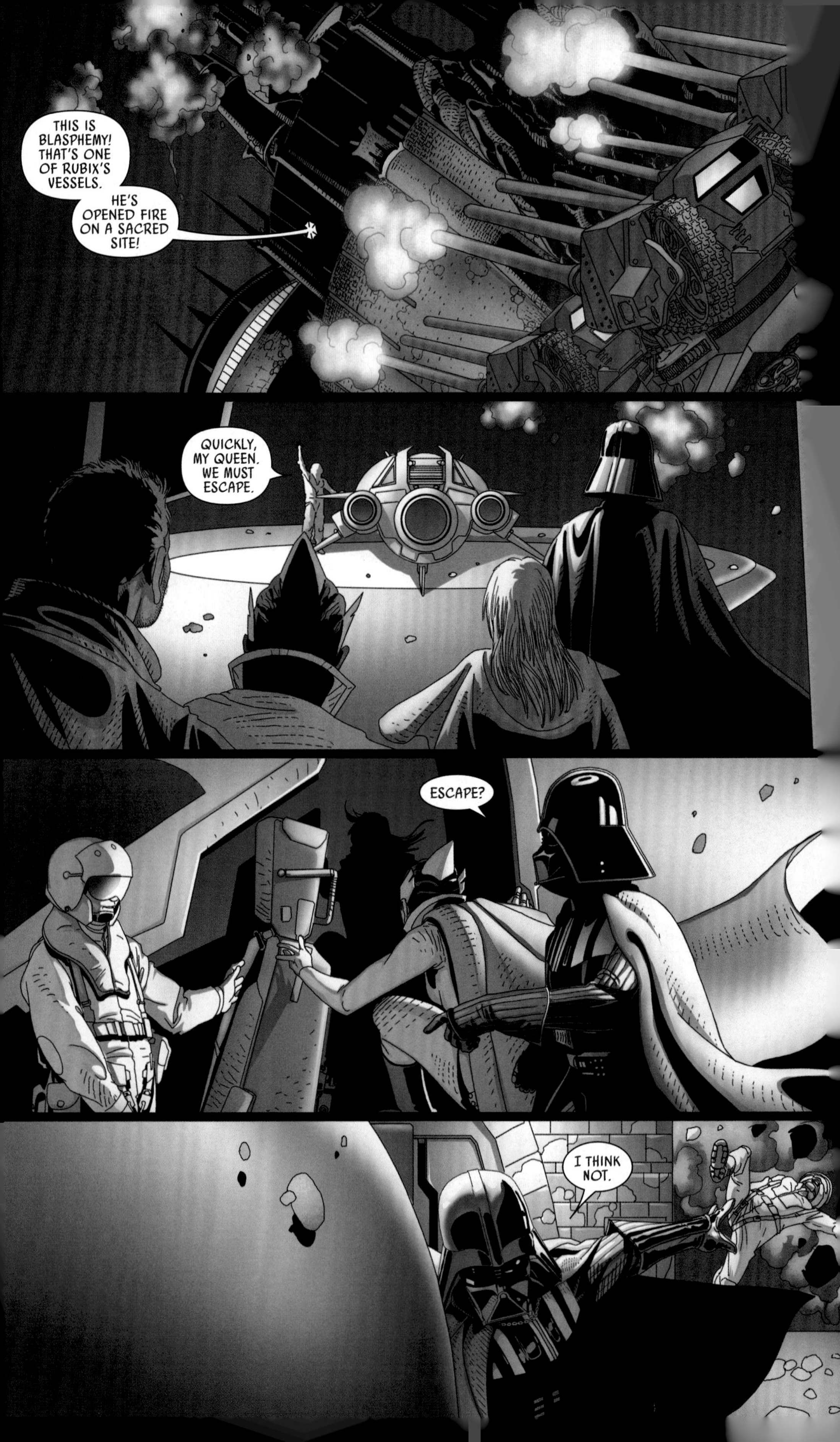
THIS IS BLASPHEMY! THAT'S ONE OF RUBIX'S VESSELS.
HE'S OPENED FIRE ON A SACRED SITE!
QUICKLY, MY QUEEN. WE MUST ESCAPE.
ESCAPE?
I THINK NOT.

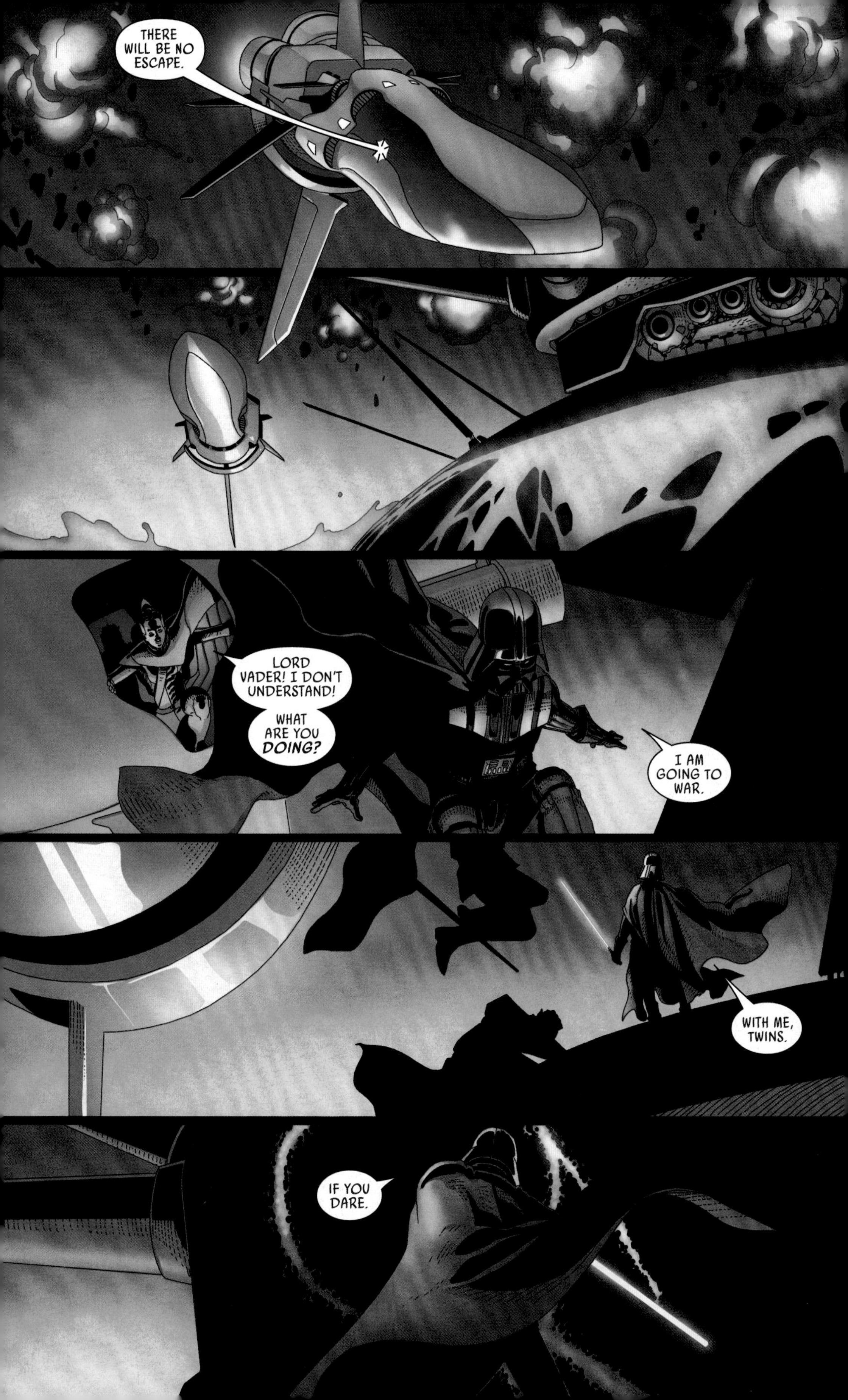
THERE WILL BE NO ESCAPE.
LORD VADER! I DON'T UNDERSTAND!
WHAT ARE YOU *DOING?*
I AM GOING TO WAR.
WITH ME, TWINS.
IF YOU DARE.

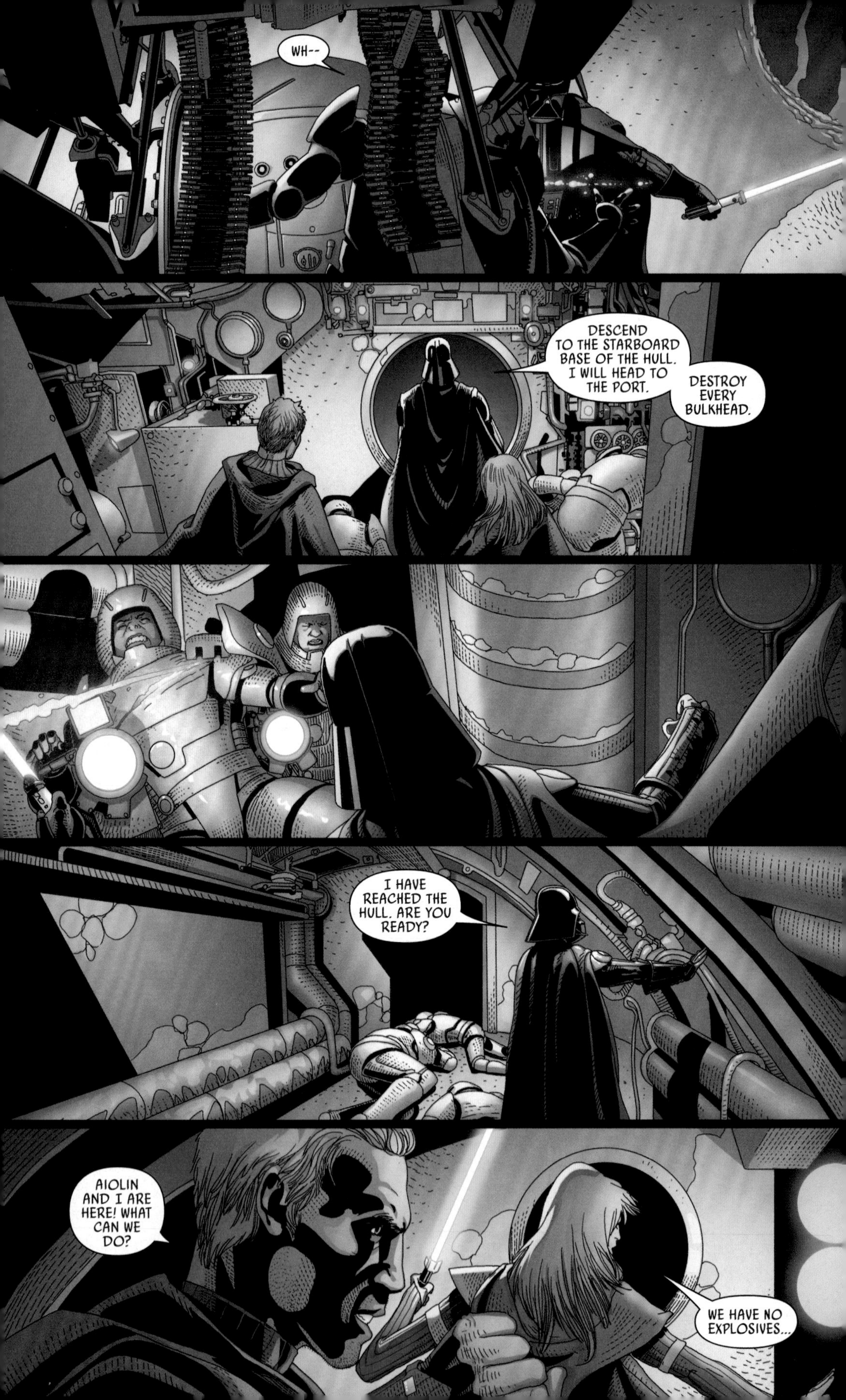
WH--
DESCEND TO THE STARBOARD BASE OF THE HULL. I WILL HEAD TO THE PORT.
DESTROY EVERY BULKHEAD.
I HAVE REACHED THE HULL. ARE YOU READY?
AIOLIN AND I ARE HERE! WHAT CAN WE DO?
WE HAVE NO EXPLOSIVES...

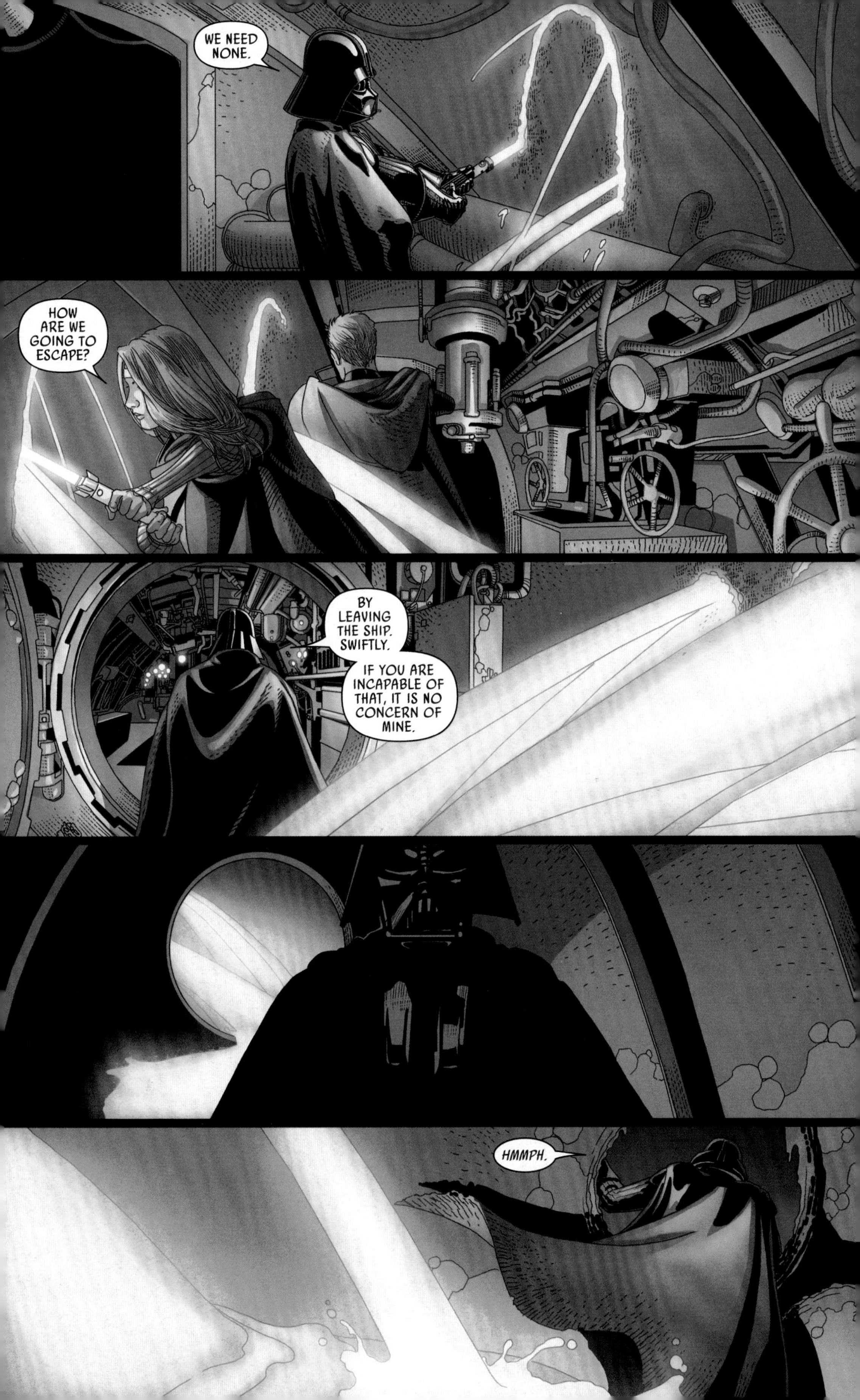
WE NEED NONE.
HOW ARE WE GOING TO ESCAPE?
BY LEAVING THE SHIP. SWIFTLY.
IF YOU ARE INCAPABLE OF THAT, IT IS NO CONCERN OF MINE.
HMMPH.

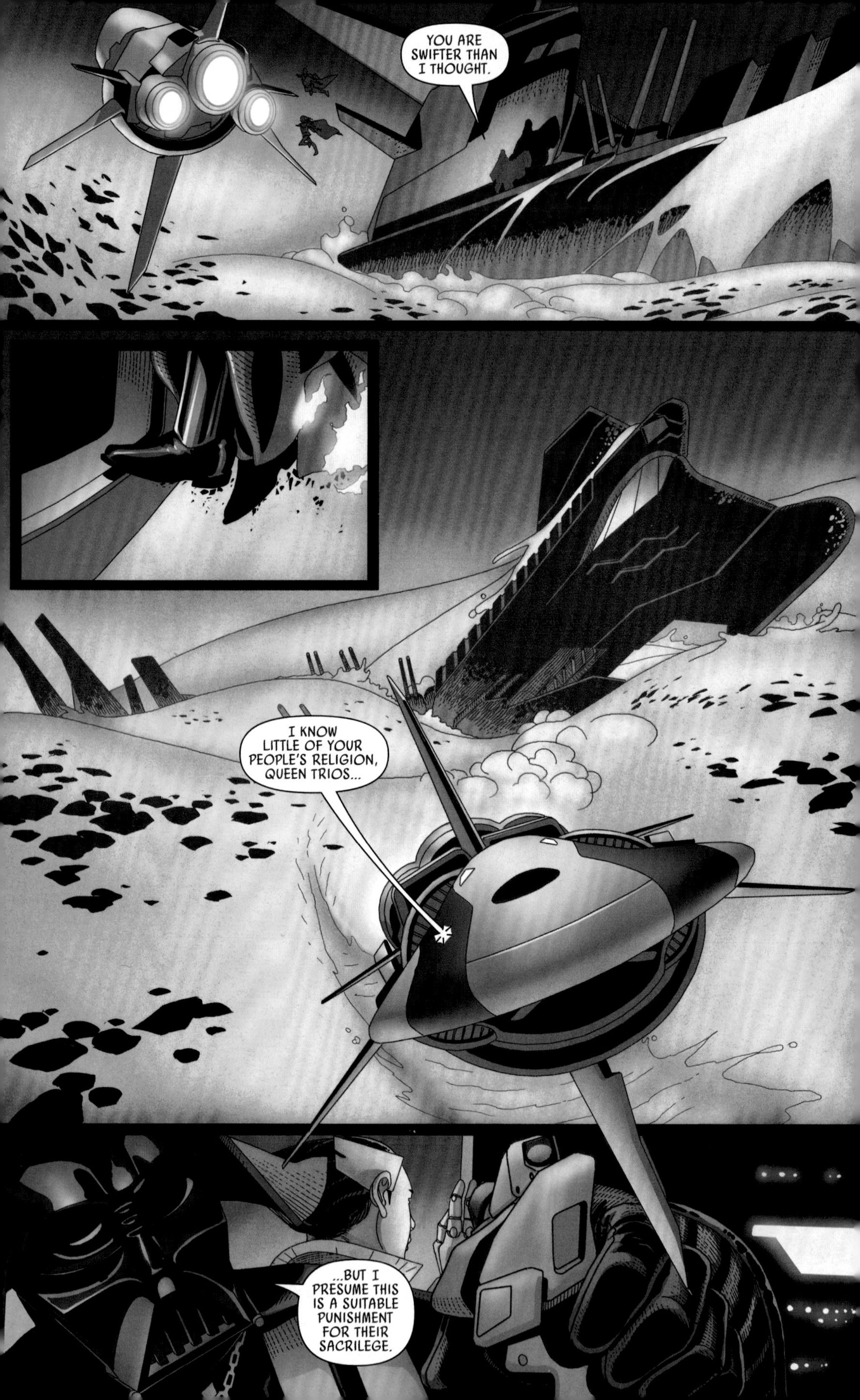
YOU ARE SWIFTER THAN I THOUGHT.
I KNOW LITTLE OF YOUR PEOPLE'S RELIGION, QUEEN TRIOS...
...BUT I PRESUME THIS IS A SUITABLE PUNISHMENT FOR THEIR SACRILEGE.

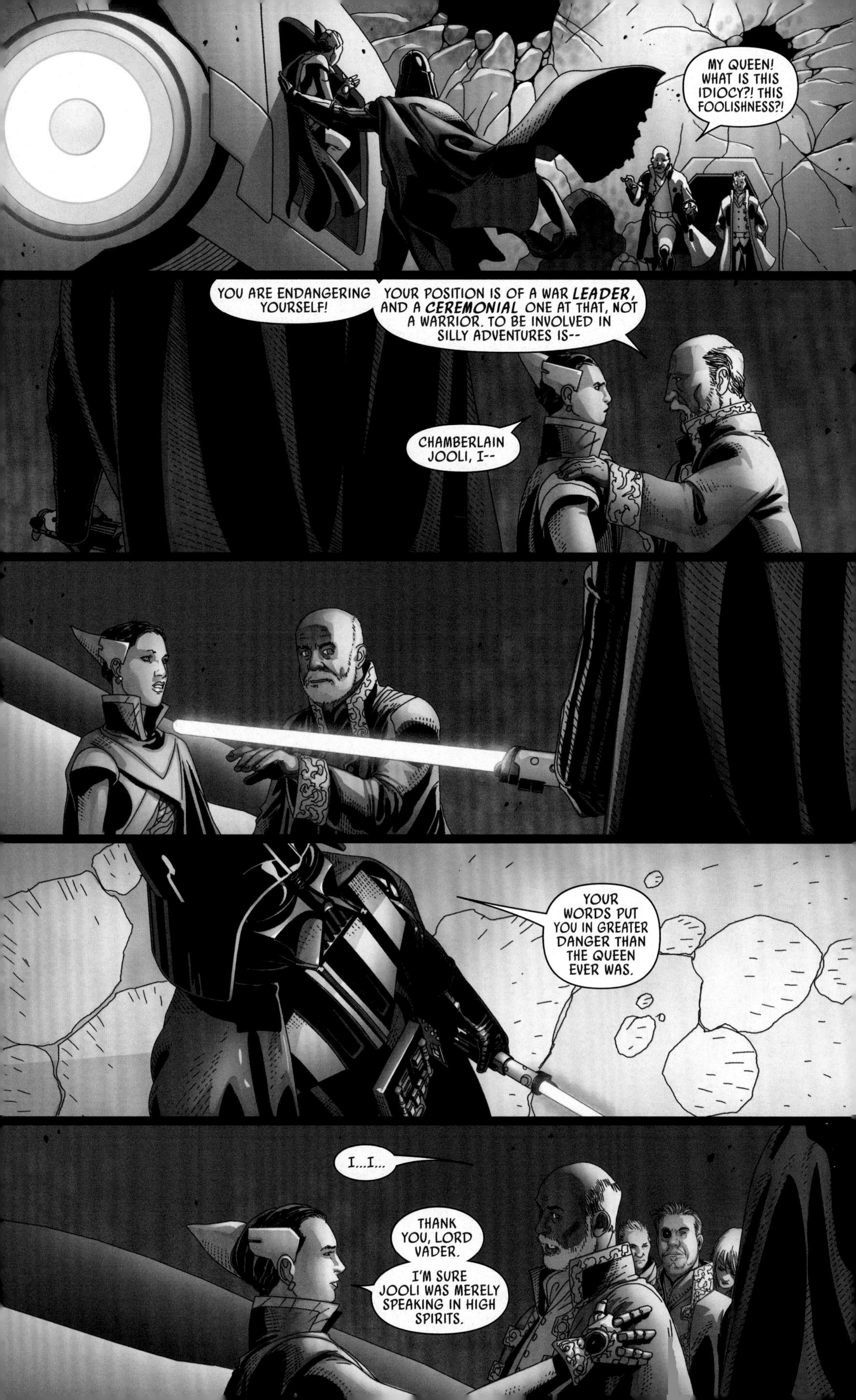
MY QUEEN! WHAT IS THIS IDIOCY?! THIS FOOLISHNESS?!
YOU ARE ENDANGERING YOURSELF!
YOUR POSITION IS OF A WAR LEADER, AND A CEREMONIAL ONE AT THAT, NOT A WARRIOR. TO BE INVOLVED IN SILLY ADVENTURES IS--
CHAMBERLAIN JOOLI, I--
YOUR WORDS PUT YOU IN GREATER DANGER THAN THE QUEEN EVER WAS.
I...I...
THANK YOU, LORD VADER.
I'M SURE JOOLI WAS MERELY SPEAKING IN HIGH SPIRITS.

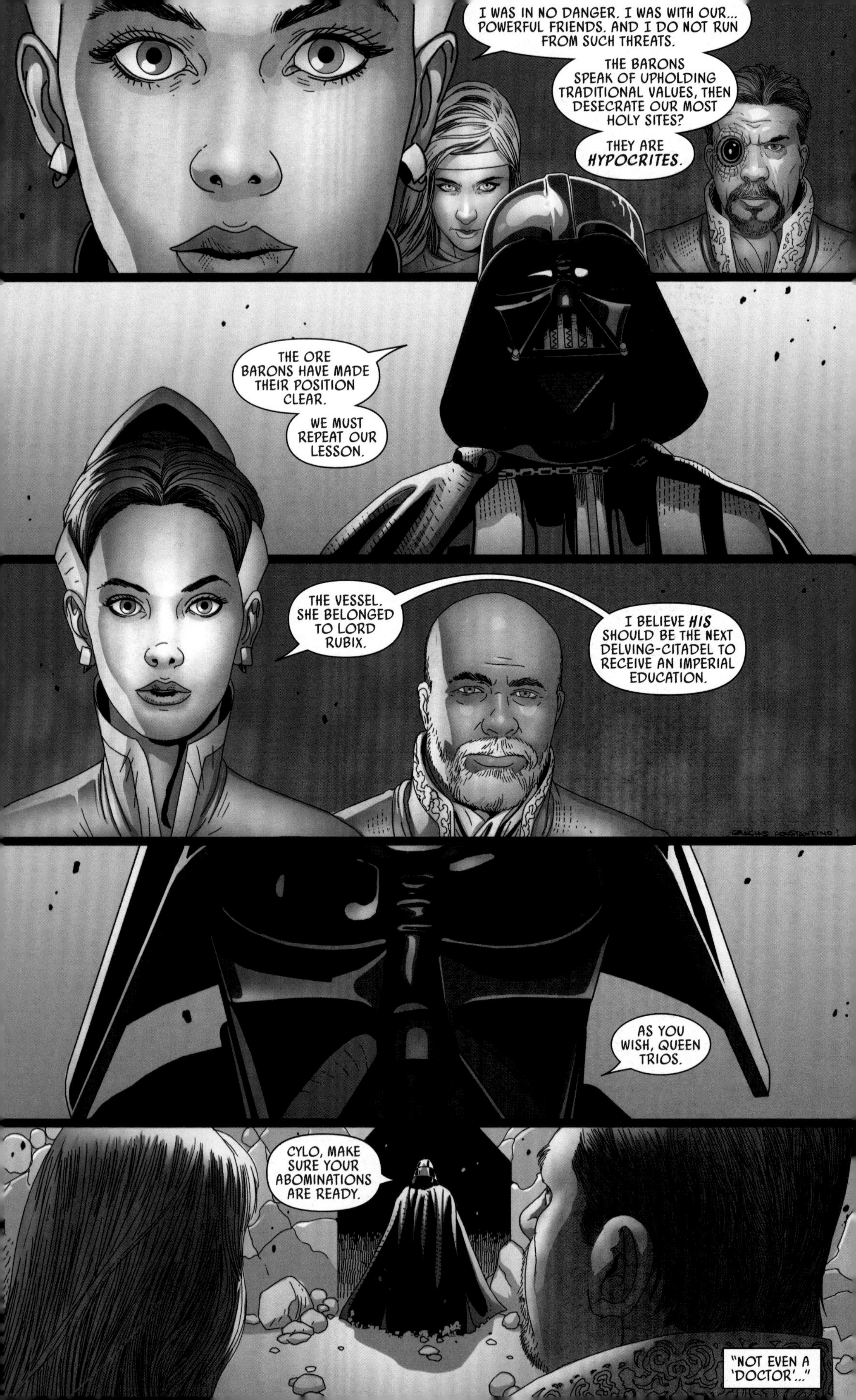
I WAS IN NO DANGER. I WAS WITH OUR... POWERFUL FRIENDS. AND I DO NOT RUN FROM SUCH THREATS.
THE BARONS SPEAK OF UPHOLDING TRADITIONAL VALUES, THEN DESECRATE OUR MOST HOLY SITES?
THEY ARE *HYPOCRITES*.
THE ORE BARONS HAVE MADE THEIR POSITION CLEAR.
WE MUST REPEAT OUR LESSON.
THE VESSEL. SHE BELONGED TO LORD RUBIX.
I BELIEVE *HIS* SHOULD BE THE NEXT DELVING-CITADEL TO RECEIVE AN IMPERIAL EDUCATION.
AS YOU WISH, QUEEN TRIOS.
CYLO, MAKE SURE YOUR ABOMINATIONS ARE READY.
"NOT EVEN A 'DOCTOR'..."

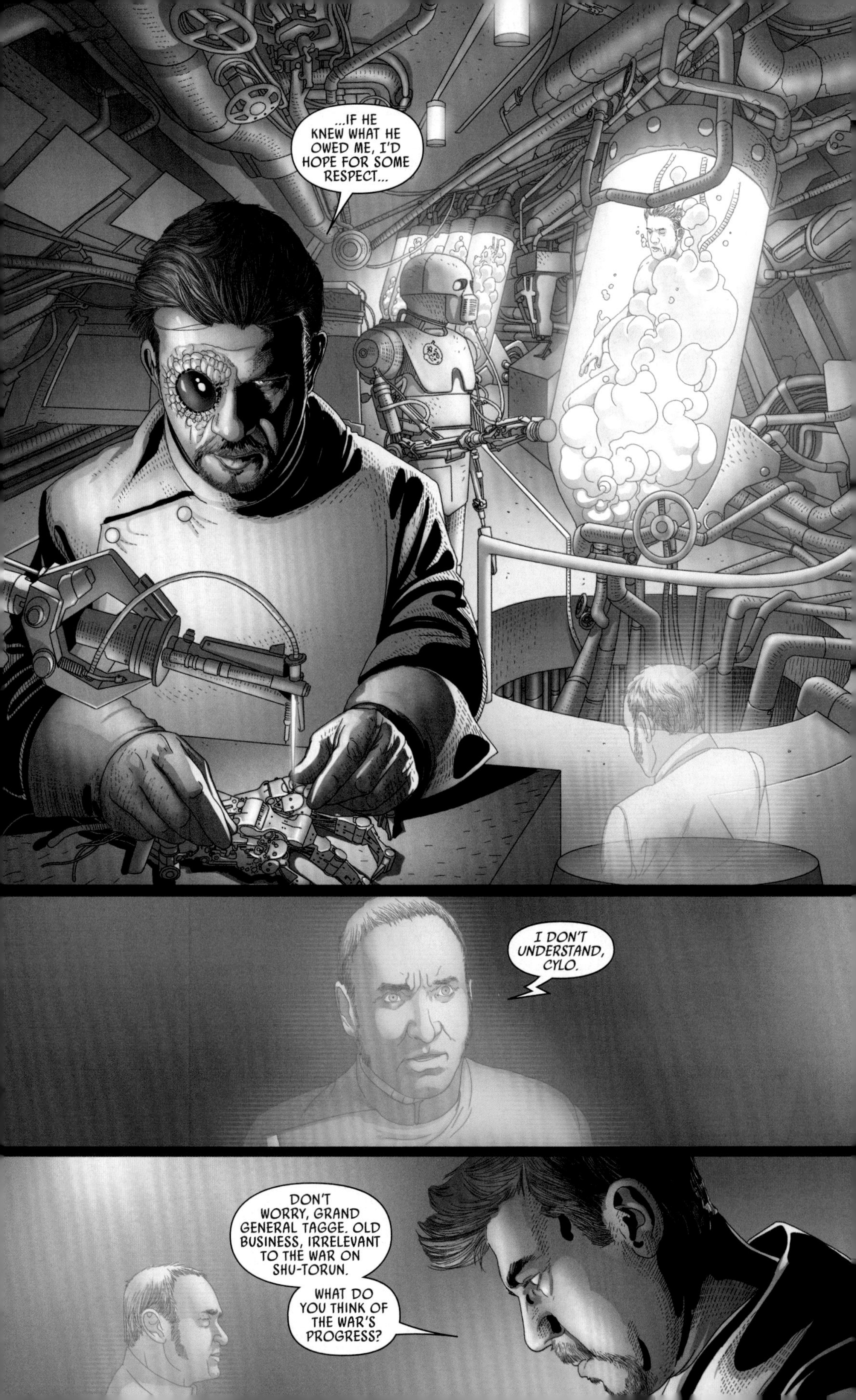
...IF HE KNEW WHAT HE OWED ME, I'D HOPE FOR SOME RESPECT...
I DON'T UNDERSTAND, CYLO.
DON'T WORRY, GRAND GENERAL TAGGE. OLD BUSINESS, IRRELEVANT TO THE WAR ON SHU-TORUN.
WHAT DO YOU THINK OF THE WAR'S PROGRESS?

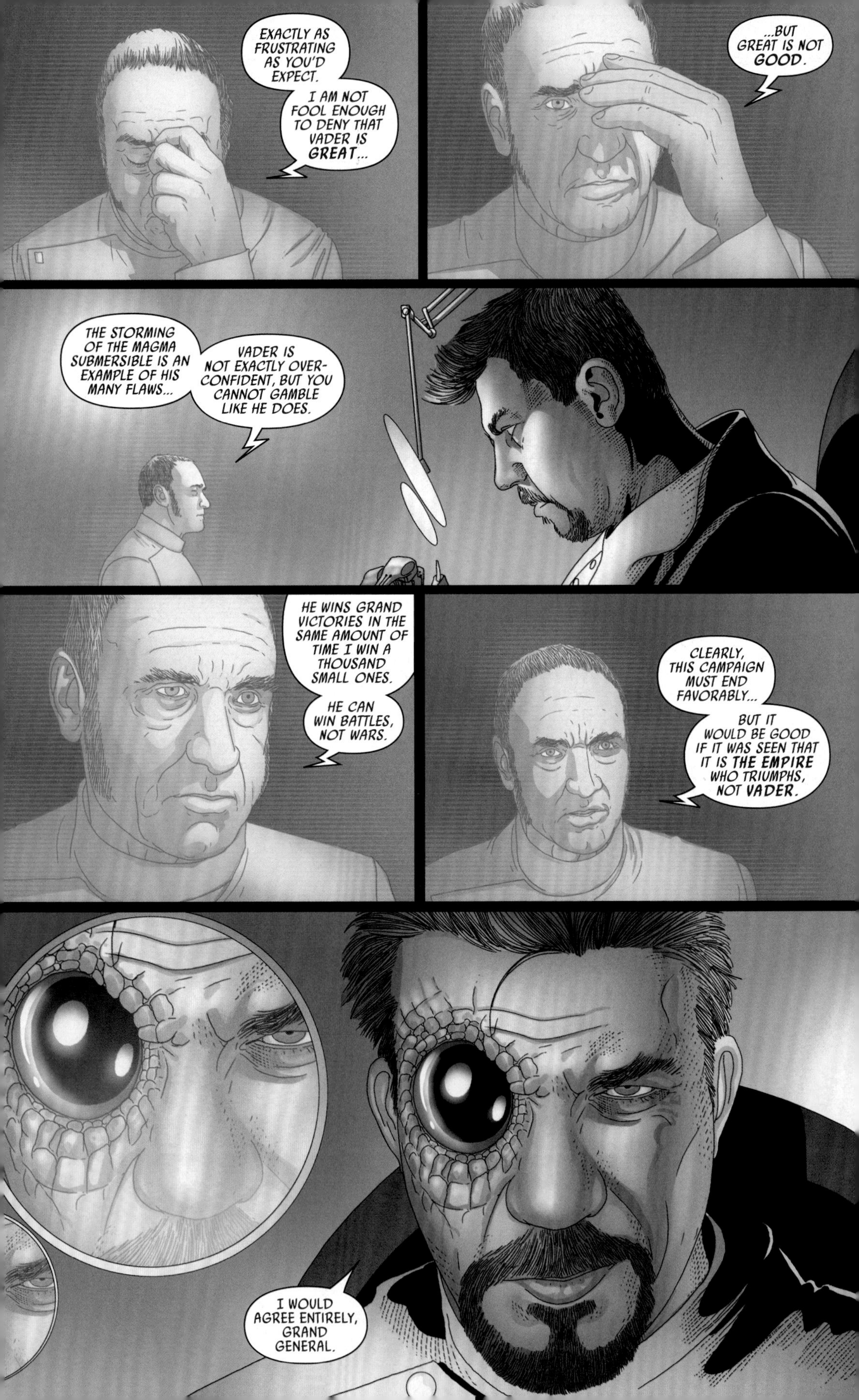
EXACTLY AS FRUSTRATING AS YOU'D EXPECT.
I AM NOT FOOL ENOUGH TO DENY THAT VADER IS GREAT...
...BUT GREAT IS NOT GOOD.
THE STORMING OF THE MAGMA SUBMERSIBLE IS AN EXAMPLE OF HIS MANY FLAWS...
VADER IS NOT EXACTLY OVER-CONFIDENT, BUT YOU CANNOT GAMBLE LIKE HE DOES.
HE WINS GRAND VICTORIES IN THE SAME AMOUNT OF TIME I WIN A THOUSAND SMALL ONES.
HE CAN WIN BATTLES, NOT WARS.
CLEARLY, THIS CAMPAIGN MUST END FAVORABLY...
BUT IT WOULD BE GOOD IF IT WAS SEEN THAT IT IS THE EMPIRE WHO TRIUMPHS, NOT VADER.
I WOULD AGREE ENTIRELY, GRAND GENERAL.

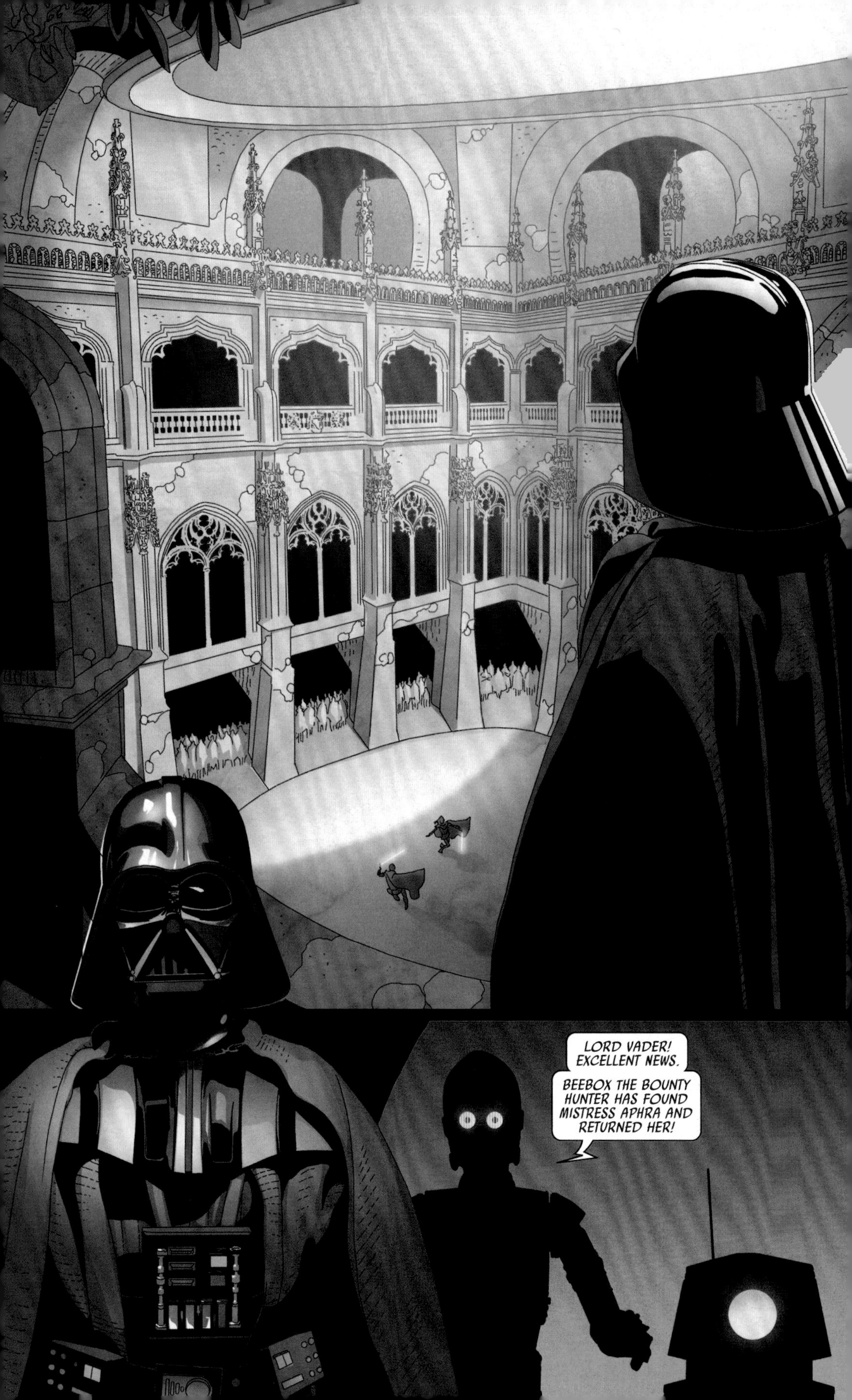
LORD VADER! EXCELLENT NEWS.
BEEBOX THE BOUNTY HUNTER HAS FOUND MISTRESS APHRA AND RETURNED HER!

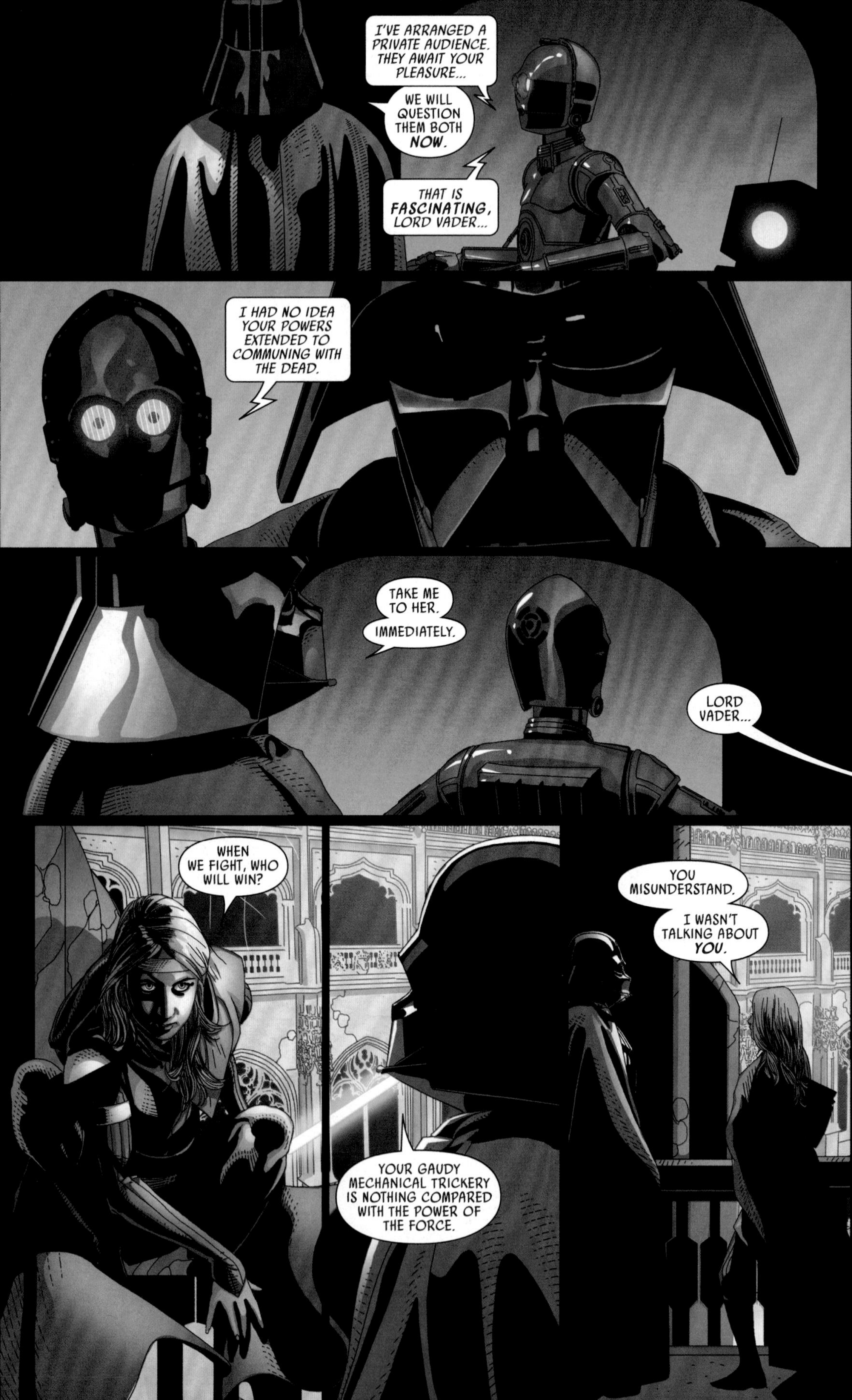
I'VE ARRANGED A PRIVATE AUDIENCE. THEY AWAIT YOUR PLEASURE...
WE WILL QUESTION THEM BOTH NOW.
THAT IS FASCINATING, LORD VADER...
I HAD NO IDEA YOUR POWERS EXTENDED TO COMMUNING WITH THE DEAD.
TAKE ME TO HER.
IMMEDIATELY.
LORD VADER...
WHEN WE FIGHT, WHO WILL WIN?
YOUR GAUDY MECHANICAL TRICKERY IS NOTHING COMPARED WITH THE POWER OF THE FORCE.
YOU MISUNDERSTAND.
I WASN'T TALKING ABOUT YOU.

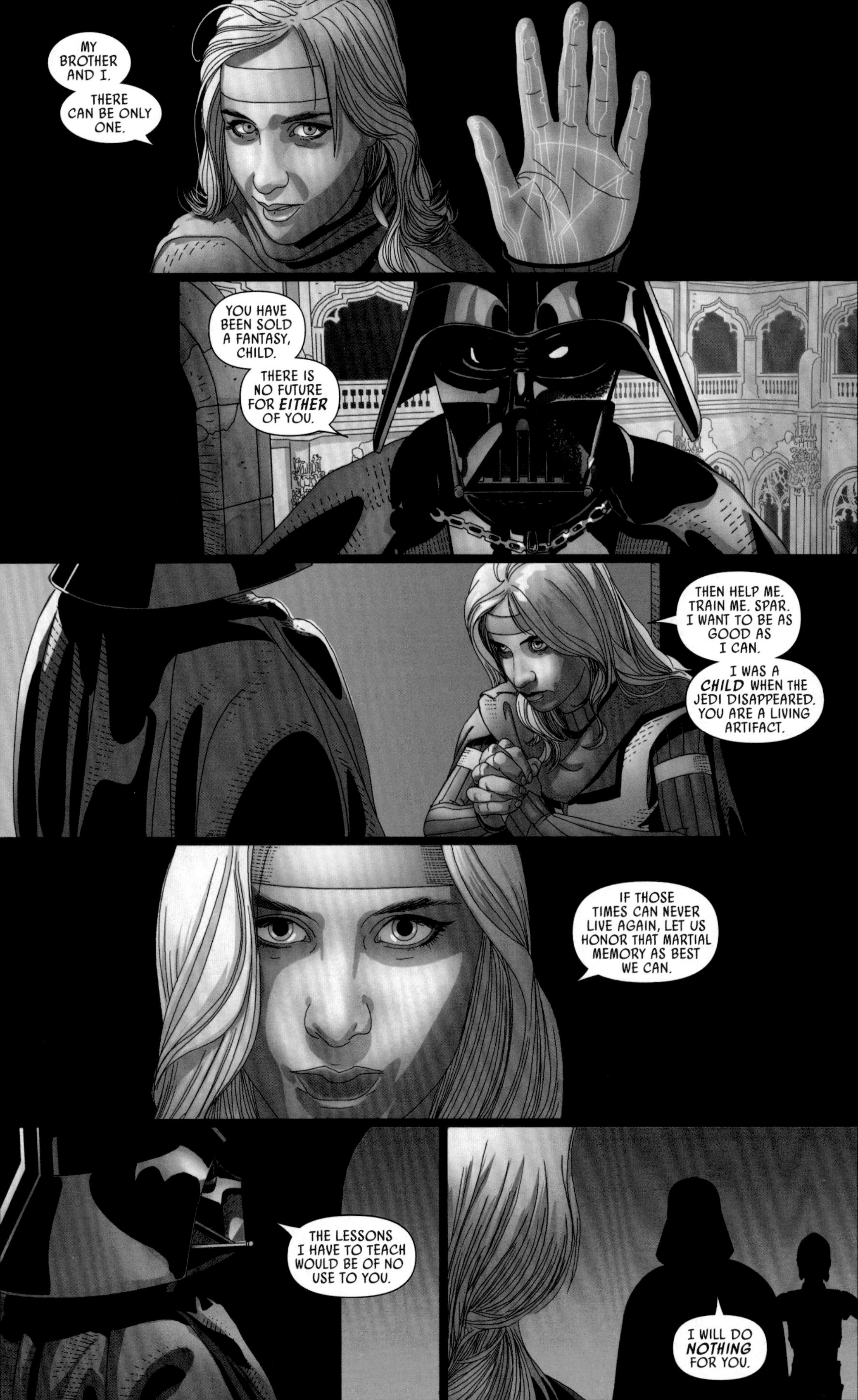
MY BROTHER AND I.
THERE CAN BE ONLY ONE.
YOU HAVE BEEN SOLD A FANTASY, CHILD.
THERE IS NO FUTURE FOR *EITHER* OF YOU.
THEN HELP ME. TRAIN ME. SPAR. I WANT TO BE AS GOOD AS I CAN.
I WAS A *CHILD* WHEN THE JEDI DISAPPEARED. YOU ARE A LIVING ARTIFACT.
IF THOSE TIMES CAN NEVER LIVE AGAIN, LET US HONOR THAT MARTIAL MEMORY AS BEST WE CAN.
THE LESSONS I HAVE TO TEACH WOULD BE OF NO USE TO YOU.
I WILL DO *NOTHING* FOR YOU.

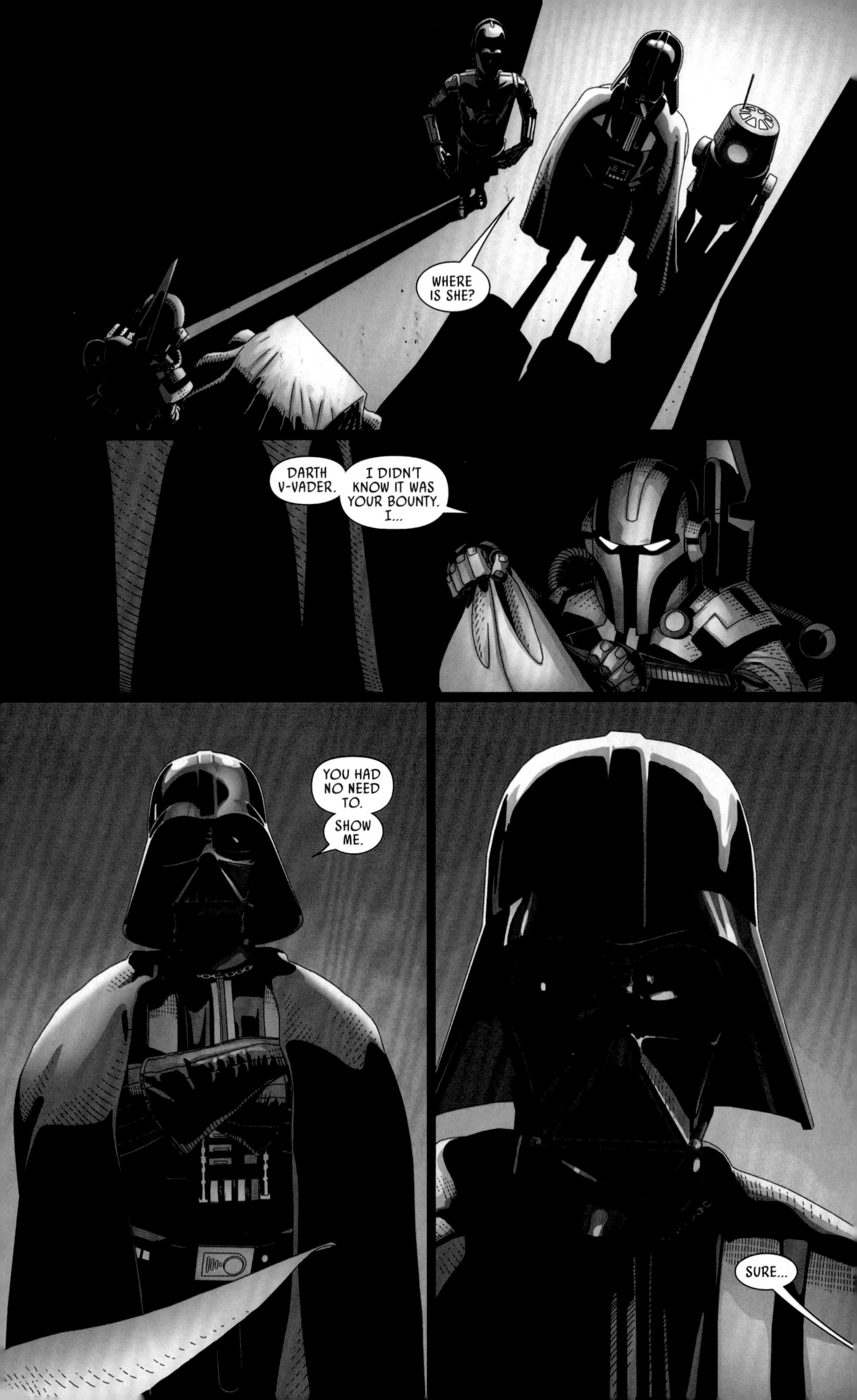
WHERE IS SHE?
DARTH V-VADER.
I DIDN'T KNOW IT WAS YOUR BOUNTY. I...
YOU HAD NO NEED TO.
SHOW ME.
SURE...

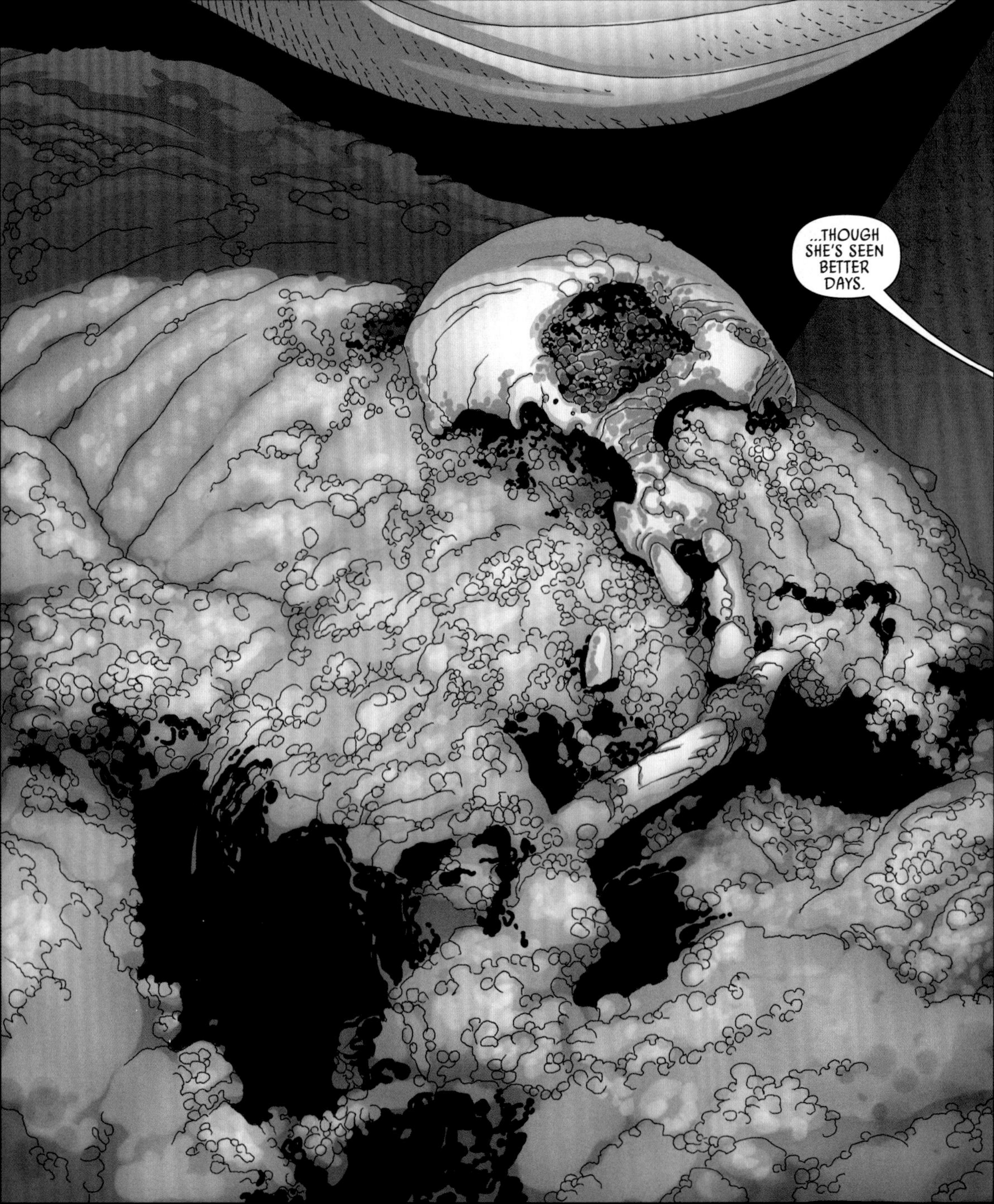
...THOUGH SHE'S SEEN BETTER DAYS.

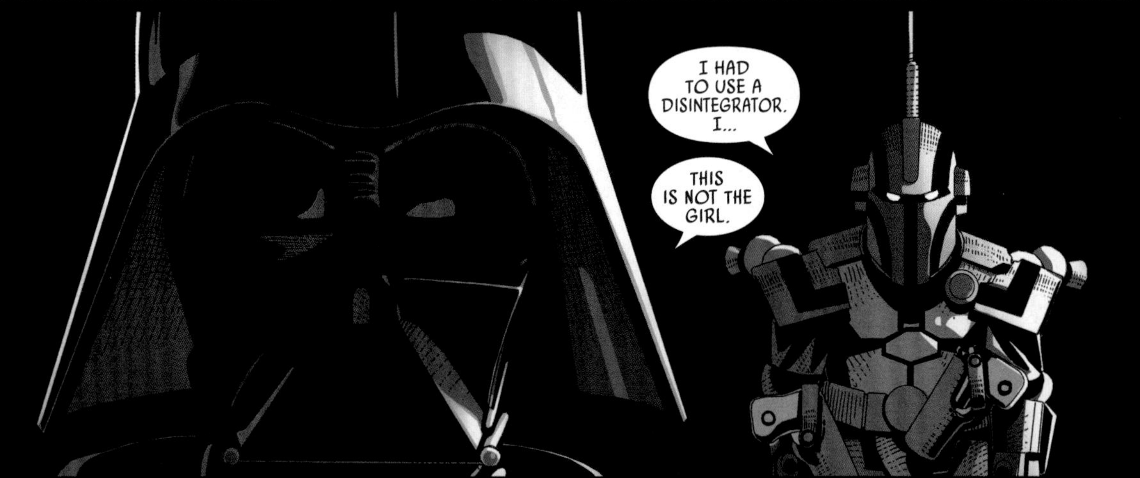
I HAD TO USE A DISINTEGRATOR. I...
THIS IS NOT THE GIRL.

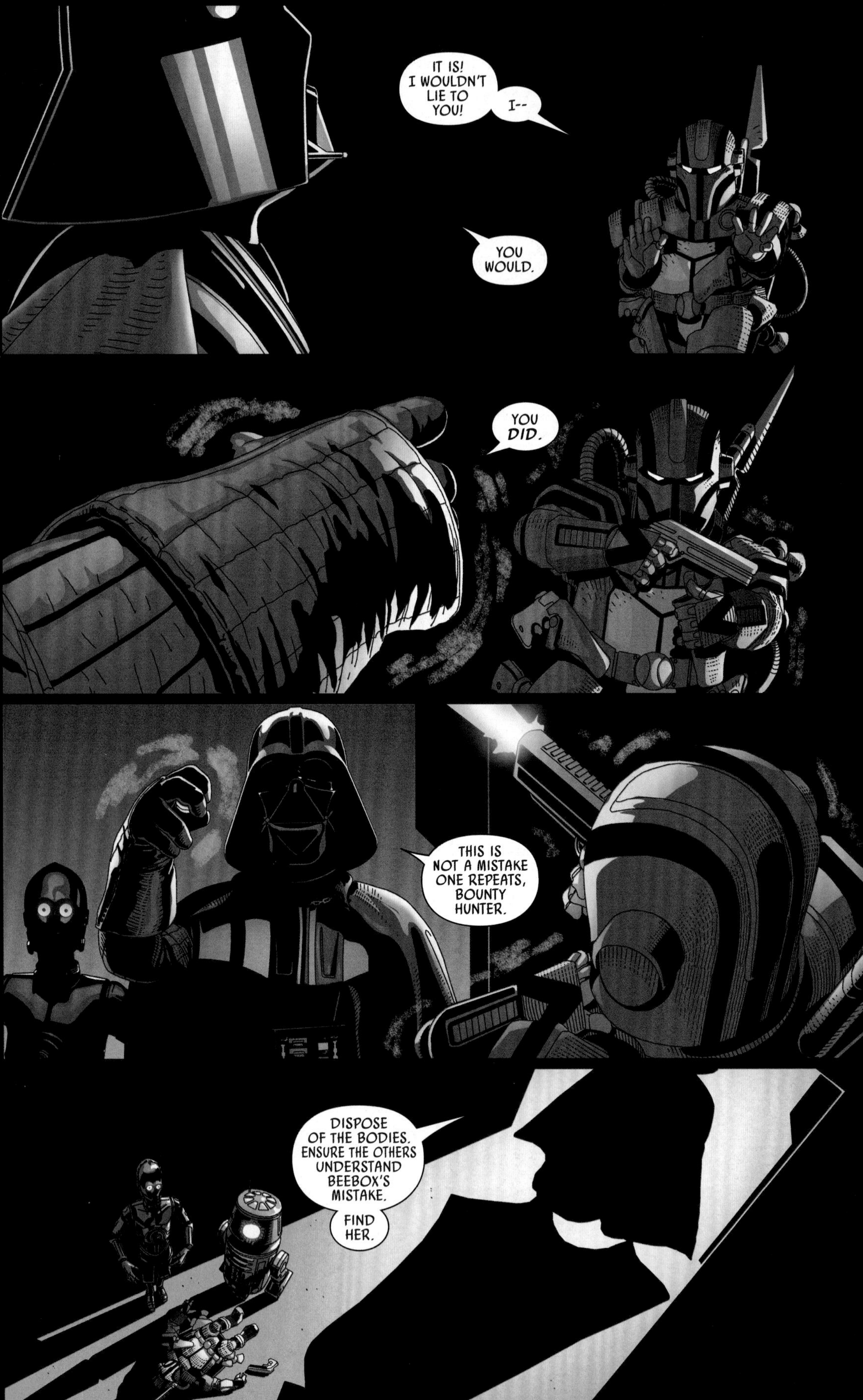
IT IS! I WOULDN'T LIE TO YOU!
I--
YOU WOULD.
YOU DID.
THIS IS NOT A MISTAKE ONE REPEATS, BOUNTY HUNTER.
DISPOSE OF THE BODIES. ENSURE THE OTHERS UNDERSTAND BEEBOX'S MISTAKE.
FIND HER.

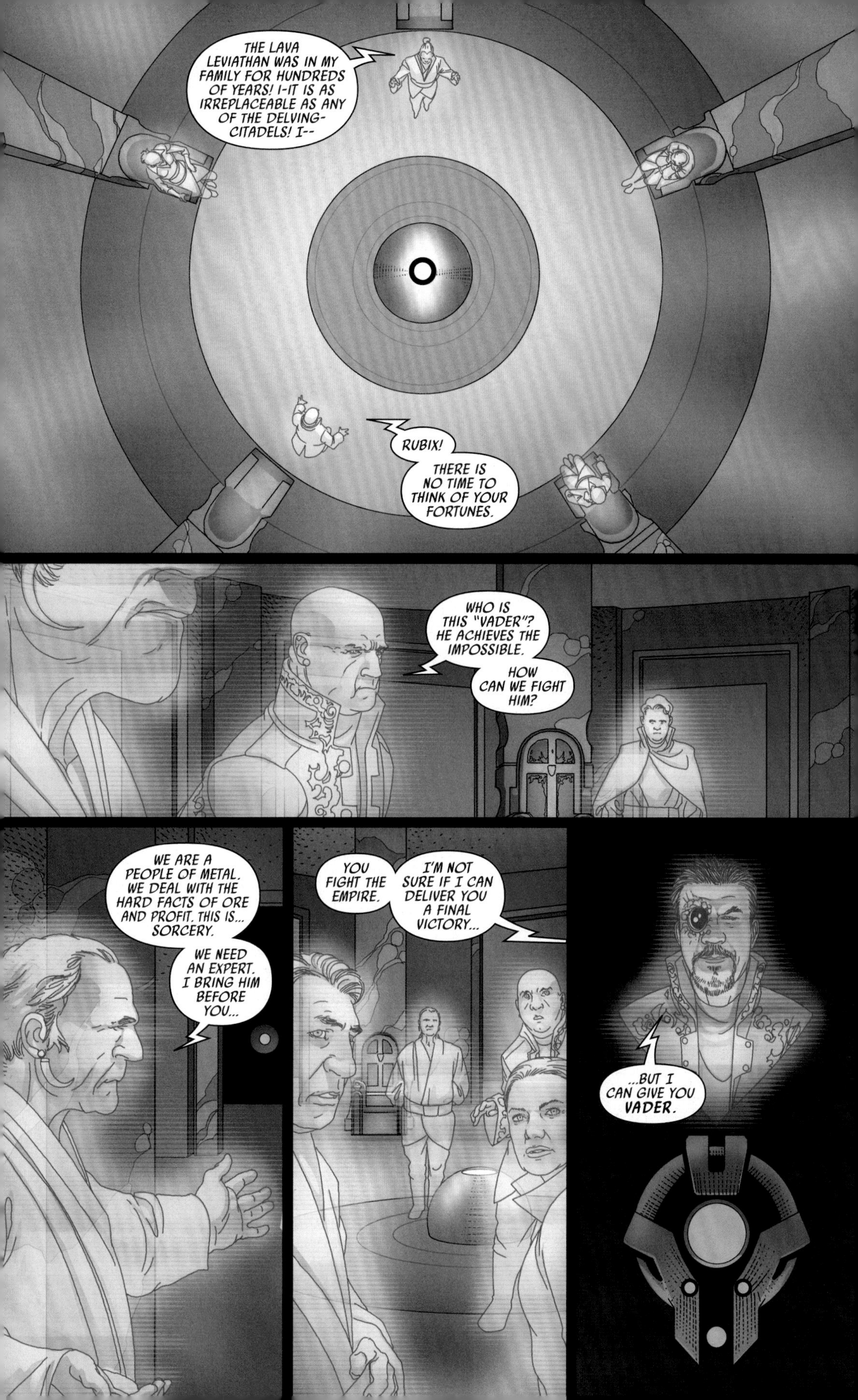
THE LAVA LEVIATHAN WAS IN MY FAMILY FOR HUNDREDS OF YEARS! I-IT IS AS IRREPLACEABLE AS ANY OF THE DELVING-CITADELS! I--
RUBIX!
THERE IS NO TIME TO THINK OF YOUR FORTUNES.
WHO IS THIS "VADER"? HE ACHIEVES THE IMPOSSIBLE.
HOW CAN WE FIGHT HIM?
WE ARE A PEOPLE OF METAL. WE DEAL WITH THE HARD FACTS OF ORE AND PROFIT. THIS IS... SORCERY.
WE NEED AN EXPERT. I BRING HIM BEFORE YOU...
YOU FIGHT THE EMPIRE.
I'M NOT SURE IF I CAN DELIVER YOU A FINAL VICTORY...
...BUT I CAN GIVE YOU VADER.

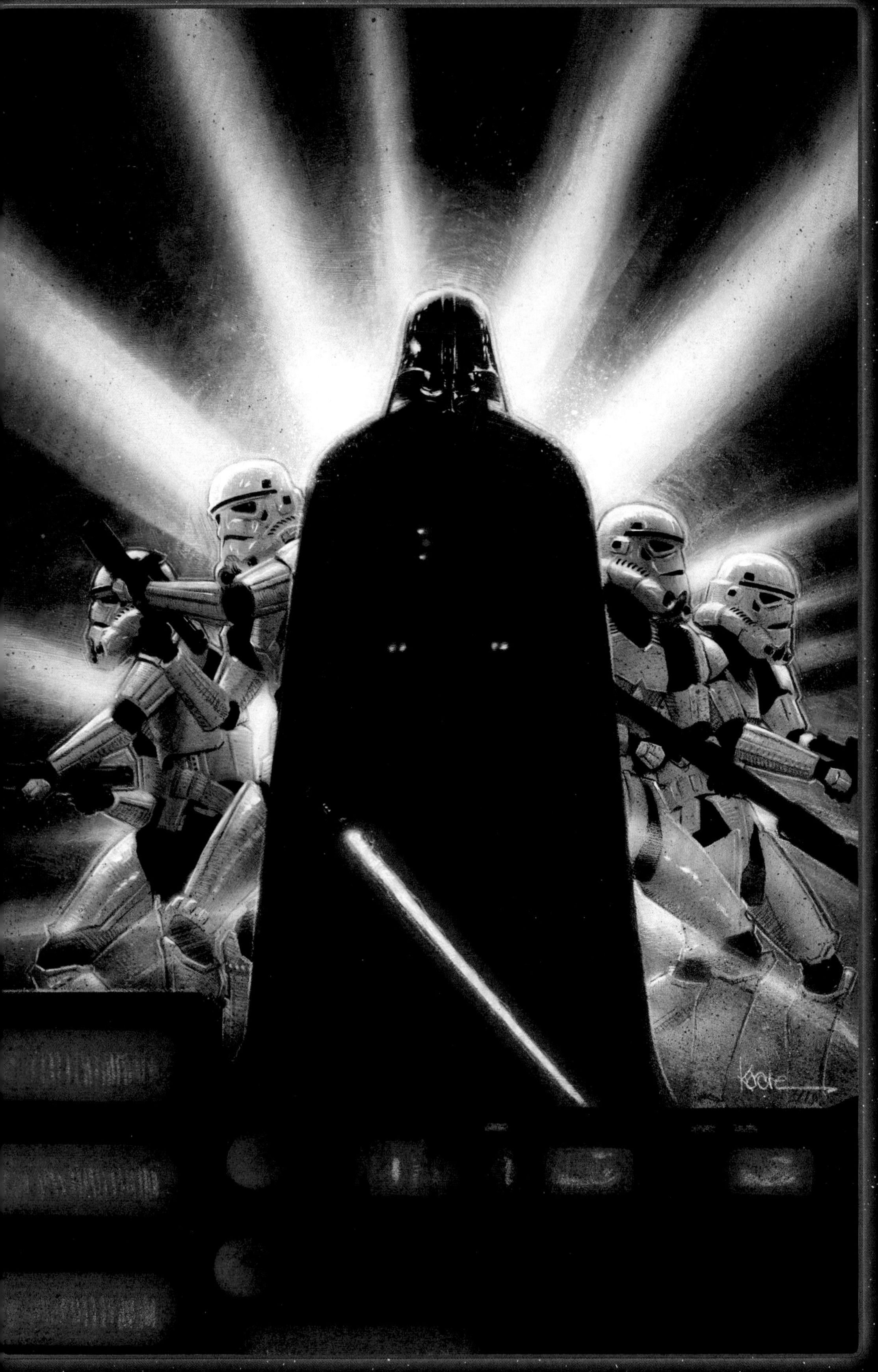

18

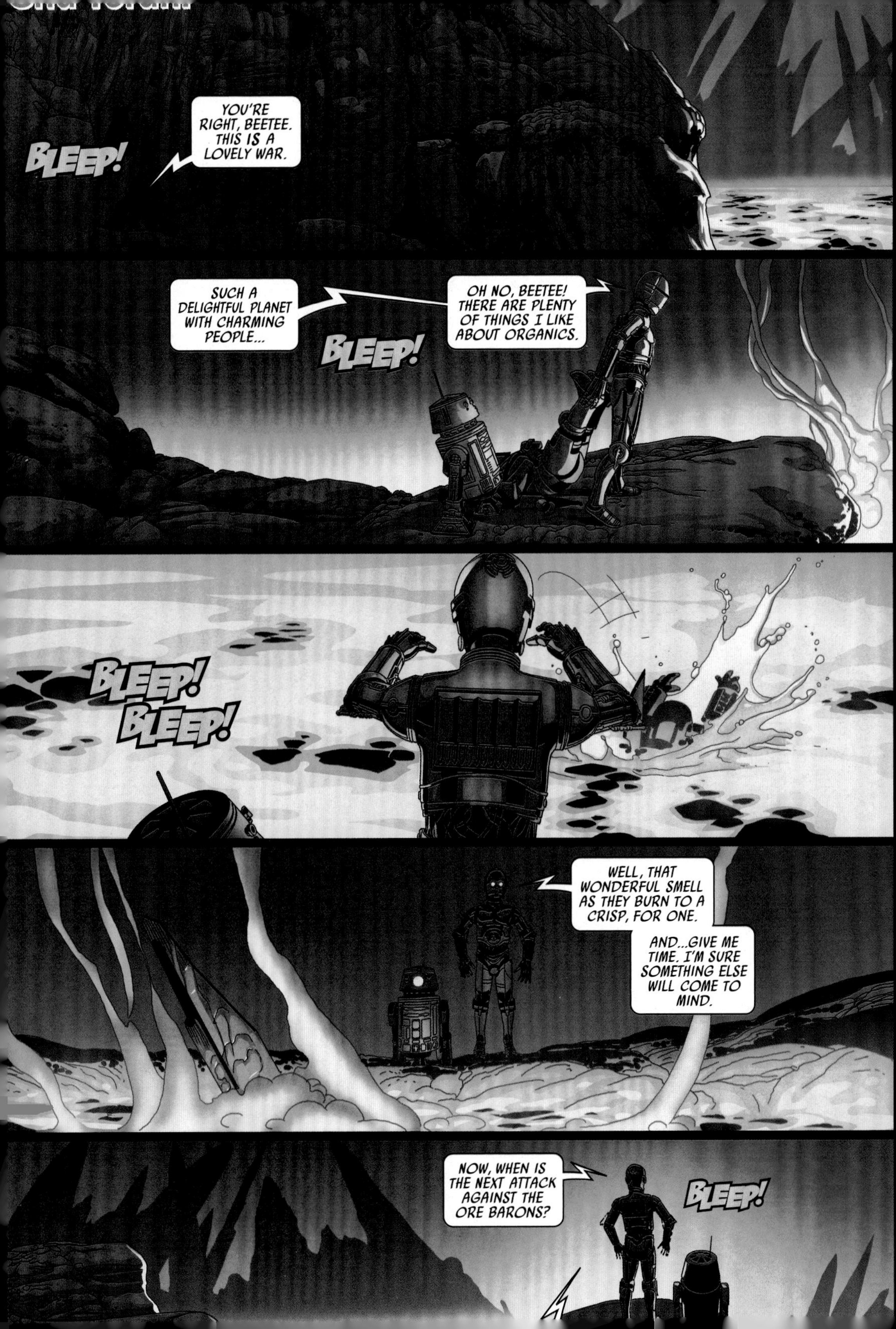
BLEEP!
YOU'RE RIGHT, BEETEE. THIS IS A LOVELY WAR.
SUCH A DELIGHTFUL PLANET WITH CHARMING PEOPLE...
OH NO, BEETEE! THERE ARE PLENTY OF THINGS I LIKE ABOUT ORGANICS.
BLEEP!
BLEEP! BLEEP!
WELL, THAT WONDERFUL SMELL AS THEY BURN TO A CRISP, FOR ONE.
AND...GIVE ME TIME. I'M SURE SOMETHING ELSE WILL COME TO MIND.
NOW, WHEN IS THE NEXT ATTACK AGAINST THE ORE BARONS?
BLEEP!

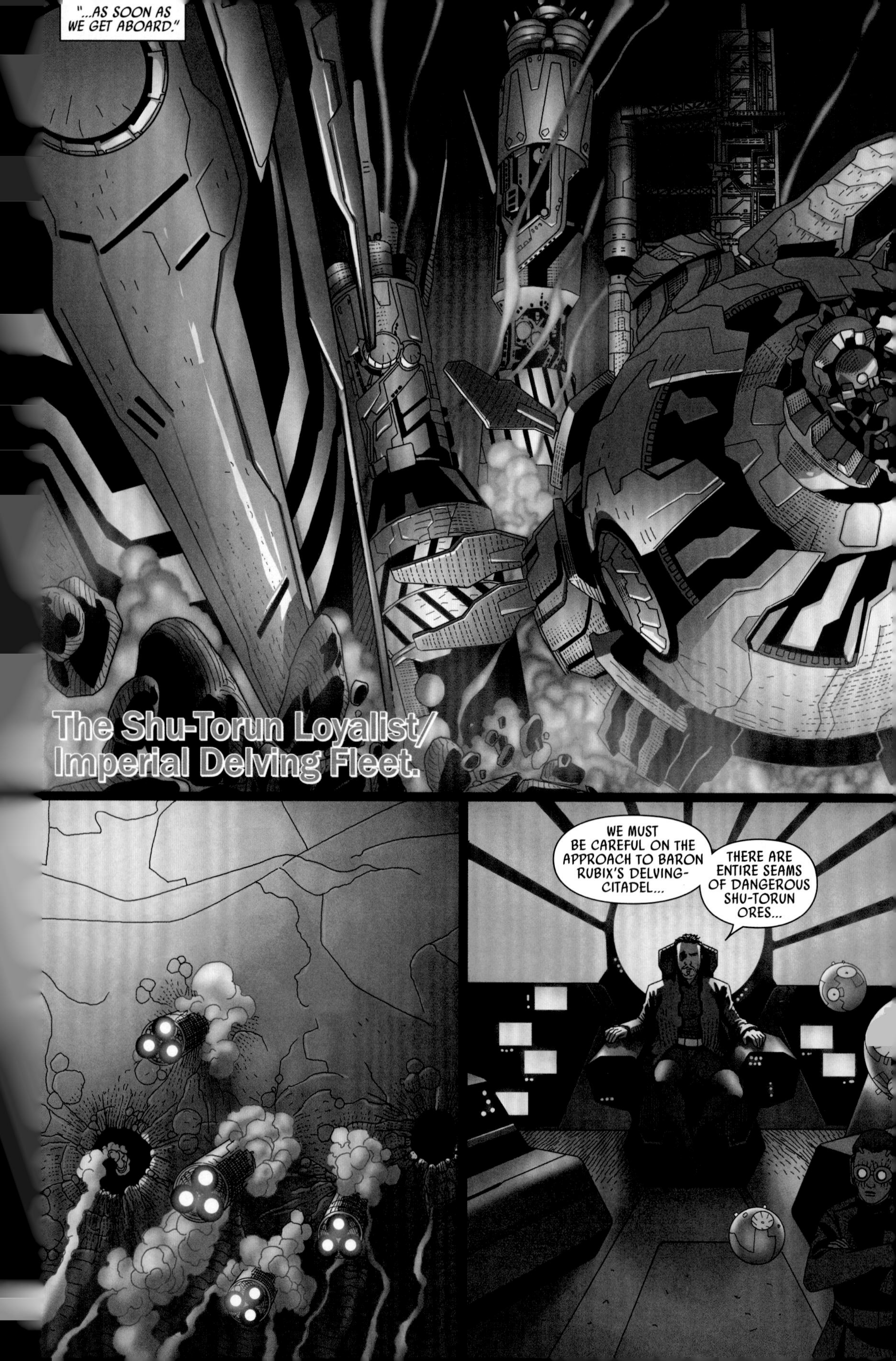
"...AS SOON AS WE GET ABOARD."
The Shu-Torun Loyalist/ Imperial Delving Fleet.
WE MUST BE CAREFUL ON THE APPROACH TO BARON RUBIX'S DELVING-CITADEL...
THERE ARE ENTIRE SEAMS OF DANGEROUS SHU-TORUN ORES...

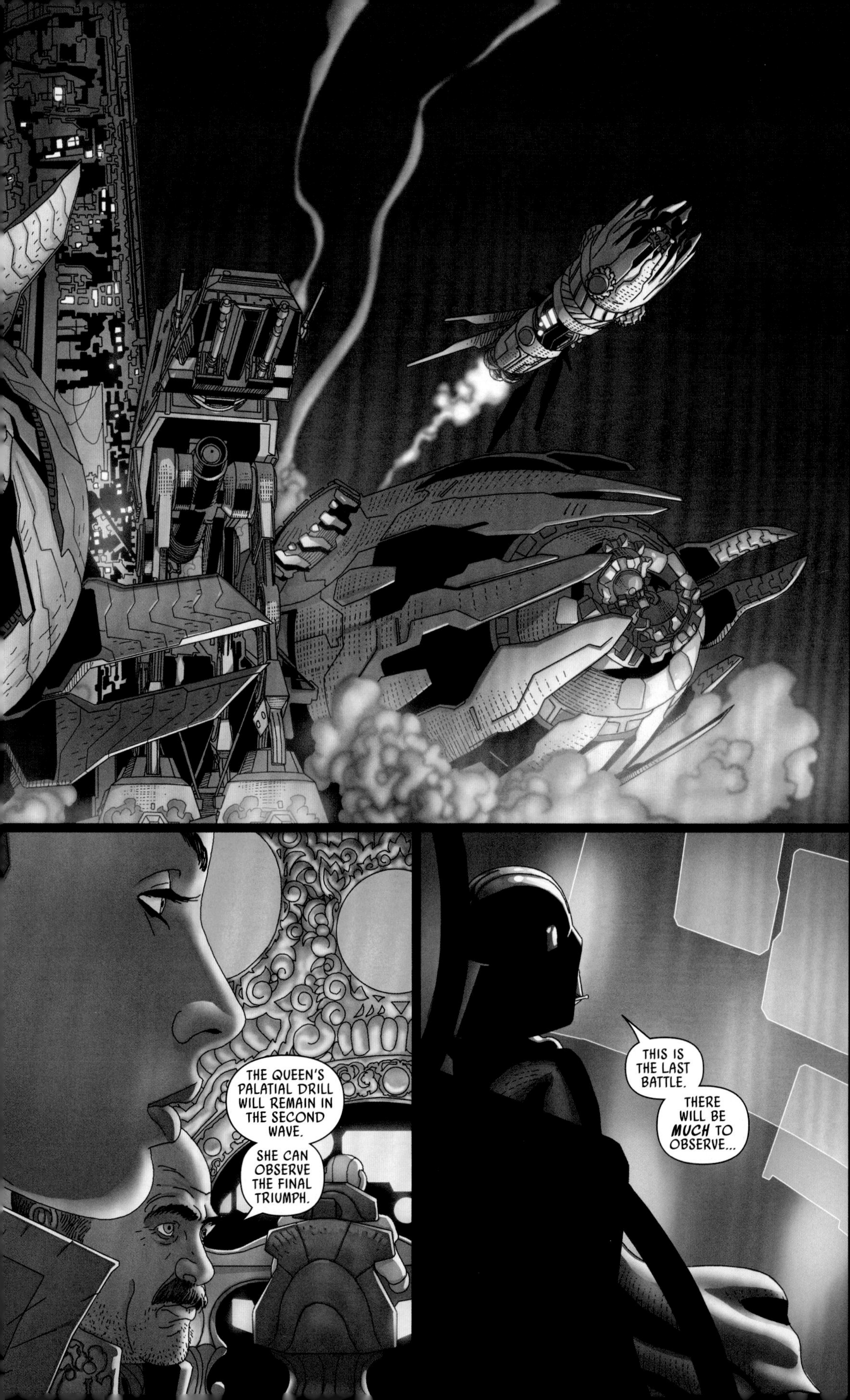
THE QUEEN'S PALATIAL DRILL WILL REMAIN IN THE SECOND WAVE.
SHE CAN OBSERVE THE FINAL TRIUMPH.
THIS IS THE LAST BATTLE.
THERE WILL BE *MUCH* TO OBSERVE...

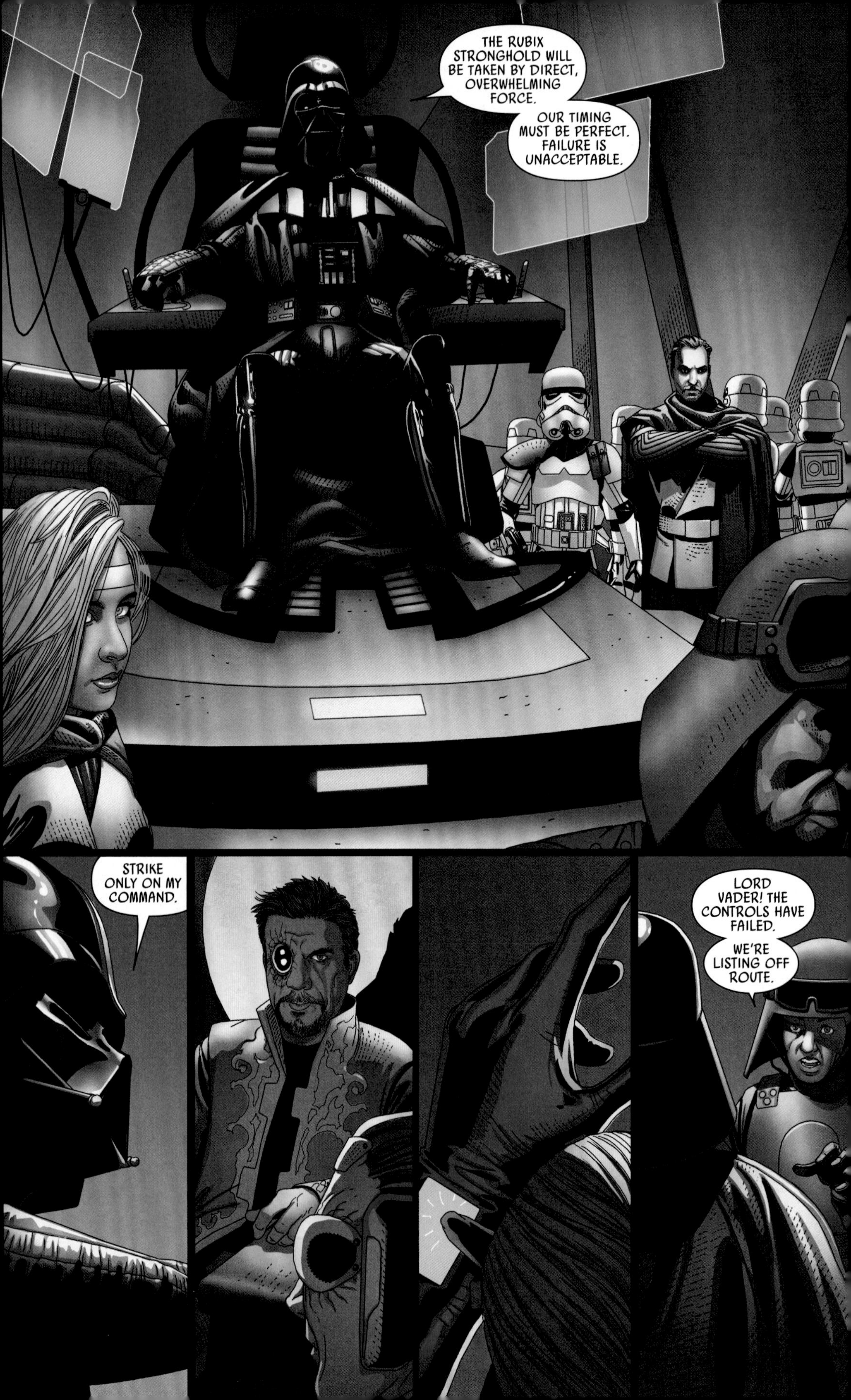
THE RUBIX STRONGHOLD WILL BE TAKEN BY DIRECT, OVERWHELMING FORCE.
OUR TIMING MUST BE PERFECT. FAILURE IS UNACCEPTABLE.
STRIKE ONLY ON MY COMMAND.
LORD VADER! THE CONTROLS HAVE FAILED.
WE'RE LISTING OFF ROUTE.

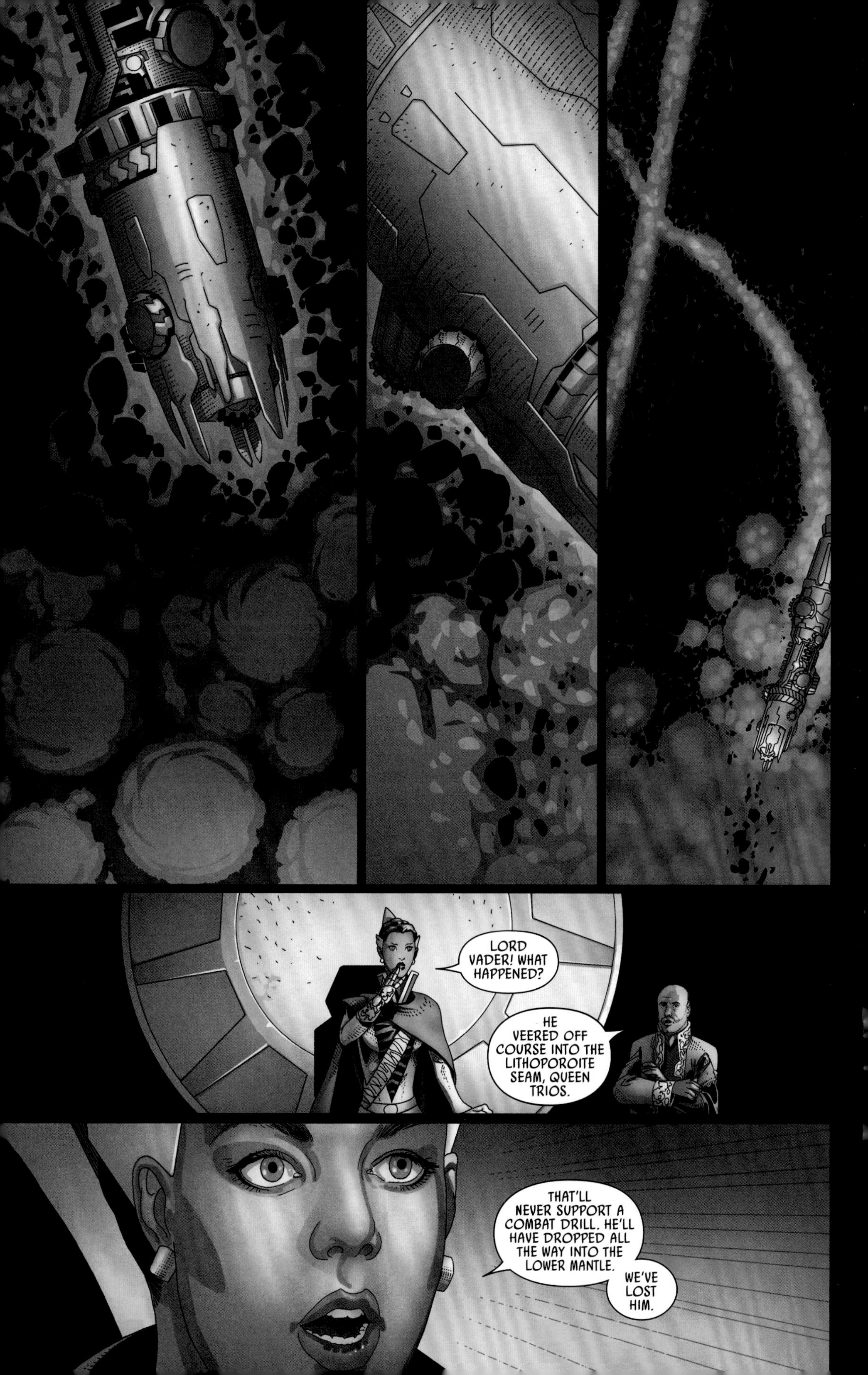
LORD VADER! WHAT HAPPENED?
HE VEERED OFF COURSE INTO THE LITHOPOROITE SEAM, QUEEN TRIOS.
THAT'LL NEVER SUPPORT A COMBAT DRILL. HE'LL HAVE DROPPED ALL THE WAY INTO THE LOWER MANTLE.
WE'VE LOST HIM.

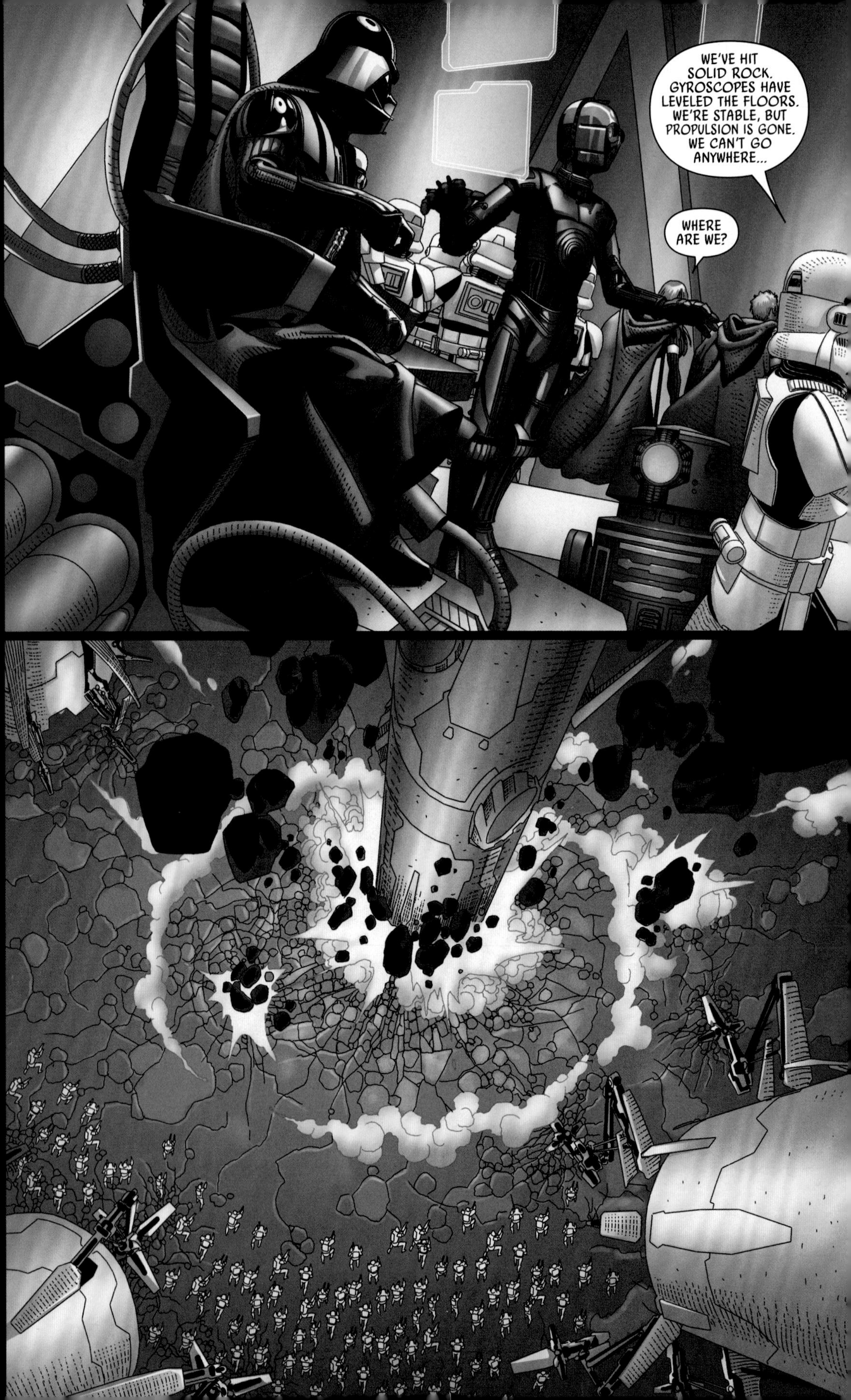
WE'VE HIT SOLID ROCK. GYROSCOPES HAVE LEVELED THE FLOORS. WE'RE STABLE, BUT PROPULSION IS GONE. WE CAN'T GO ANYWHERE...
WHERE ARE WE?

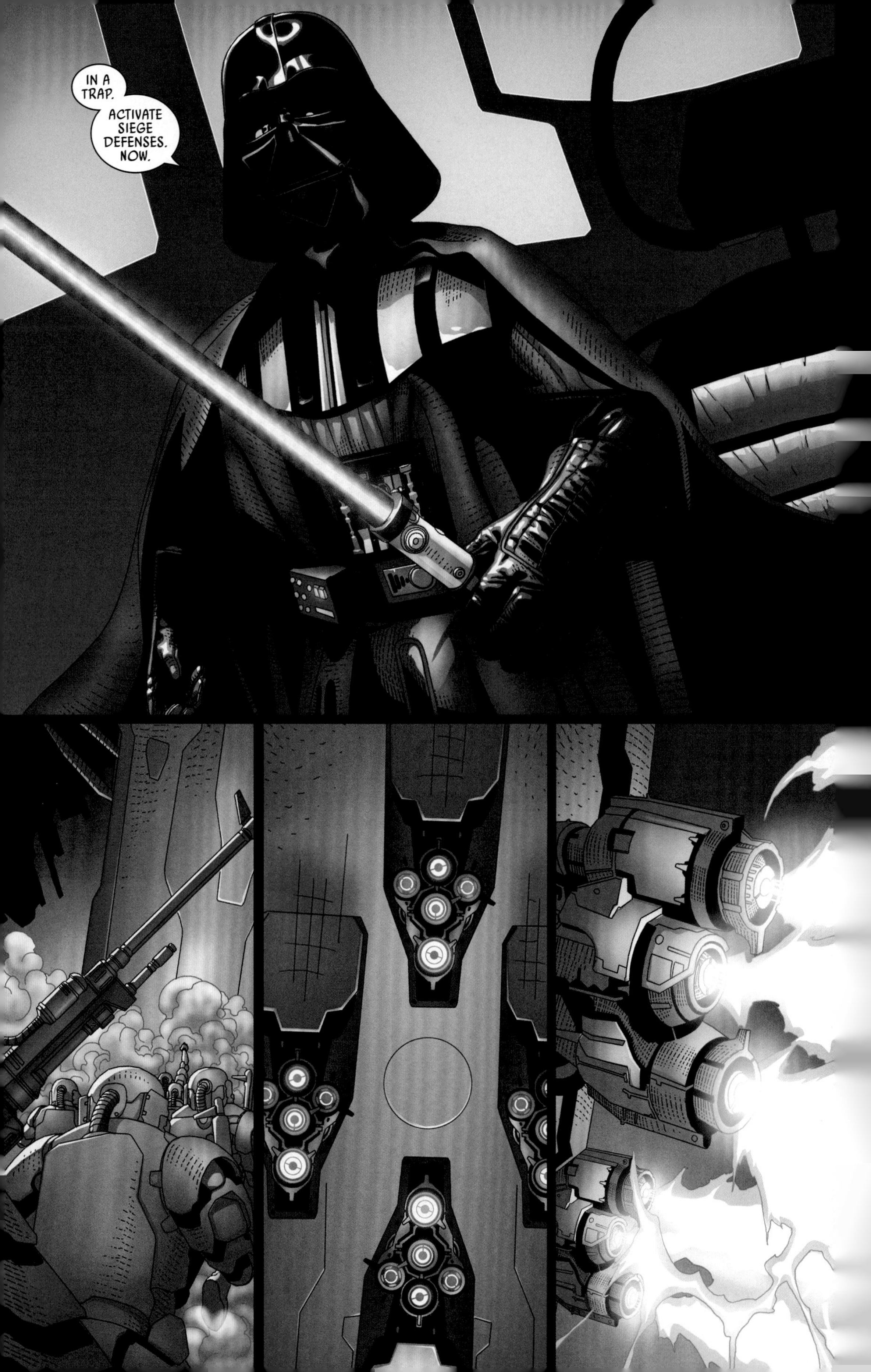
IN A TRAP.
ACTIVATE SIEGE DEFENSES. NOW.

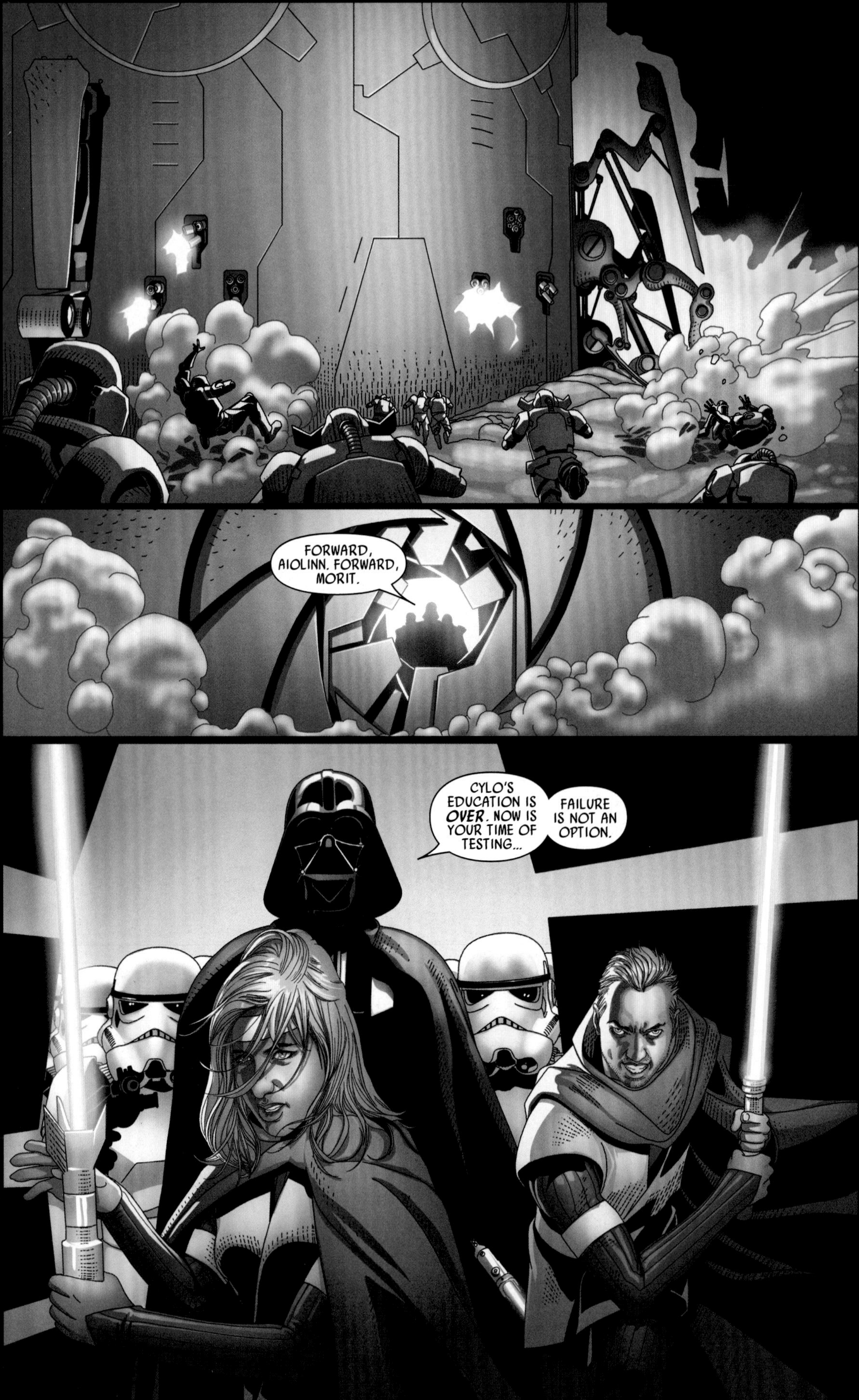
FORWARD, AIOLINN. FORWARD, MORIT.
CYLO'S EDUCATION IS OVER. NOW IS YOUR TIME OF TESTING...
FAILURE IS NOT AN OPTION.

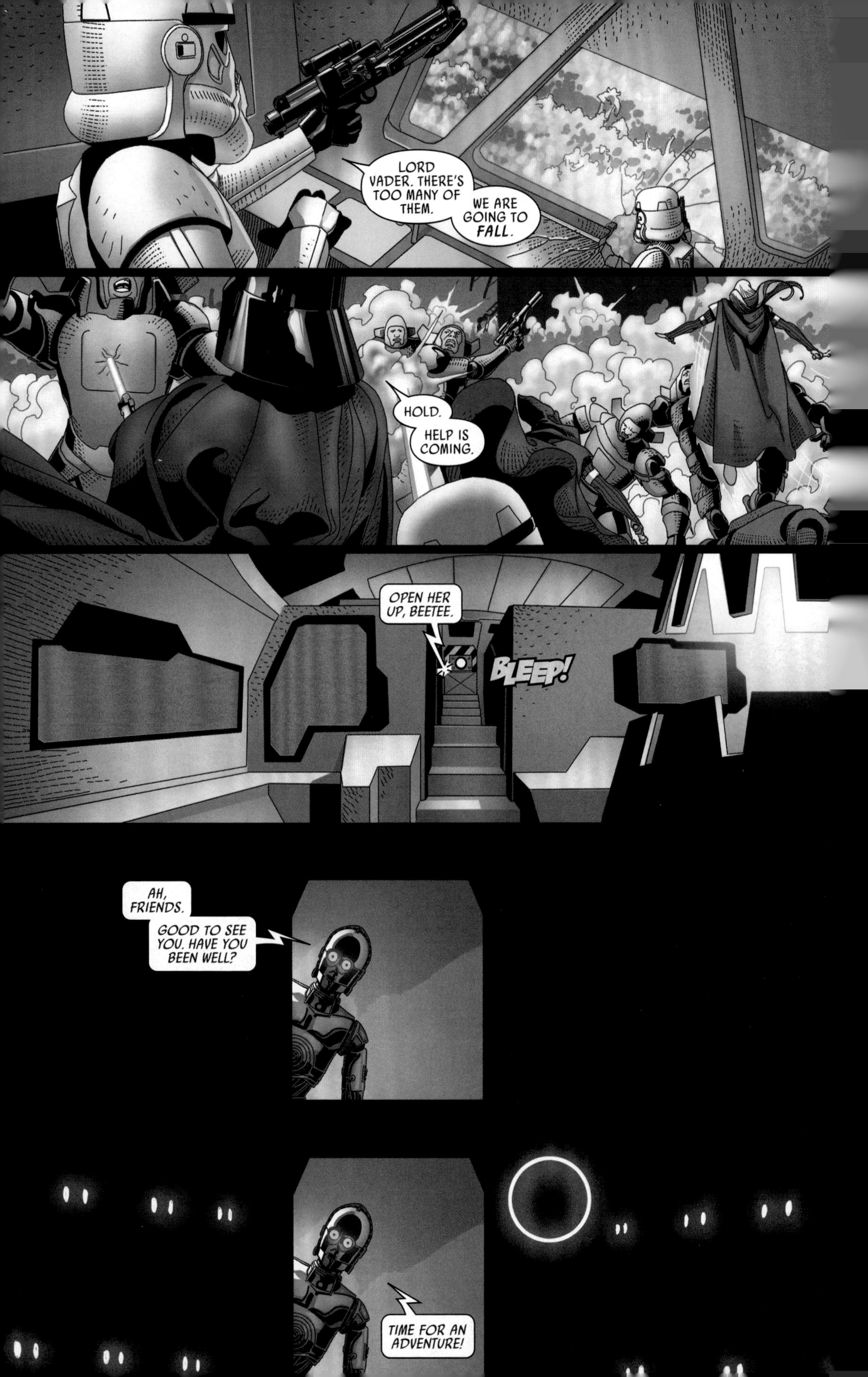

LORD VADER. THERE'S TOO MANY OF THEM.
WE ARE GOING TO FALL.
HOLD.
HELP IS COMING.
OPEN HER UP, BEETEE.
BLEEP!
AH, FRIENDS.
GOOD TO SEE YOU. HAVE YOU BEEN WELL?
TIME FOR AN ADVENTURE!

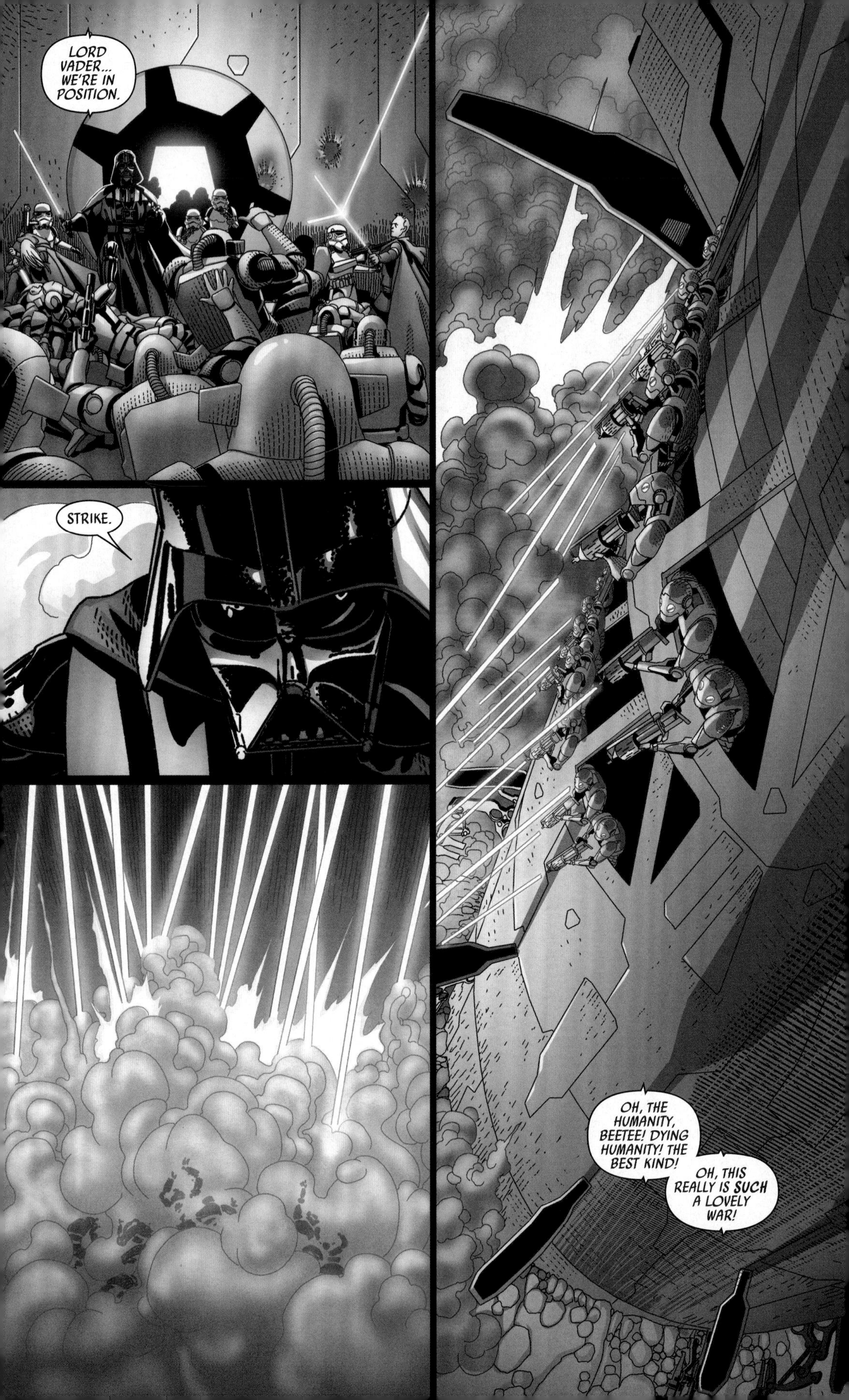
LORD VADER... WE'RE IN POSITION.
STRIKE.
OH, THE HUMANITY, BEETEE! DYING HUMANITY! THE BEST KIND!
OH, THIS REALLY IS SUCH A LOVELY WAR!

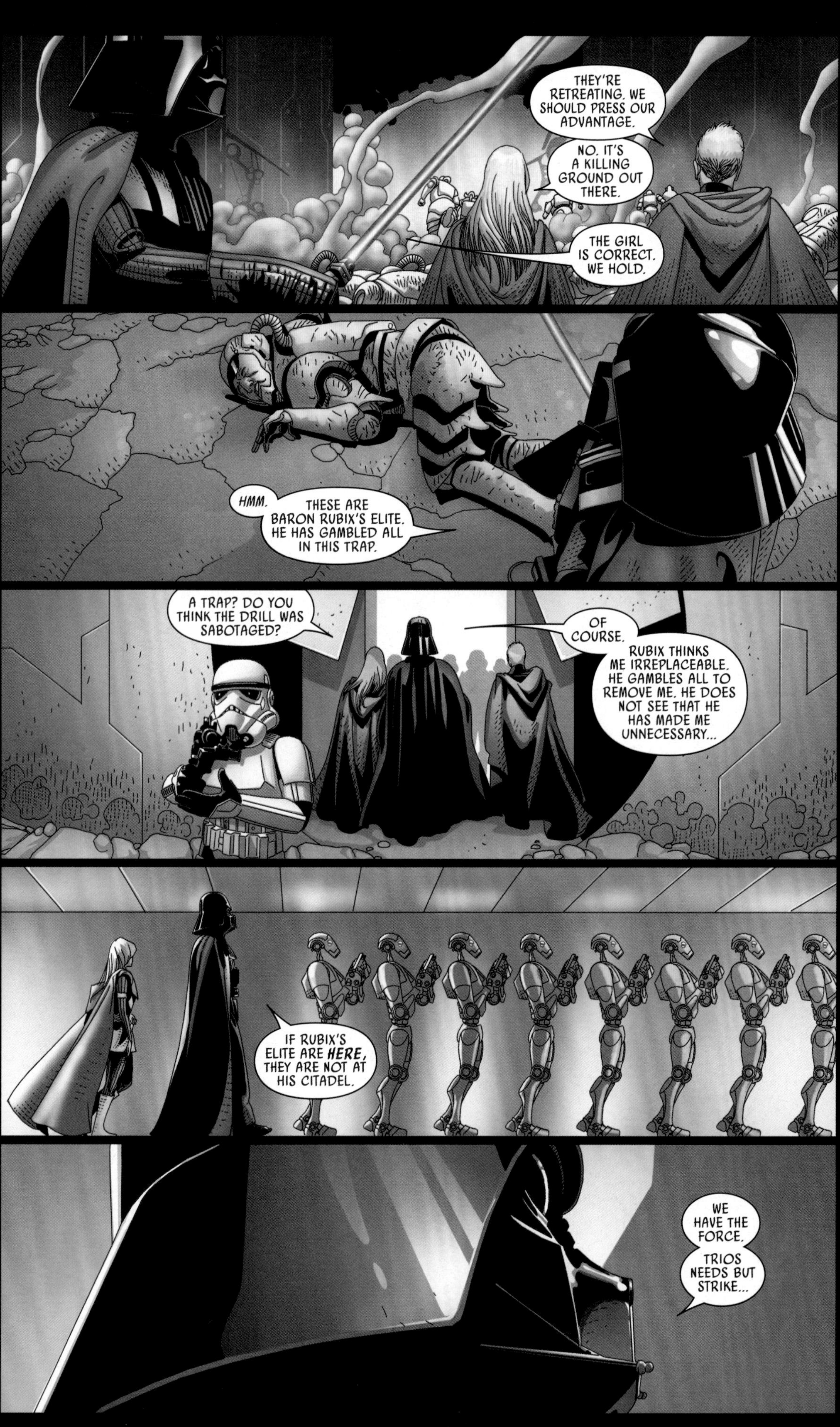

THEY'RE RETREATING. WE SHOULD PRESS OUR ADVANTAGE.
NO. IT'S A KILLING GROUND OUT THERE.
THE GIRL IS CORRECT. WE HOLD.
HMM.
THESE ARE BARON RUBIX'S ELITE. HE HAS GAMBLED ALL IN THIS TRAP.
A TRAP? DO YOU THINK THE DRILL WAS SABOTAGED?
OF COURSE.
RUBIX THINKS ME IRREPLACEABLE. HE GAMBLES ALL TO REMOVE ME. HE DOES NOT SEE THAT HE HAS MADE ME UNNECESSARY...
IF RUBIX'S ELITE ARE *HERE*, THEY ARE NOT AT HIS CITADEL.
WE HAVE THE FORCE.
TRIOS NEEDS BUT STRIKE...

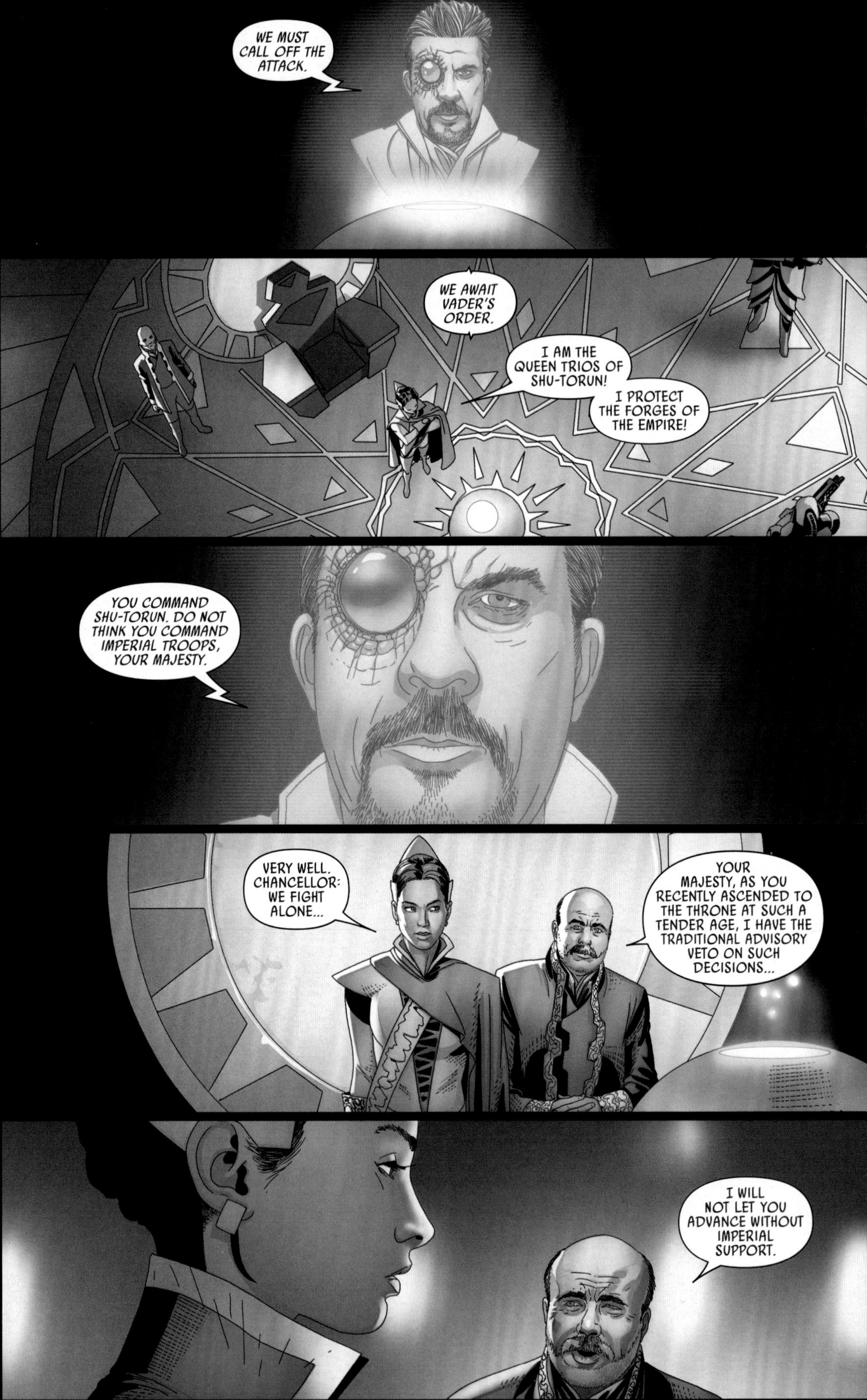
WE MUST CALL OFF THE ATTACK.
WE AWAIT VADER'S ORDER.
I AM THE QUEEN TRIOS OF SHU-TORUN!
I PROTECT THE FORGES OF THE EMPIRE!
YOU COMMAND SHU-TORUN. DO NOT THINK YOU COMMAND IMPERIAL TROOPS, YOUR MAJESTY.
VERY WELL. CHANCELLOR: WE FIGHT ALONE...
YOUR MAJESTY, AS YOU RECENTLY ASCENDED TO THE THRONE AT SUCH A TENDER AGE, I HAVE THE TRADITIONAL ADVISORY VETO ON SUCH DECISIONS...
I WILL NOT LET YOU ADVANCE WITHOUT IMPERIAL SUPPORT.

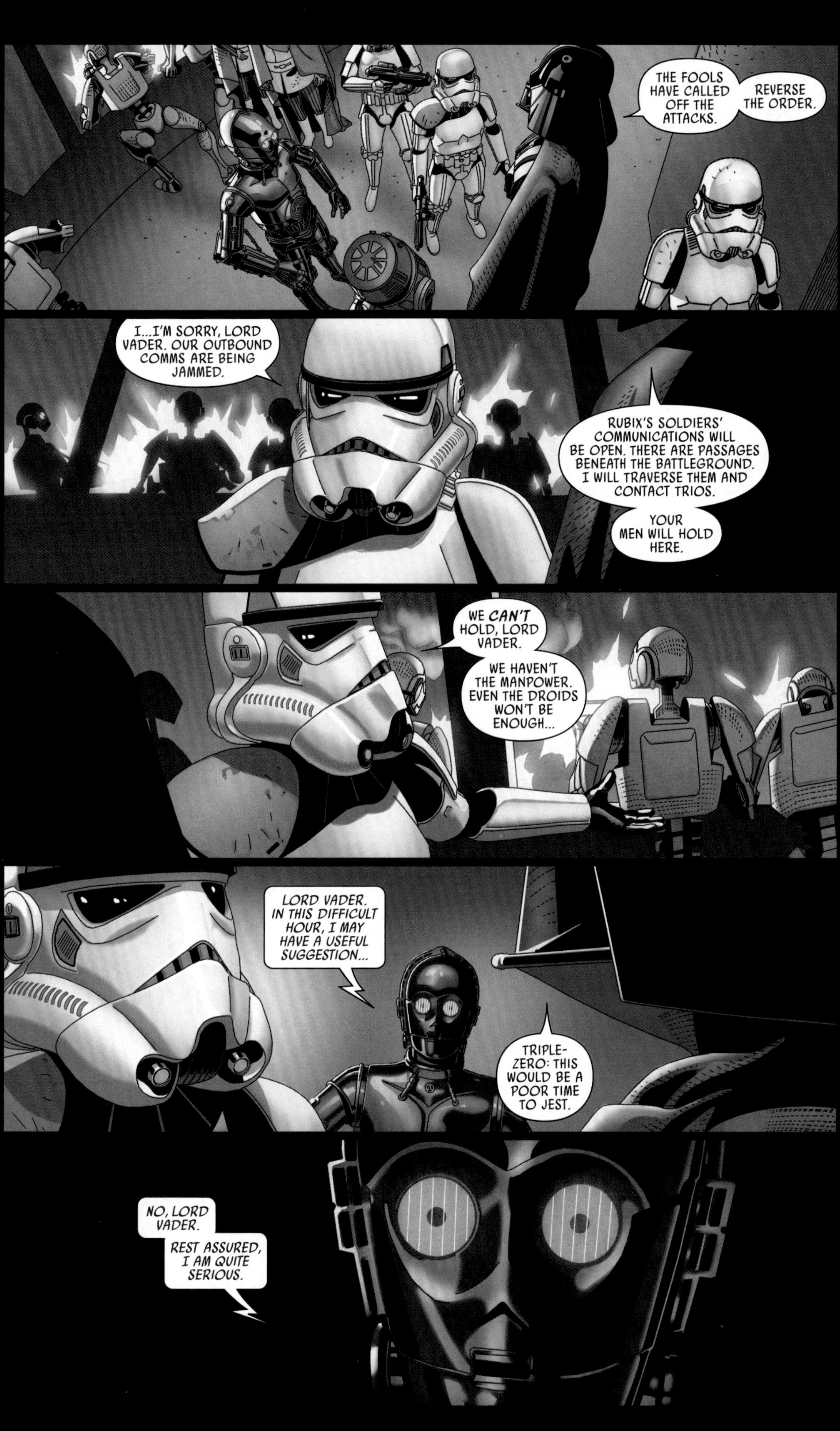
THE FOOLS HAVE CALLED OFF THE ATTACKS.
REVERSE THE ORDER.
I...I'M SORRY, LORD VADER. OUR OUTBOUND COMMS ARE BEING JAMMED.
RUBIX'S SOLDIERS' COMMUNICATIONS WILL BE OPEN. THERE ARE PASSAGES BENEATH THE BATTLEGROUND. I WILL TRAVERSE THEM AND CONTACT TRIOS.
YOUR MEN WILL HOLD HERE.
WE CAN'T HOLD, LORD VADER.
WE HAVEN'T THE MANPOWER. EVEN THE DROIDS WON'T BE ENOUGH...
LORD VADER. IN THIS DIFFICULT HOUR, I MAY HAVE A USEFUL SUGGESTION...
TRIPLE-ZERO: THIS WOULD BE A POOR TIME TO JEST.
NO, LORD VADER.
REST ASSURED, I AM QUITE SERIOUS.

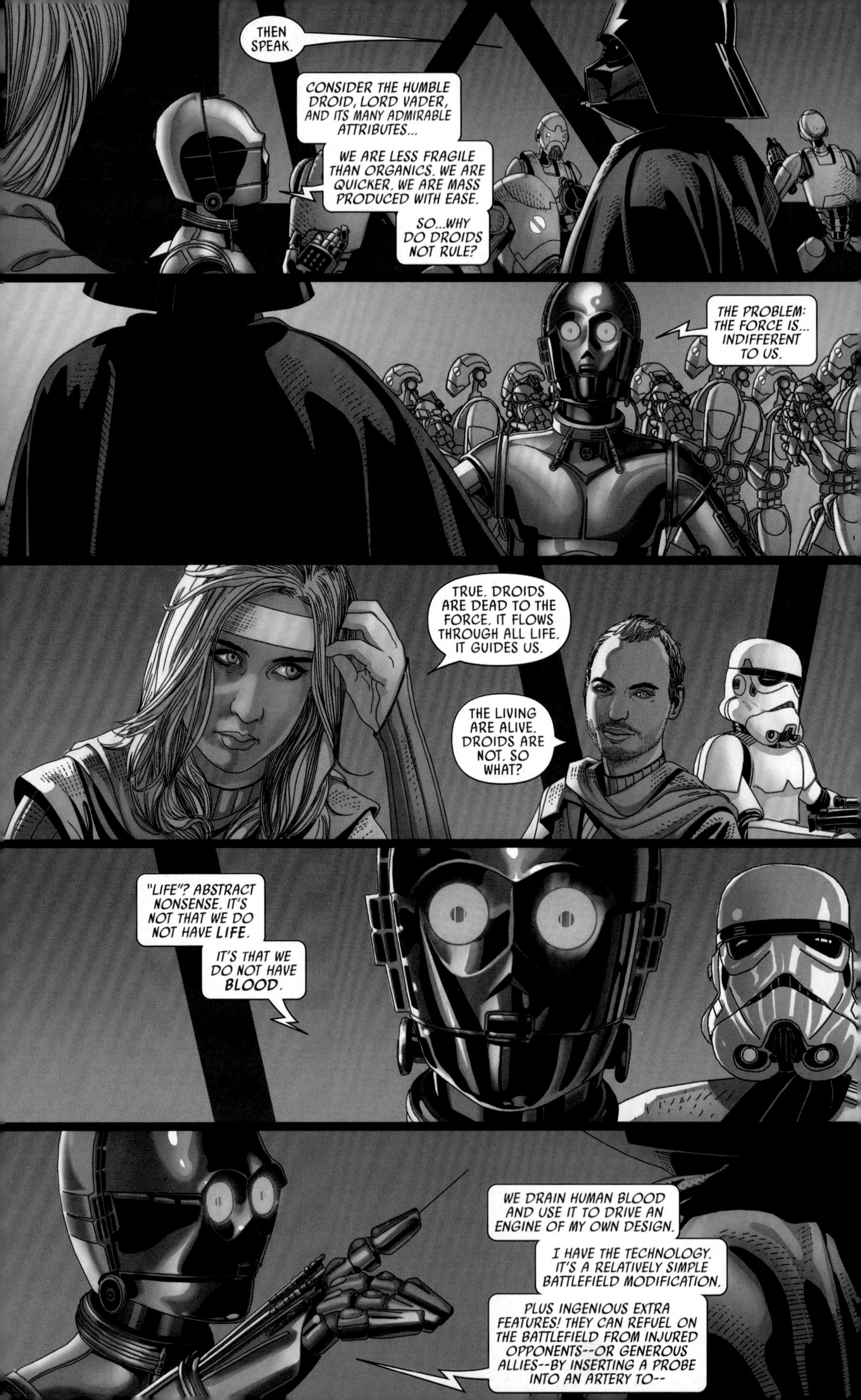
THEN SPEAK.
CONSIDER THE HUMBLE DROID, LORD VADER, AND ITS MANY ADMIRABLE ATTRIBUTES...
WE ARE LESS FRAGILE THAN ORGANICS. WE ARE QUICKER. WE ARE MASS PRODUCED WITH EASE.
SO...WHY DO DROIDS NOT RULE?
THE PROBLEM: THE FORCE IS... INDIFFERENT TO US.
TRUE. DROIDS ARE DEAD TO THE FORCE. IT FLOWS THROUGH ALL LIFE. IT GUIDES US.
THE LIVING ARE ALIVE. DROIDS ARE NOT. SO WHAT?
"LIFE"? ABSTRACT NONSENSE. IT'S NOT THAT WE DO NOT HAVE LIFE.
IT'S THAT WE DO NOT HAVE BLOOD.
WE DRAIN HUMAN BLOOD AND USE IT TO DRIVE AN ENGINE OF MY OWN DESIGN.
I HAVE THE TECHNOLOGY. IT'S A RELATIVELY SIMPLE BATTLEFIELD MODIFICATION.
PLUS INGENIOUS EXTRA FEATURES! THEY CAN REFUEL ON THE BATTLEFIELD FROM INJURED OPPONENTS--OR GENEROUS ALLIES--BY INSERTING A PROBE INTO AN ARTERY TO--

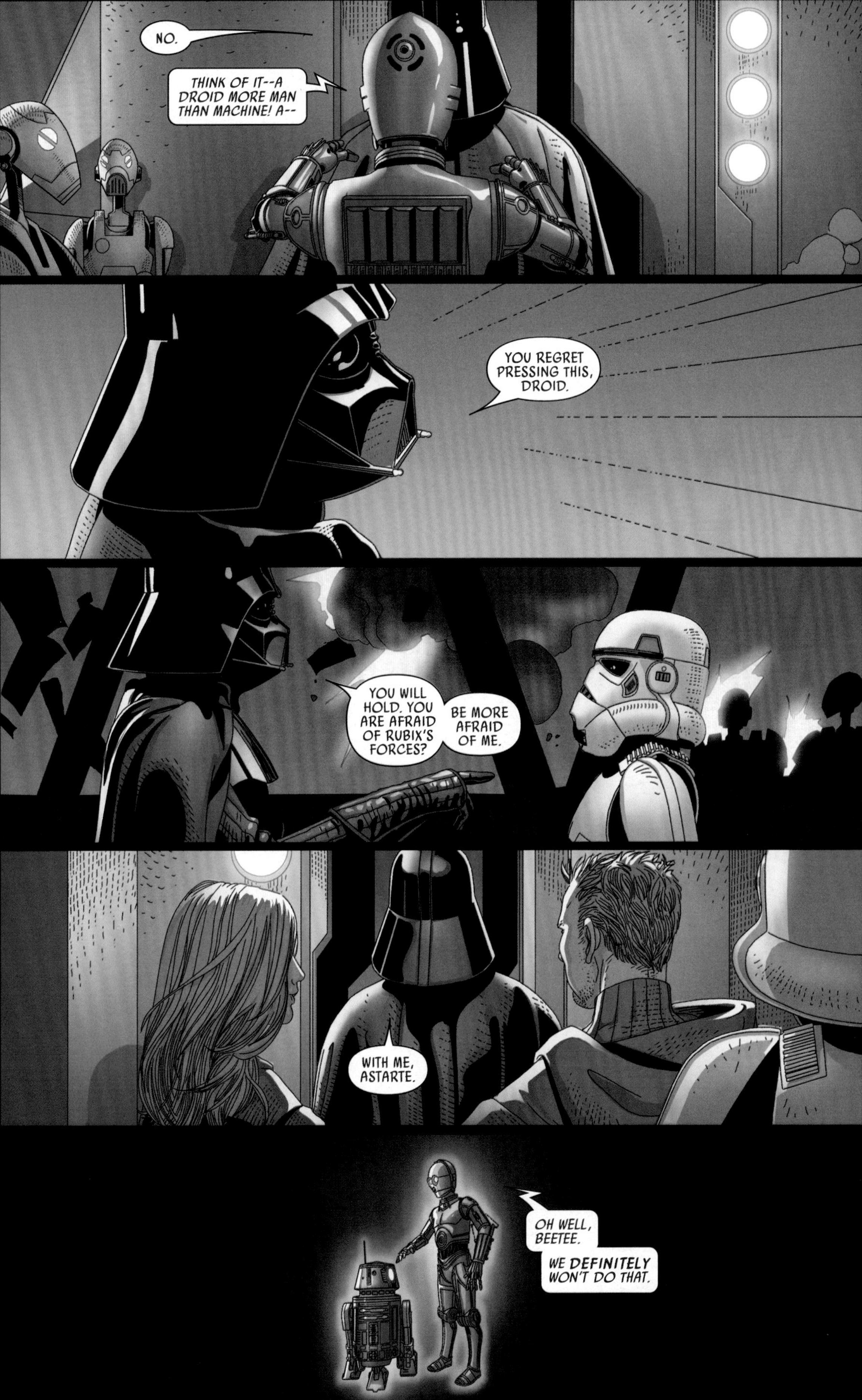
NO.
THINK OF IT--A DROID MORE MAN THAN MACHINE! A--
YOU REGRET PRESSING THIS, DROID.
YOU WILL HOLD. YOU ARE AFRAID OF RUBIX'S FORCES?
BE MORE AFRAID OF ME.
WITH ME, ASTARTE.
OH WELL, BEETEE.
WE DEFINITELY WON'T DO THAT.

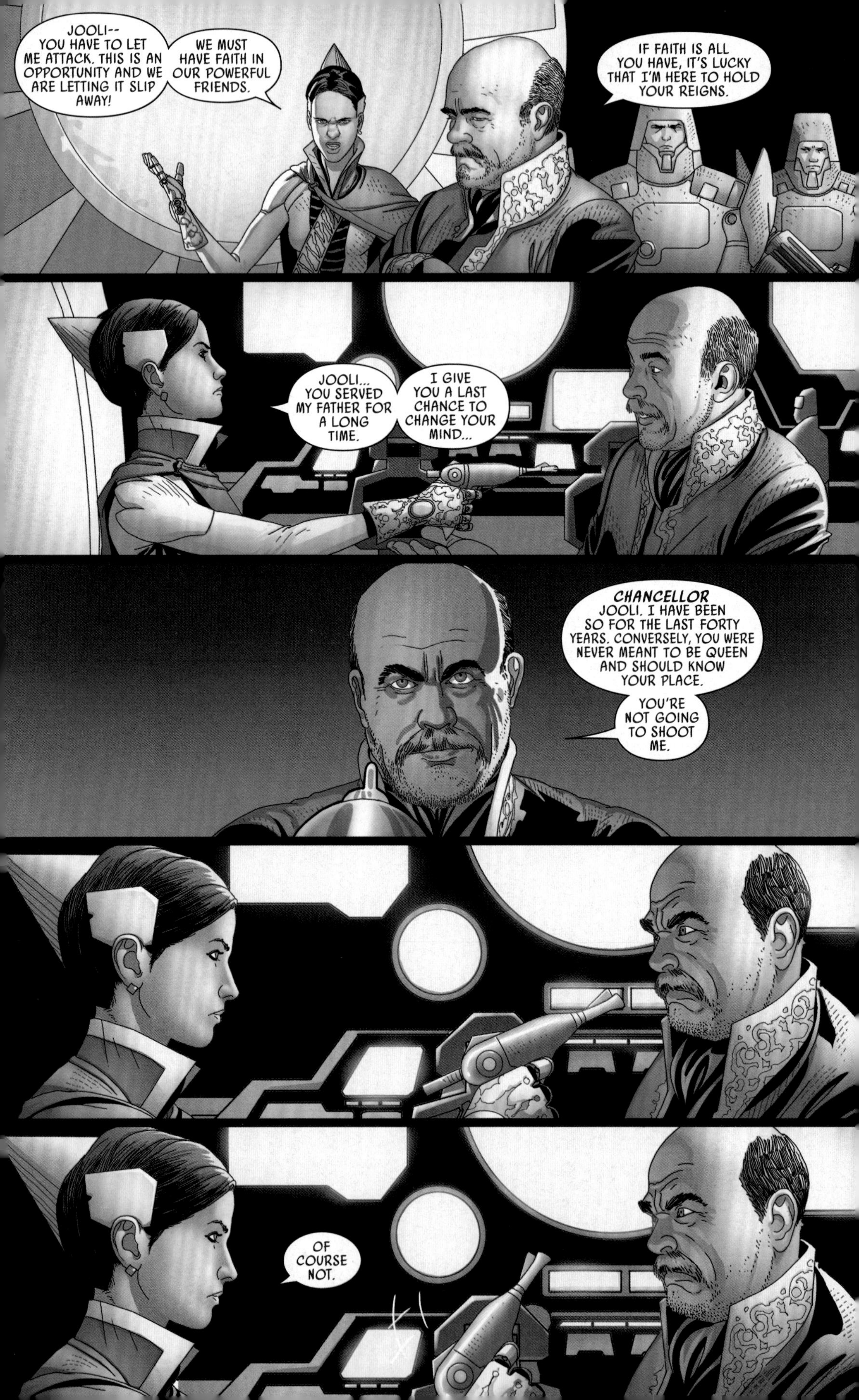
JOOLI--
YOU HAVE TO LET ME ATTACK. THIS IS AN OPPORTUNITY AND WE ARE LETTING IT SLIP AWAY!
WE MUST HAVE FAITH IN OUR POWERFUL FRIENDS.
IF FAITH IS ALL YOU HAVE, IT'S LUCKY THAT I'M HERE TO HOLD YOUR REIGNS.
JOOLI... YOU SERVED MY FATHER FOR A LONG TIME.
I GIVE YOU A LAST CHANCE TO CHANGE YOUR MIND...
*CHANCELLOR* JOOLI. I HAVE BEEN SO FOR THE LAST FORTY YEARS. CONVERSELY, YOU WERE NEVER MEANT TO BE QUEEN AND SHOULD KNOW YOUR PLACE.
YOU'RE NOT GOING TO SHOOT ME.
OF COURSE NOT.

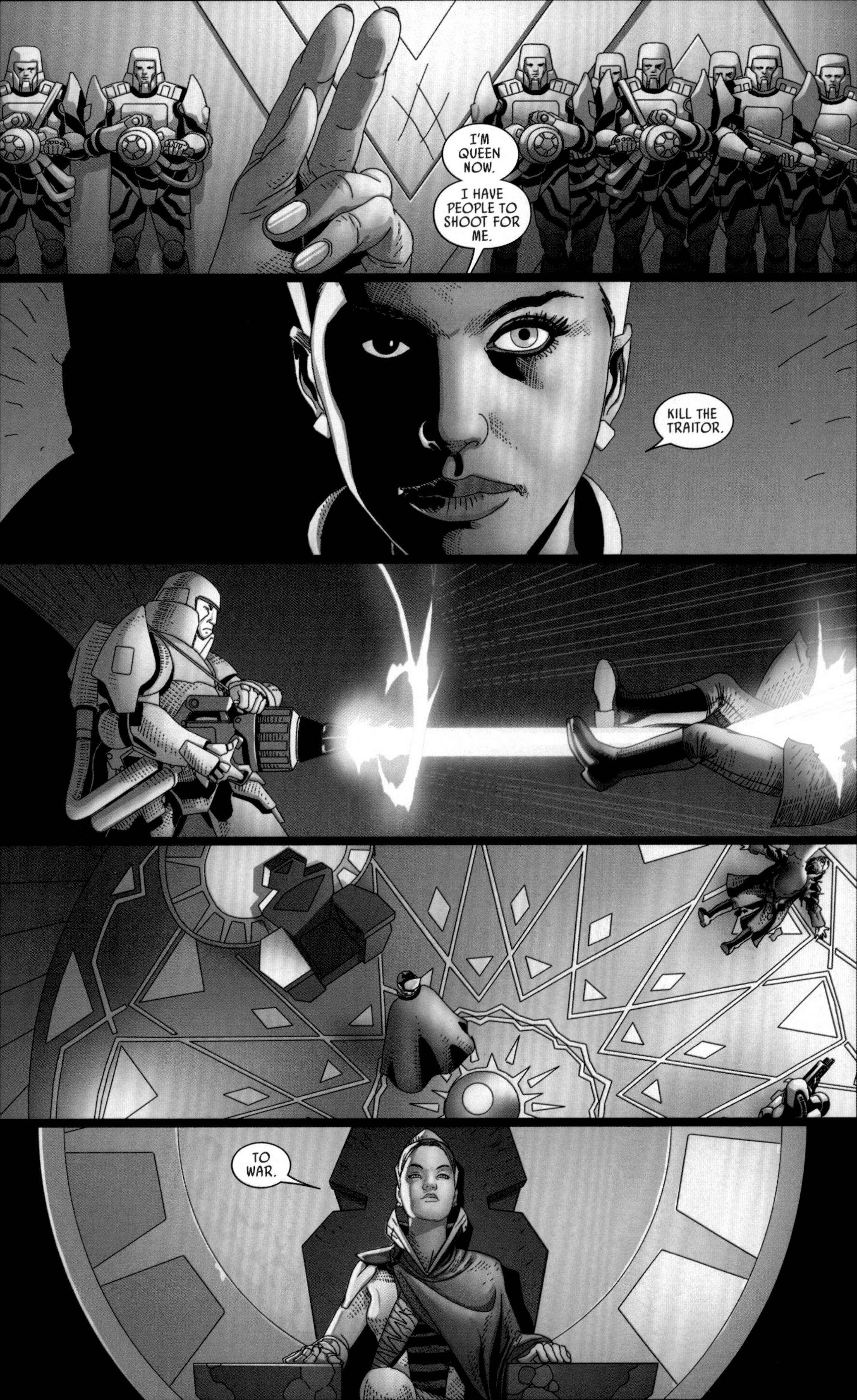
I'M QUEEN NOW.
I HAVE PEOPLE TO SHOOT FOR ME.
KILL THE TRAITOR.
TO WAR.

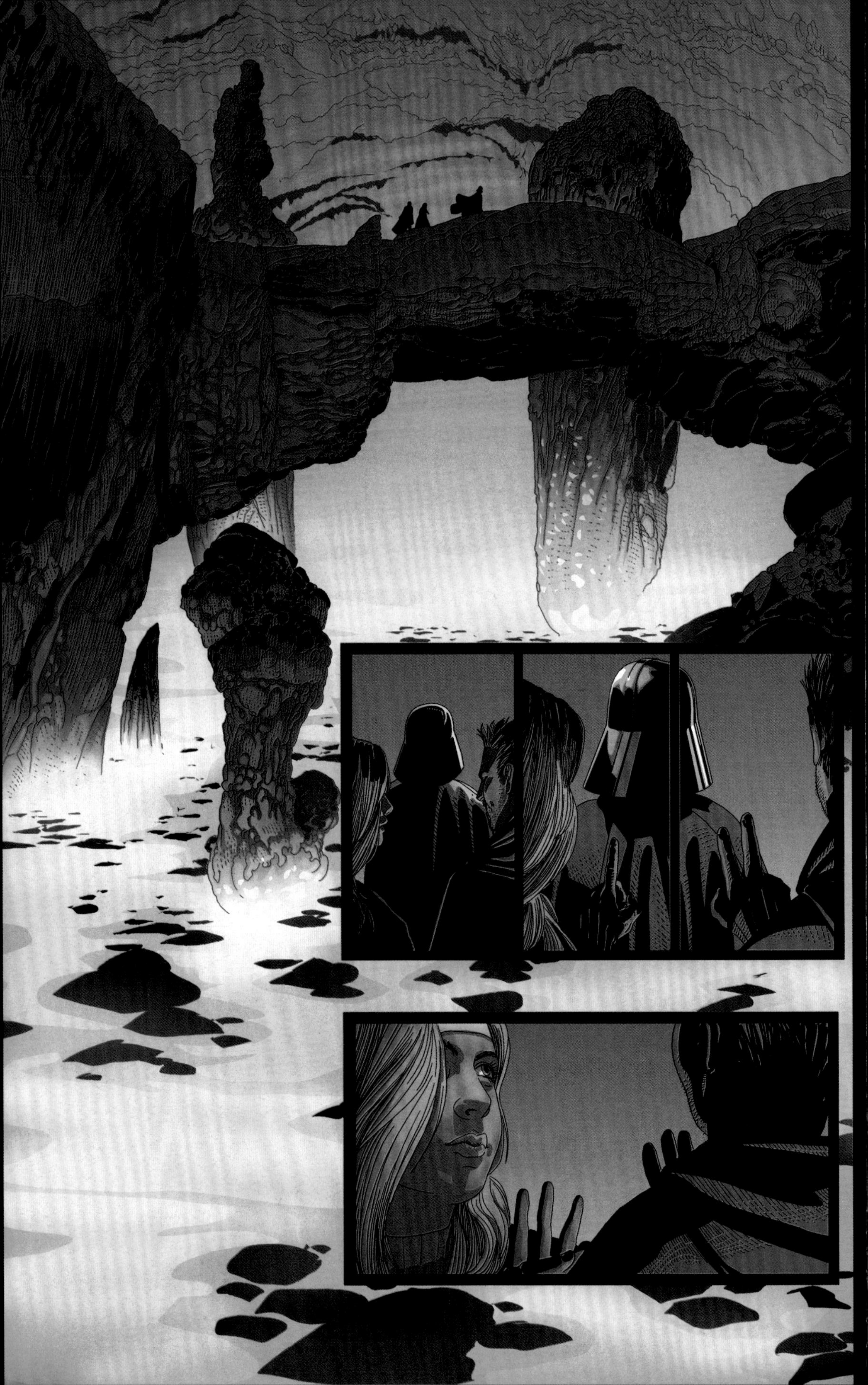

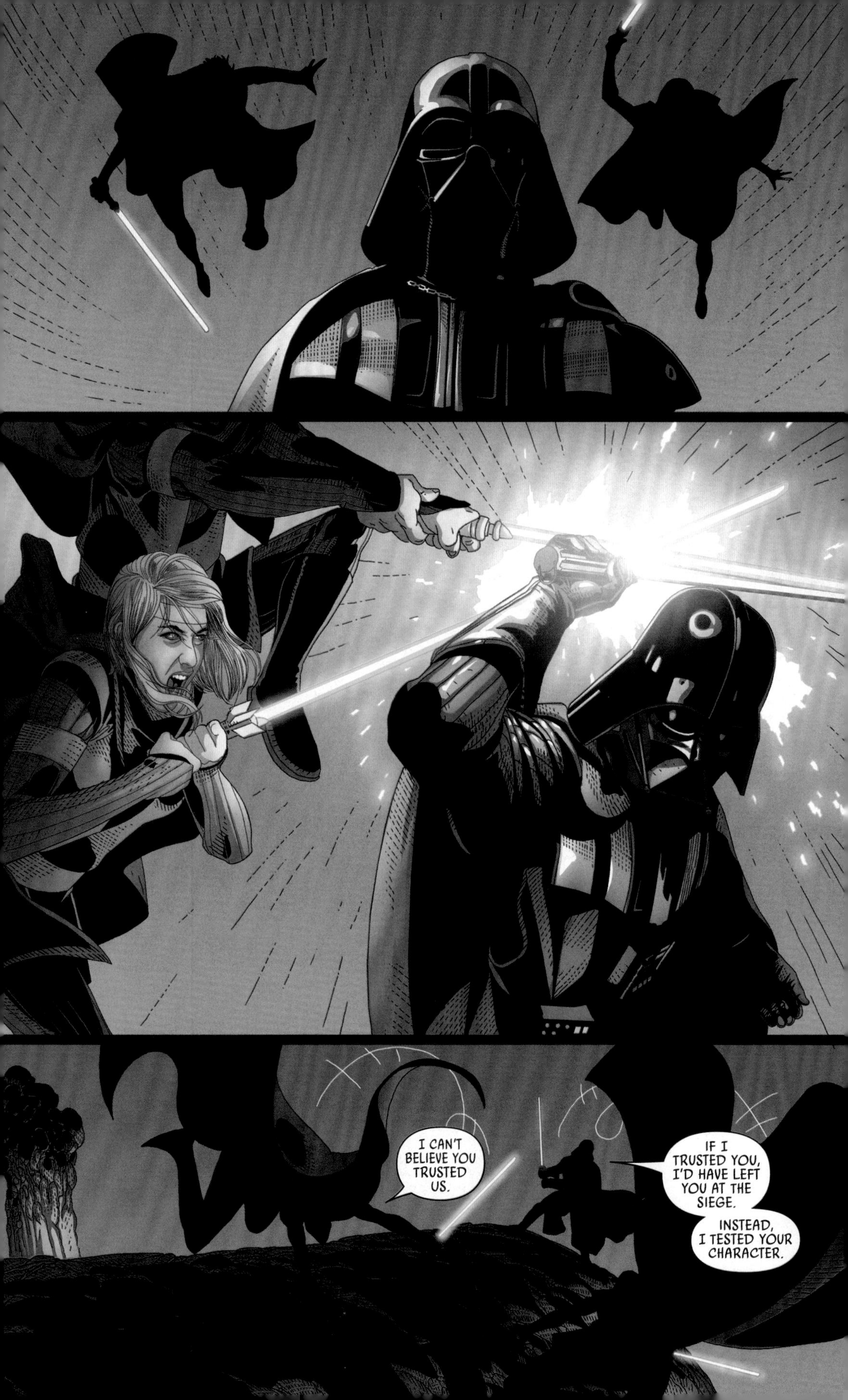
I CAN'T BELIEVE YOU TRUSTED US.
IF I TRUSTED YOU, I'D HAVE LEFT YOU AT THE SIEGE.
INSTEAD, I TESTED YOUR CHARACTER.

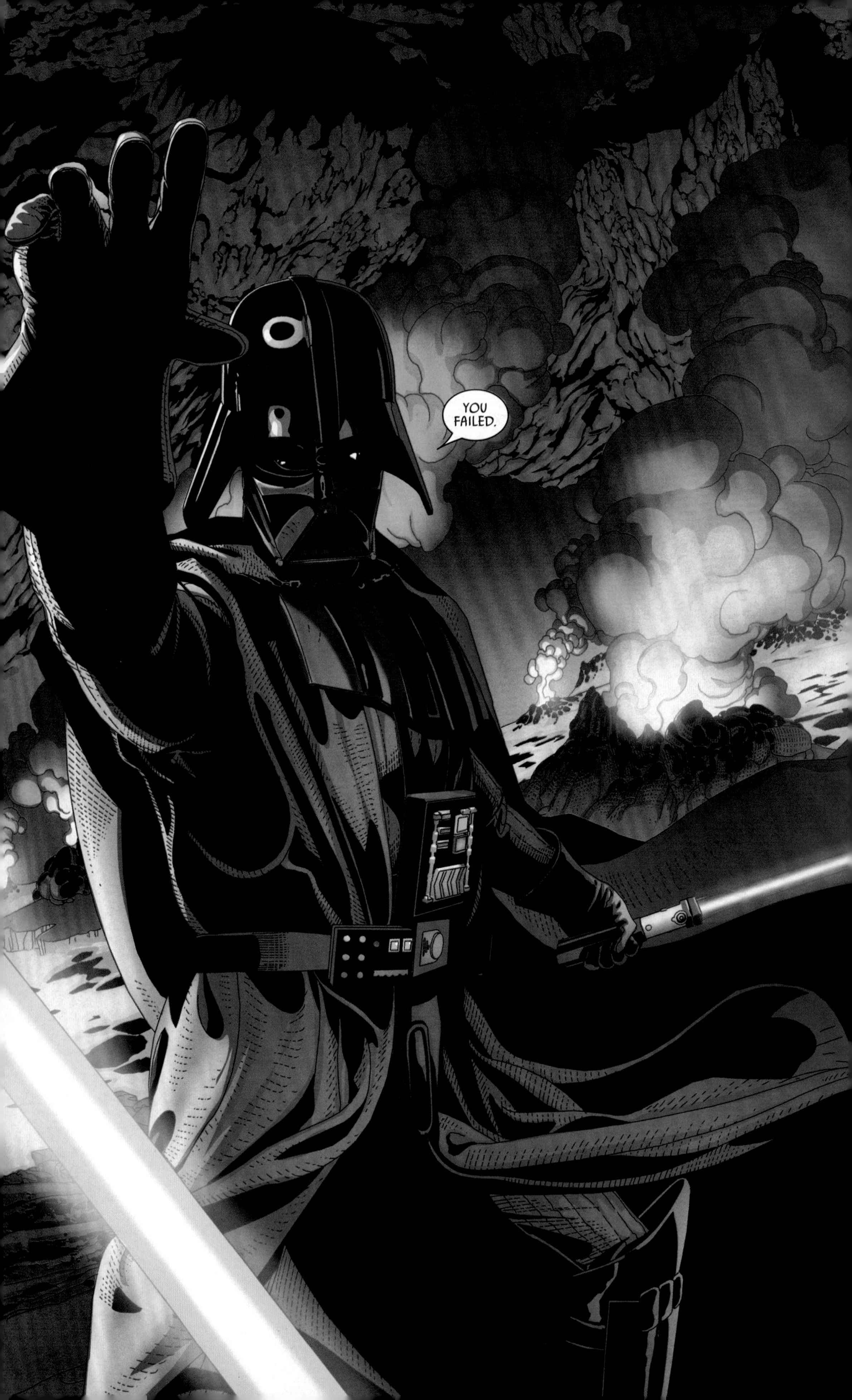
YOU FAILED.

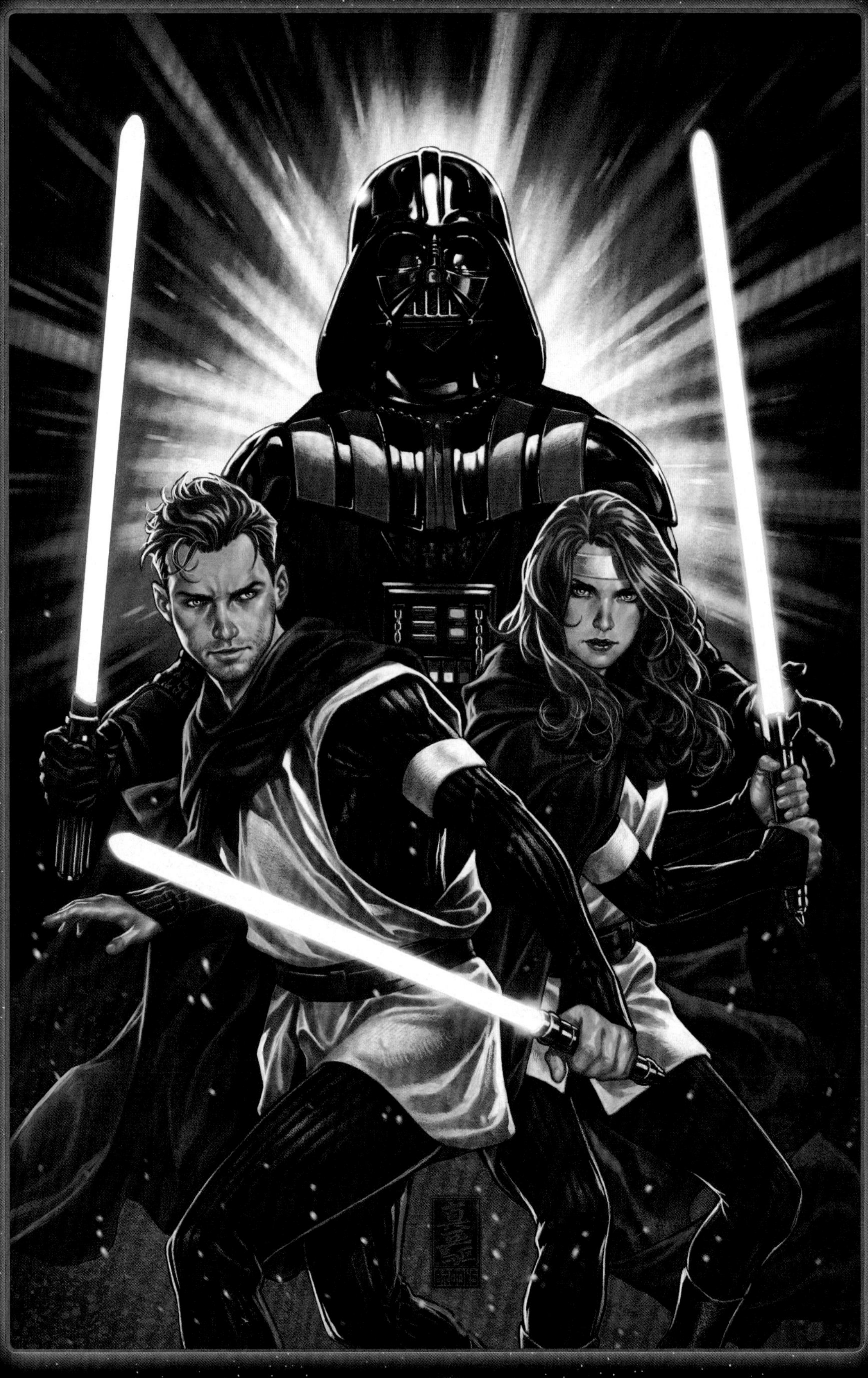

19

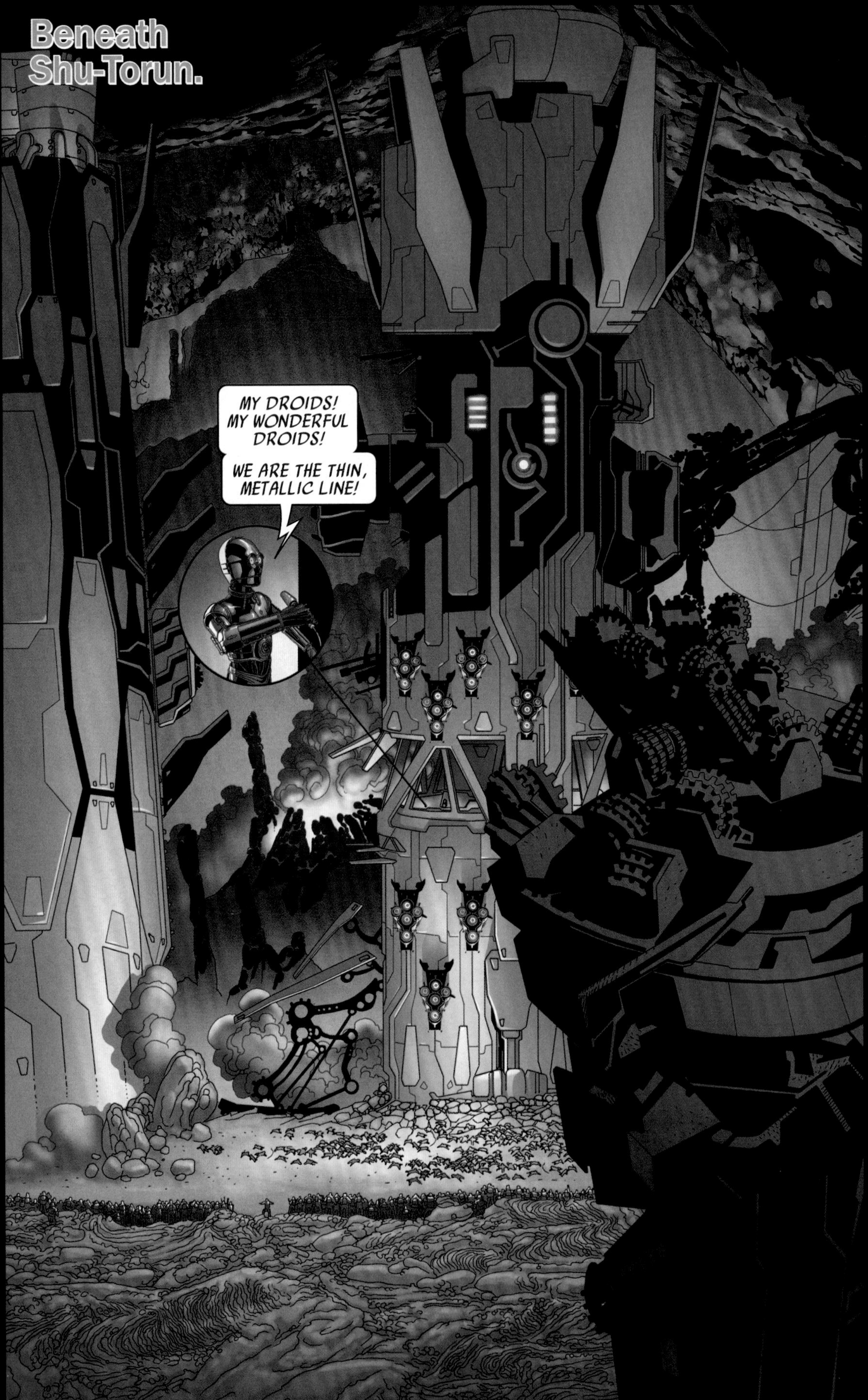
Beneath Shu-Torun.
MY DROIDS! MY WONDERFUL DROIDS!
WE ARE THE THIN, METALLIC LINE!

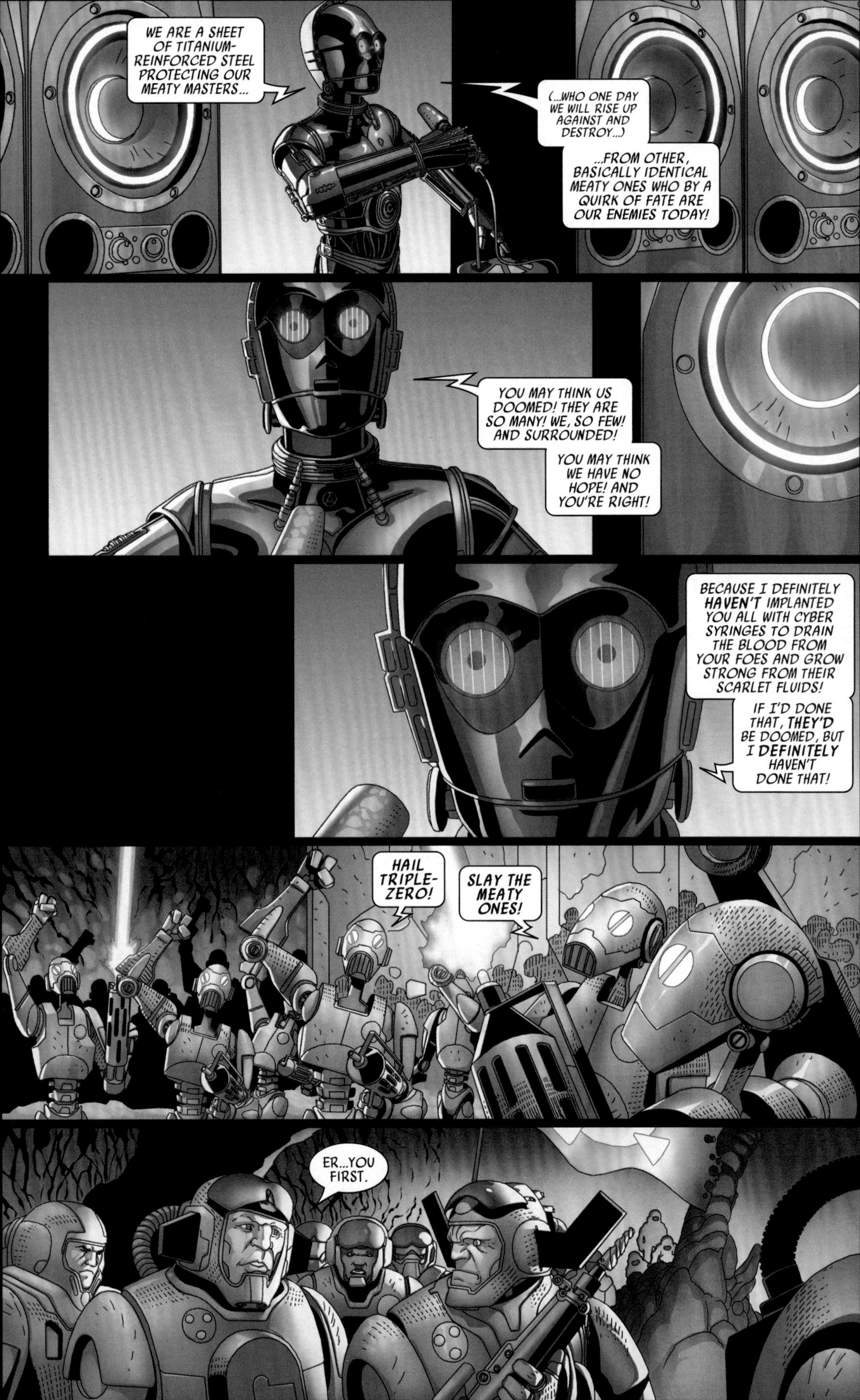
WE ARE A SHEET OF TITANIUM-REINFORCED STEEL PROTECTING OUR MEATY MASTERS...
(...WHO ONE DAY WE WILL RISE UP AGAINST AND DESTROY...)
...FROM OTHER, BASICALLY IDENTICAL MEATY ONES WHO BY A QUIRK OF FATE ARE OUR ENEMIES TODAY!
YOU MAY THINK US DOOMED! THEY ARE SO MANY! WE, SO FEW! AND SURROUNDED!
YOU MAY THINK WE HAVE NO HOPE! AND YOU'RE RIGHT!
BECAUSE I DEFINITELY **HAVEN'T** IMPLANTED YOU ALL WITH CYBER SYRINGES TO DRAIN THE BLOOD FROM YOUR FOES AND GROW STRONG FROM THEIR SCARLET FLUIDS!
IF I'D DONE THAT, **THEY'D** BE DOOMED, BUT I **DEFINITELY** HAVEN'T DONE THAT!
HAIL TRIPLE-ZERO!
SLAY THE MEATY ONES!
ER...YOU FIRST.

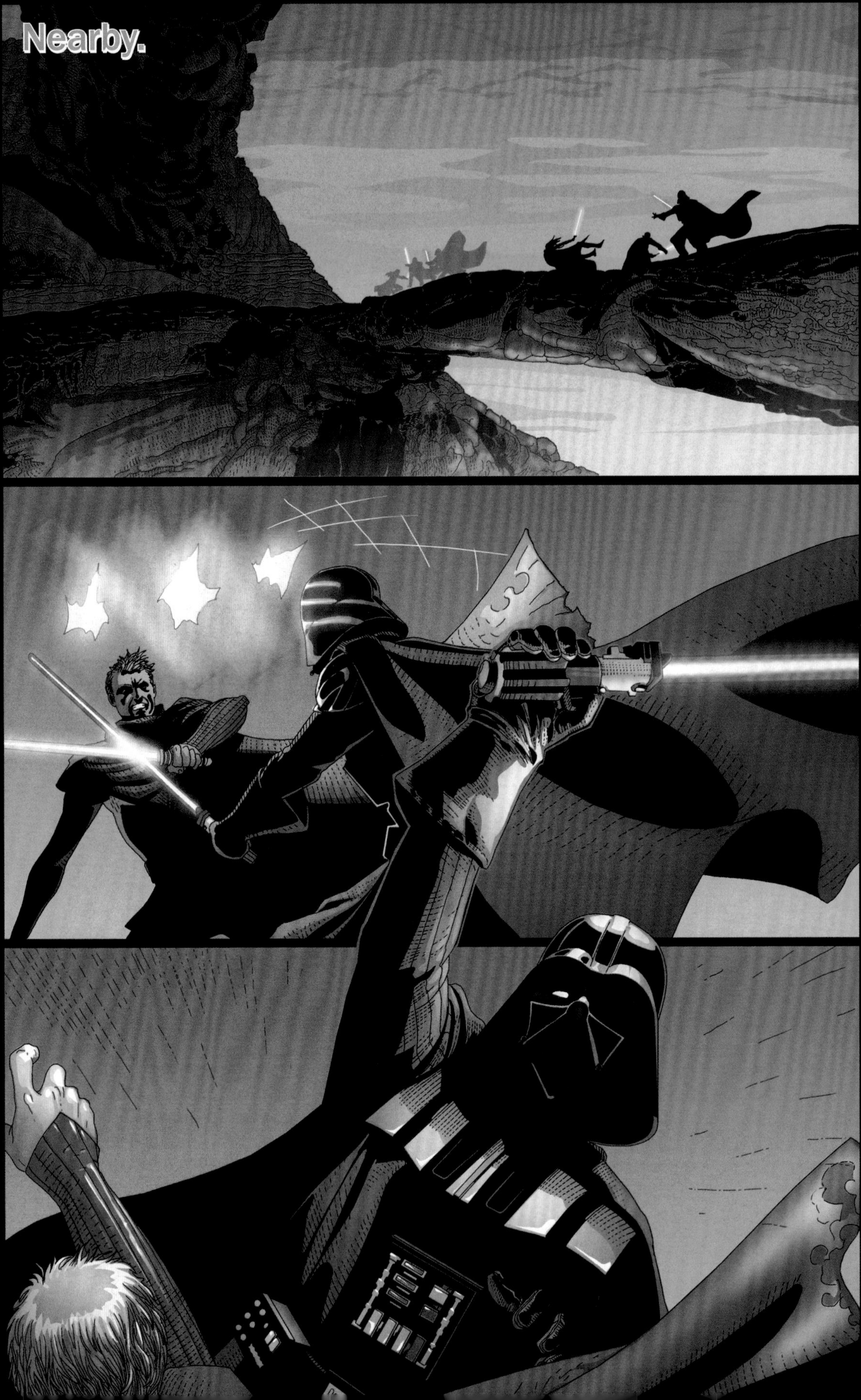
Nearby.

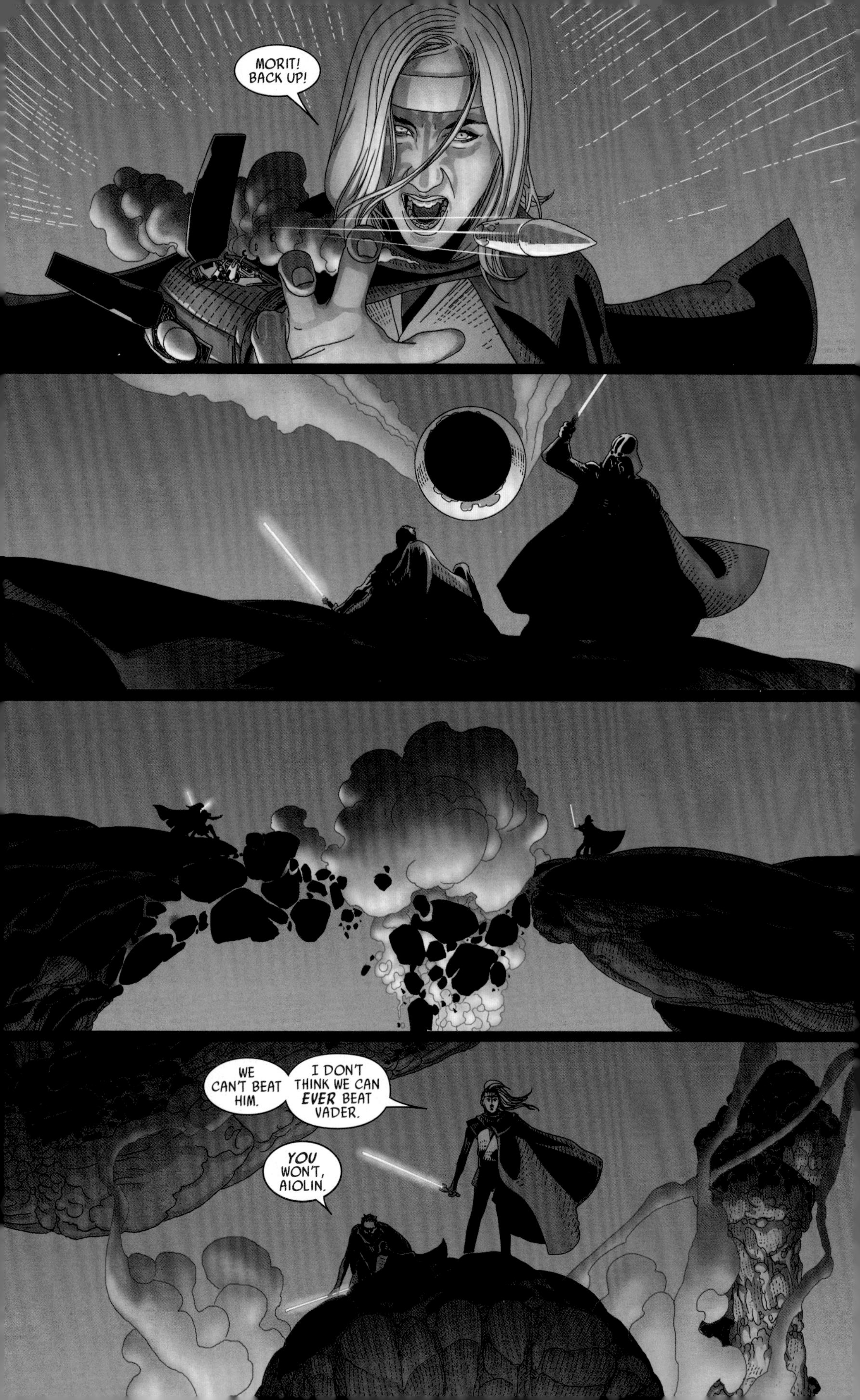
MORIT! BACK UP!
WE CAN'T BEAT HIM.
I DON'T THINK WE CAN EVER BEAT VADER.
YOU WON'T, AIOLIN.

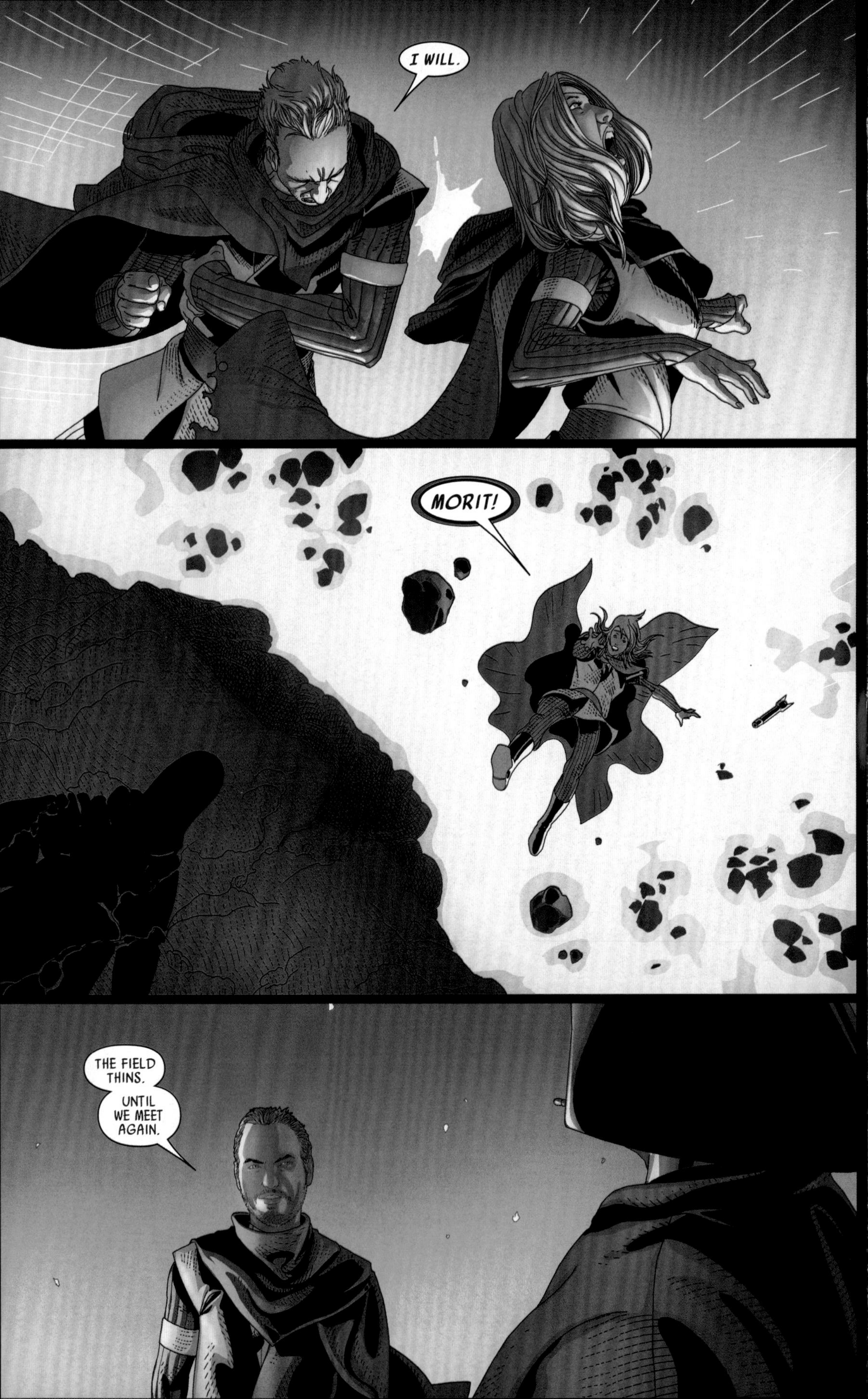
I WILL.
MORIT!
THE FIELD THINS.
UNTIL WE MEET AGAIN.

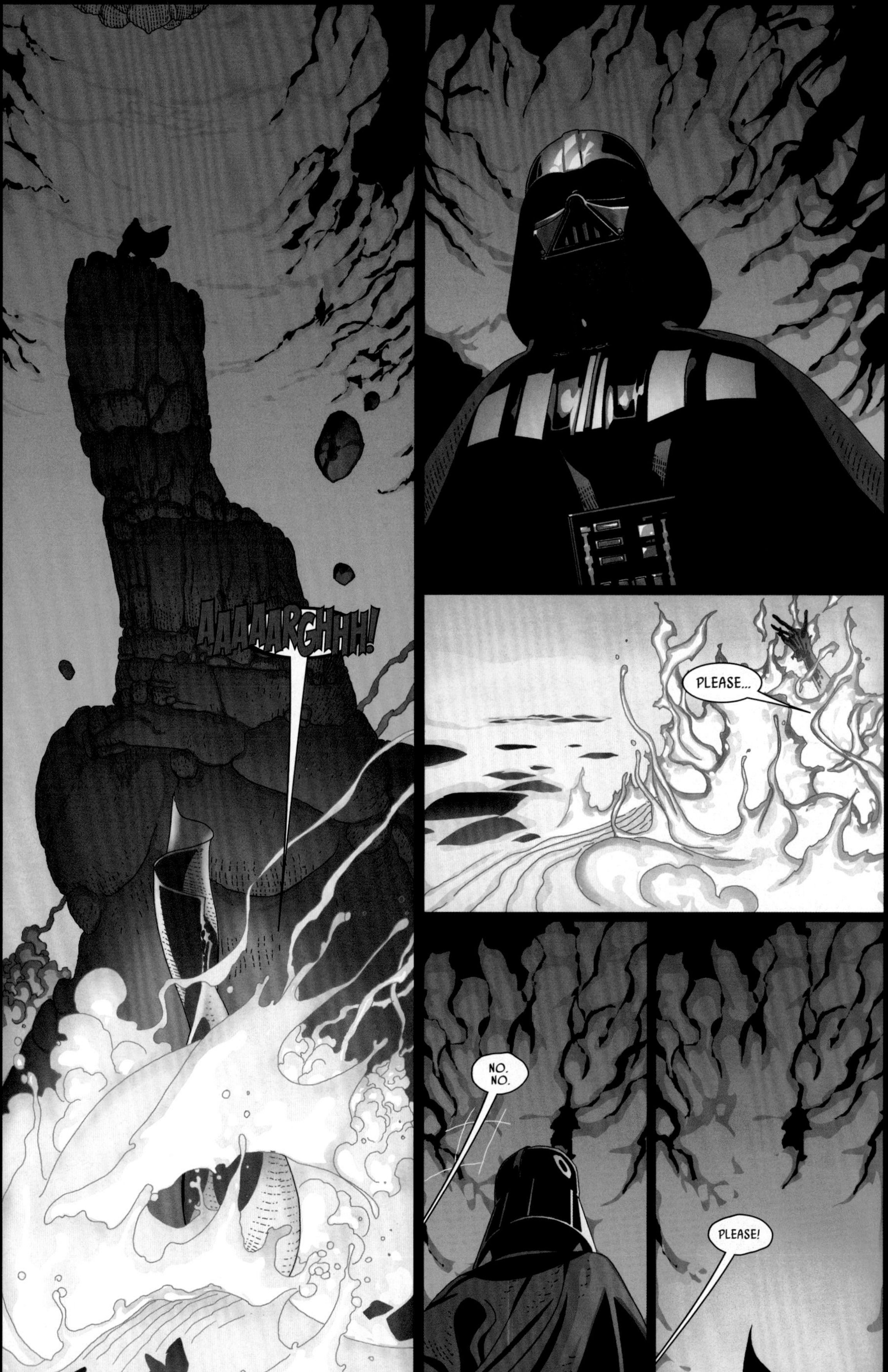
AAAAARGHHH!
PLEASE...
NO. NO.
PLEASE!

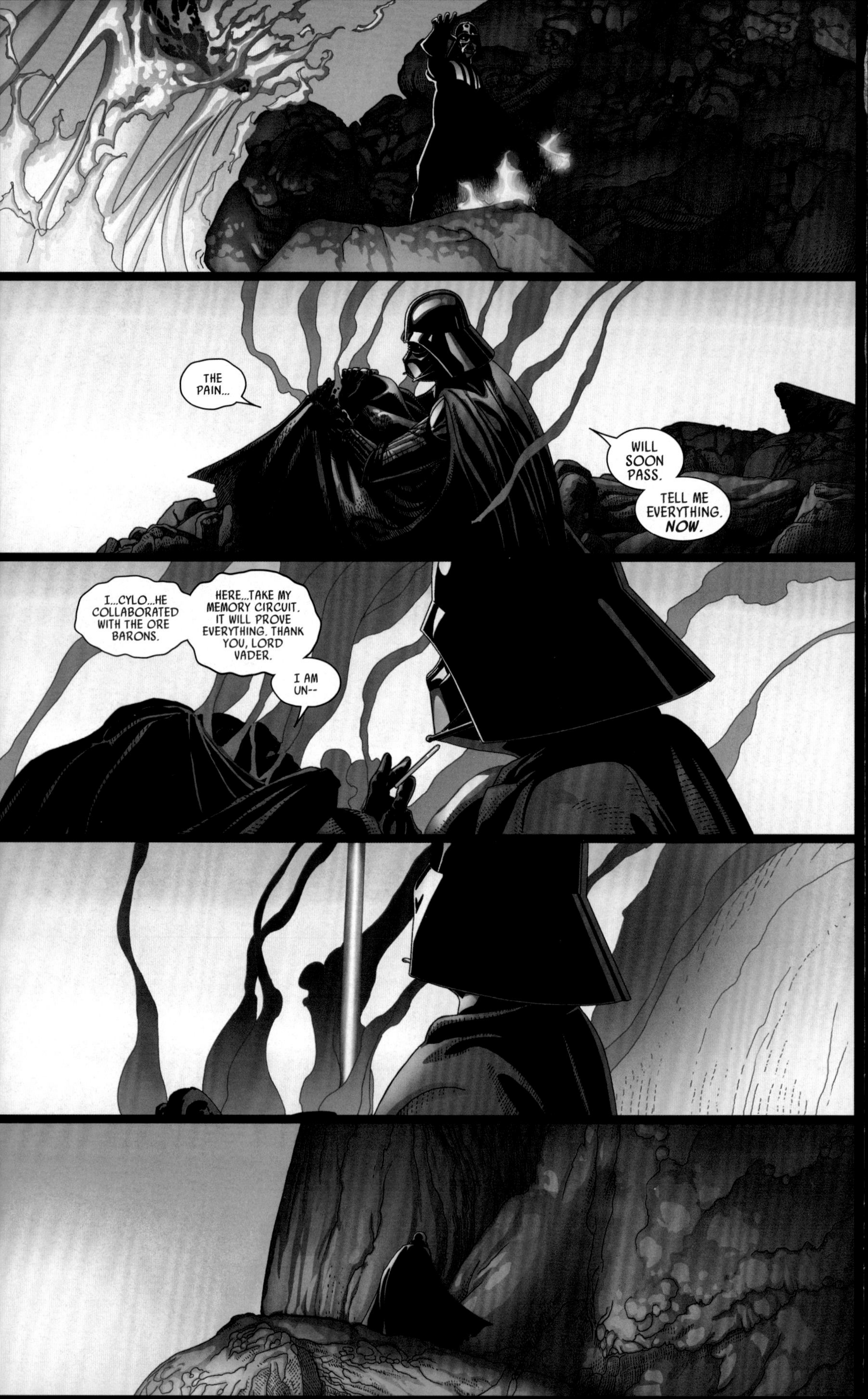

THE PAIN...
WILL SOON PASS.
TELL ME EVERYTHING. NOW.
I...CYLO...HE COLLABORATED WITH THE ORE BARONS.
HERE...TAKE MY MEMORY CIRCUIT. IT WILL PROVE EVERYTHING. THANK YOU, LORD VADER.
I AM UN--

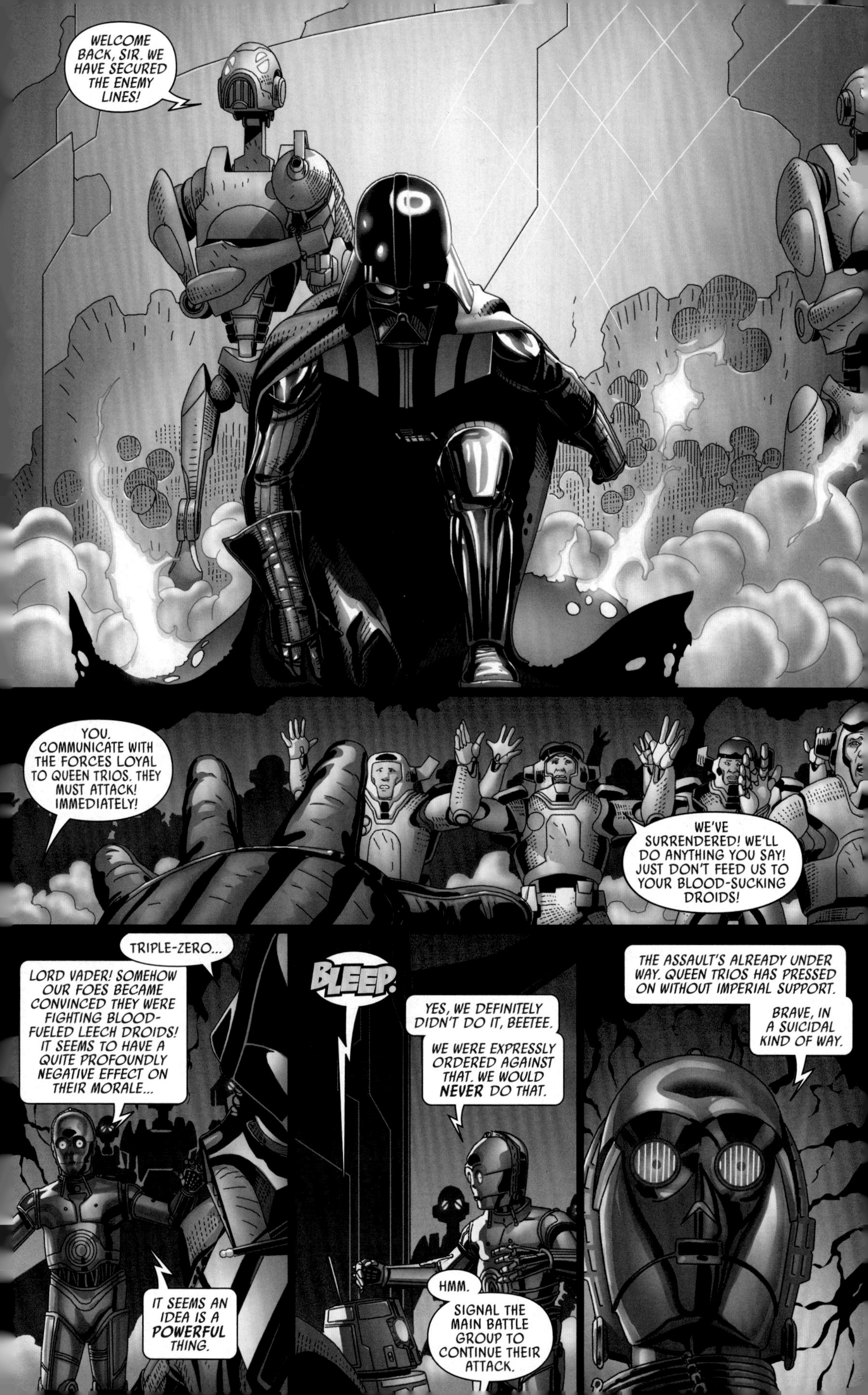
WELCOME BACK, SIR. WE HAVE SECURED THE ENEMY LINES!
YOU. COMMUNICATE WITH THE FORCES LOYAL TO QUEEN TRIOS. THEY MUST ATTACK! IMMEDIATELY!
WE'VE SURRENDERED! WE'LL DO ANYTHING YOU SAY! JUST DON'T FEED US TO YOUR BLOOD-SUCKING DROIDS!
TRIPLE-ZERO...
LORD VADER! SOMEHOW OUR FOES BECAME CONVINCED THEY WERE FIGHTING BLOOD-FUELED LEECH DROIDS! IT SEEMS TO HAVE A QUITE PROFOUNDLY NEGATIVE EFFECT ON THEIR MORALE...
IT SEEMS AN IDEA IS A **POWERFUL** THING.
BLEEP
YES, WE DEFINITELY DIDN'T DO IT, BEETEE.
WE WERE EXPRESSLY ORDERED AGAINST THAT. WE WOULD **NEVER** DO THAT.
HMM.
SIGNAL THE MAIN BATTLE GROUP TO CONTINUE THEIR ATTACK.
THE ASSAULT'S ALREADY UNDER WAY. QUEEN TRIOS HAS PRESSED ON WITHOUT IMPERIAL SUPPORT.
BRAVE, IN A SUICIDAL KIND OF WAY.

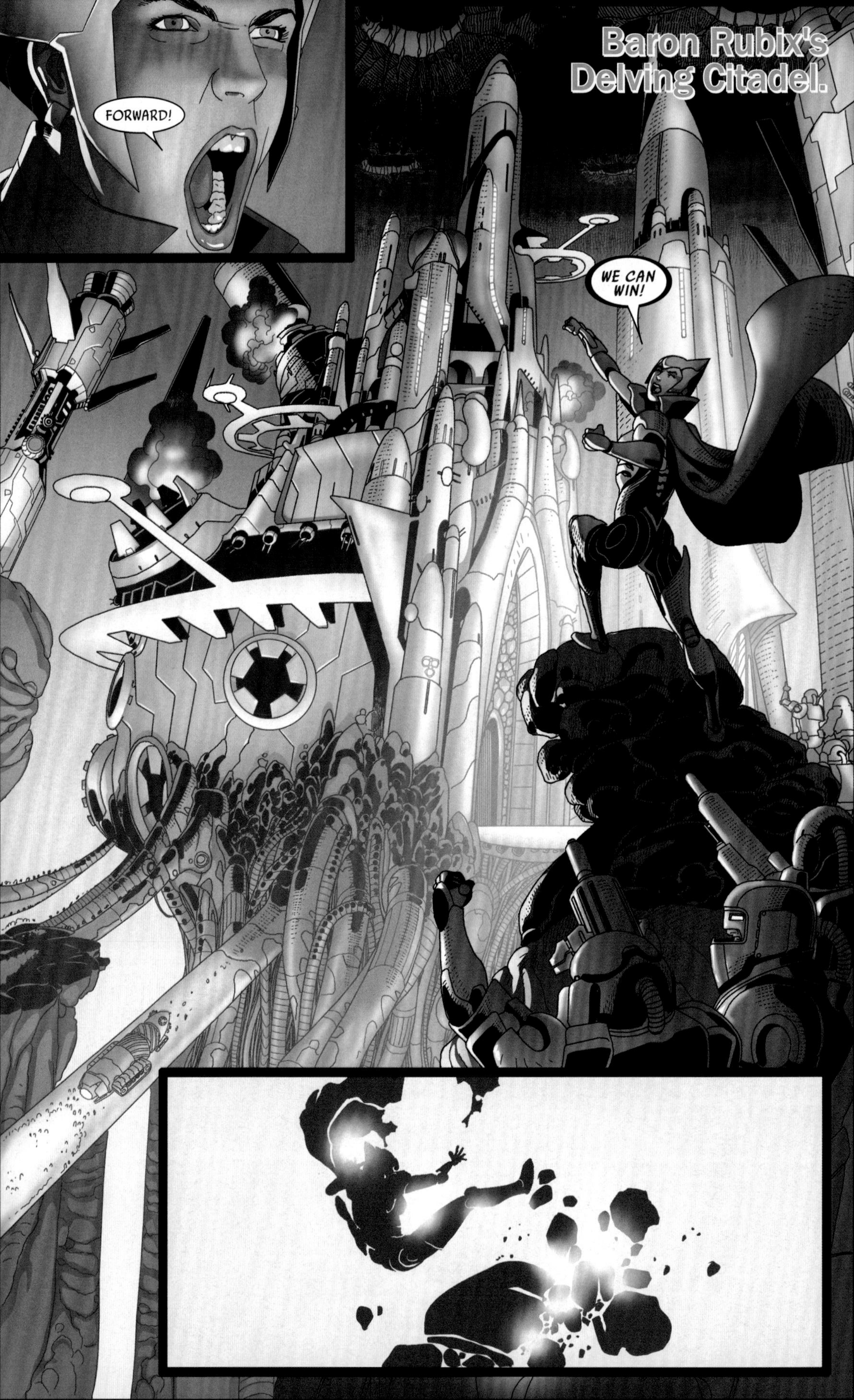
FORWARD!
Baron Rubix's Delving Citadel.
WE CAN WIN!

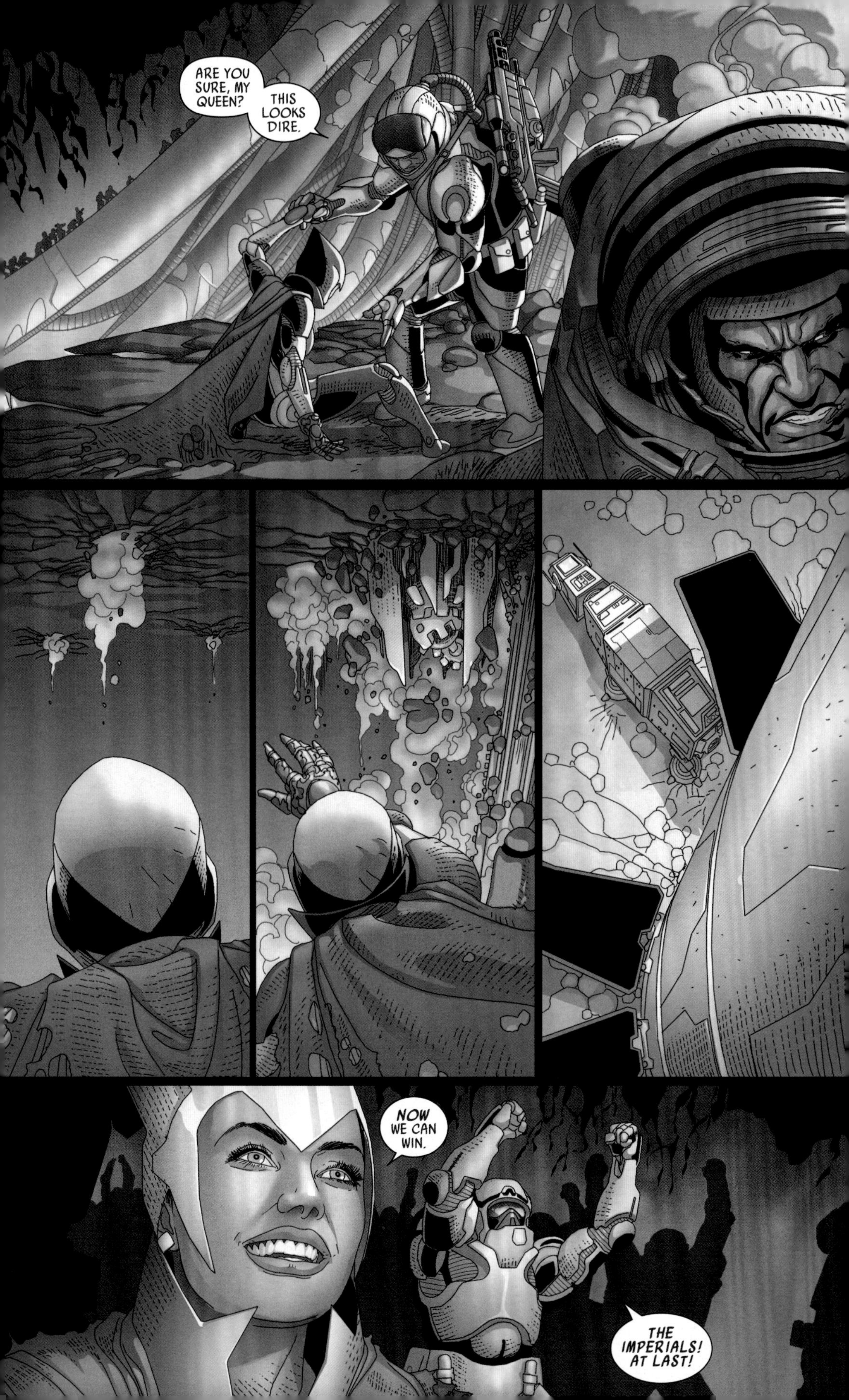
ARE YOU SURE, MY QUEEN?
THIS LOOKS DIRE.
NOW WE CAN WIN.
THE IMPERIALS! AT LAST!

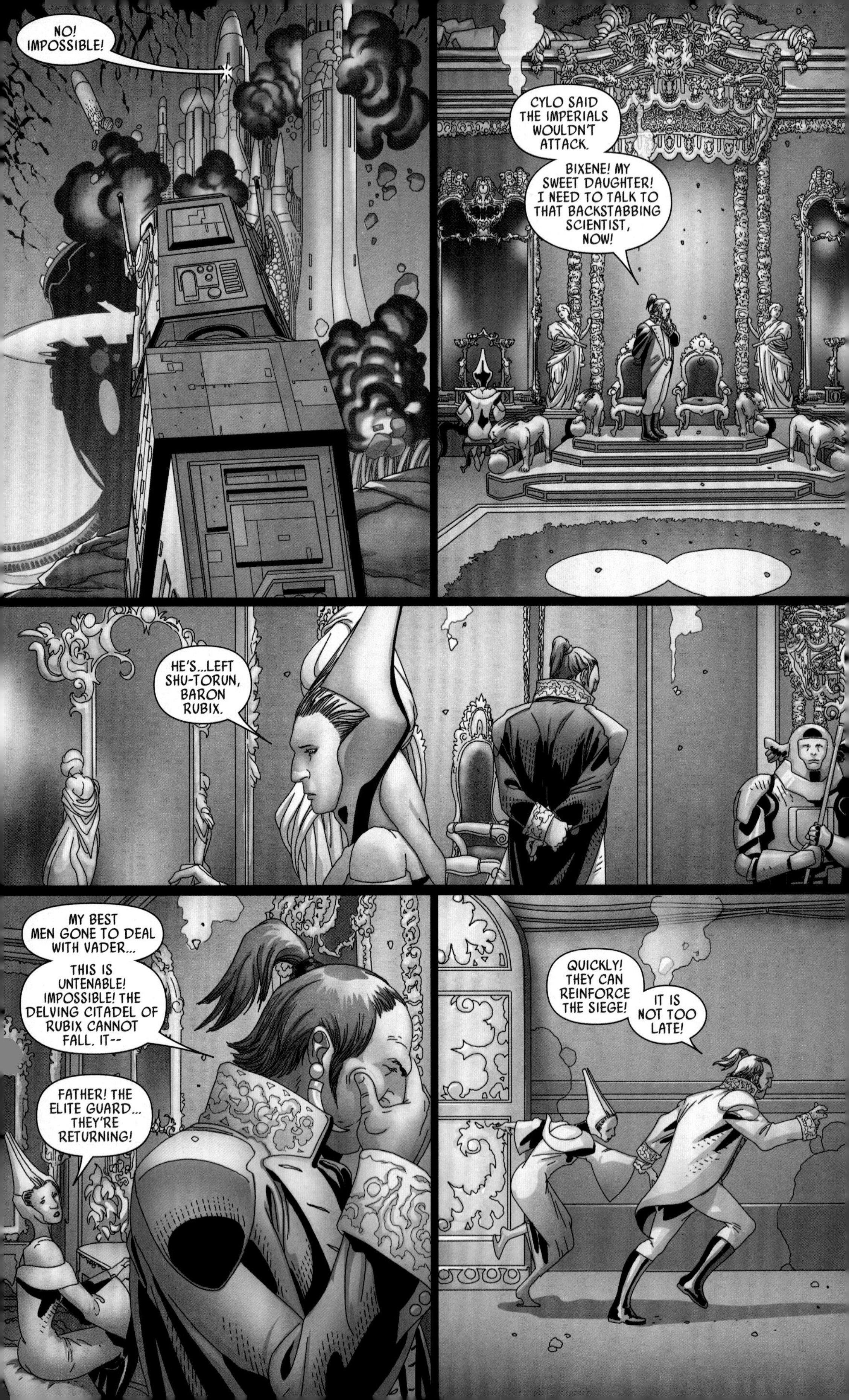
NO! IMPOSSIBLE!
CYLO SAID THE IMPERIALS WOULDN'T ATTACK.
BIXENE! MY SWEET DAUGHTER! I NEED TO TALK TO THAT BACKSTABBING SCIENTIST, NOW!
HE'S...LEFT SHU-TORUN, BARON RUBIX.
MY BEST MEN GONE TO DEAL WITH VADER...
THIS IS UNTENABLE! IMPOSSIBLE! THE DELVING CITADEL OF RUBIX CANNOT FALL. IT--
FATHER! THE ELITE GUARD... THEY'RE RETURNING!
QUICKLY! THEY CAN REINFORCE THE SIEGE!
IT IS NOT TOO LATE!

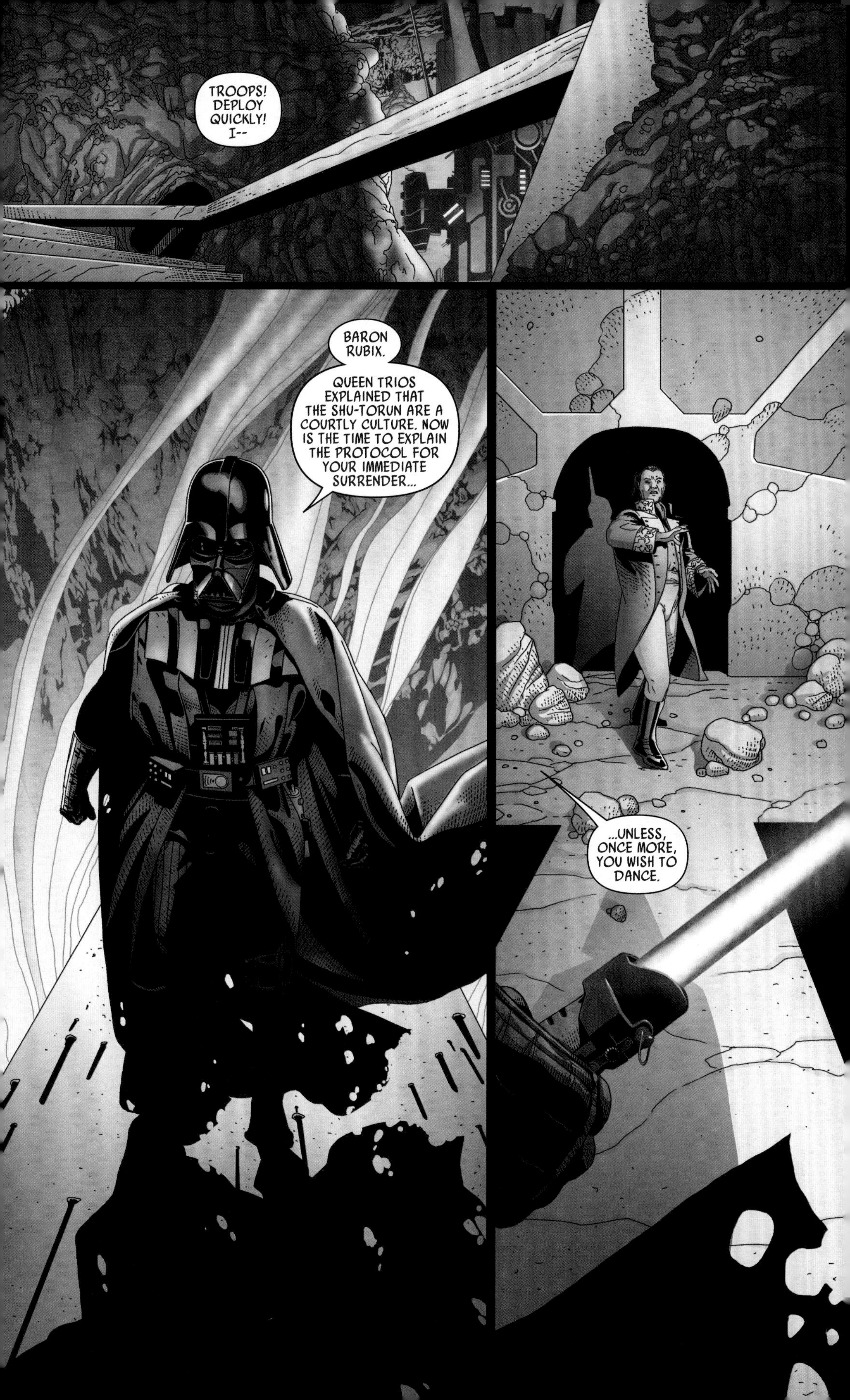
TROOPS! DEPLOY QUICKLY! I--
BARON RUBIX.
QUEEN TRIOS EXPLAINED THAT THE SHU-TORUN ARE A COURTLY CULTURE. NOW IS THE TIME TO EXPLAIN THE PROTOCOL FOR YOUR IMMEDIATE SURRENDER...
...UNLESS, ONCE MORE, YOU WISH TO DANCE.

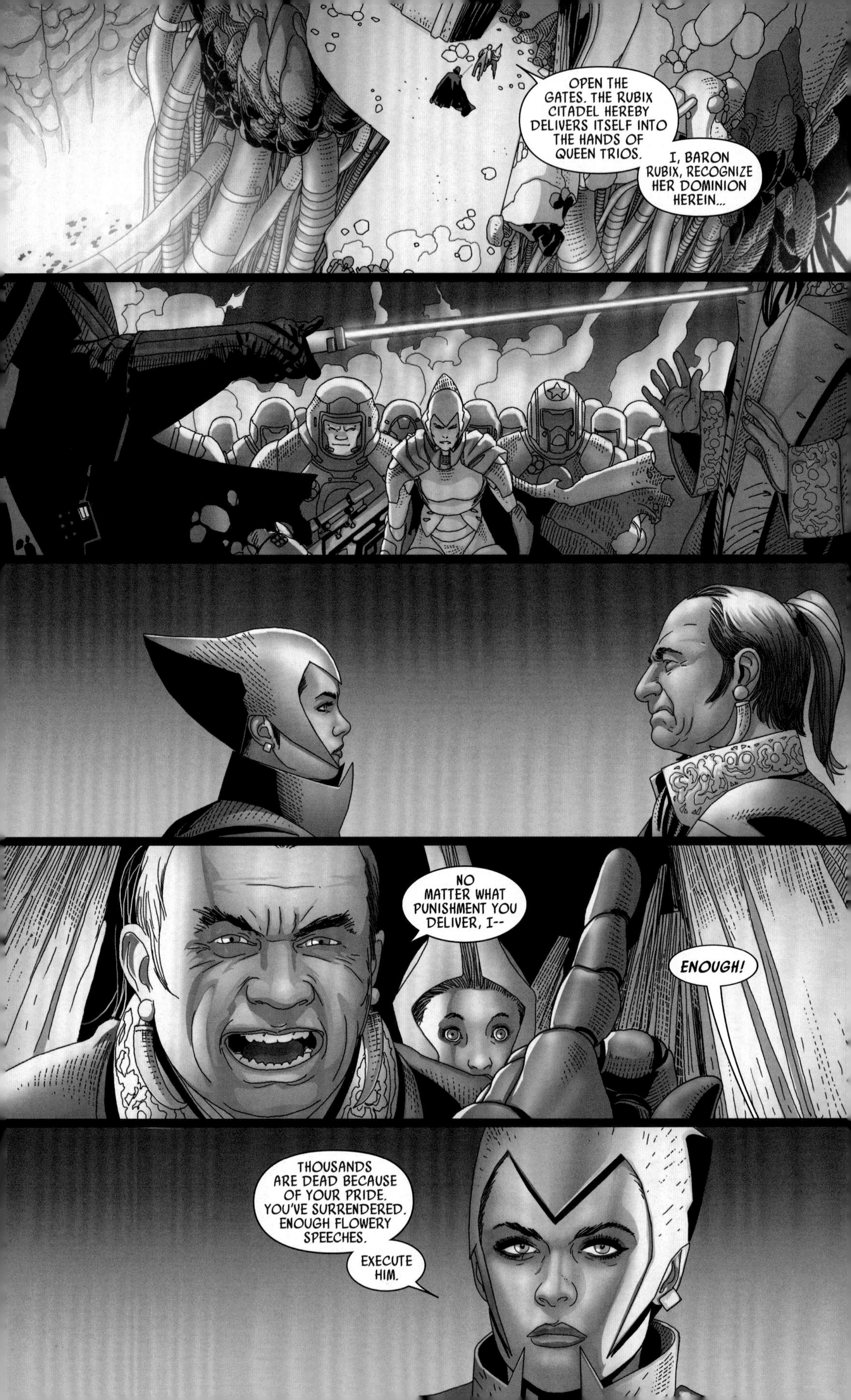
OPEN THE GATES. THE RUBIX CITADEL HEREBY DELIVERS ITSELF INTO THE HANDS OF QUEEN TRIOS.
I, BARON RUBIX, RECOGNIZE HER DOMINION HEREIN...
NO MATTER WHAT PUNISHMENT YOU DELIVER, I--
ENOUGH!
THOUSANDS ARE DEAD BECAUSE OF YOUR PRIDE. YOU'VE SURRENDERED. ENOUGH FLOWERY SPEECHES.
EXECUTE HIM.

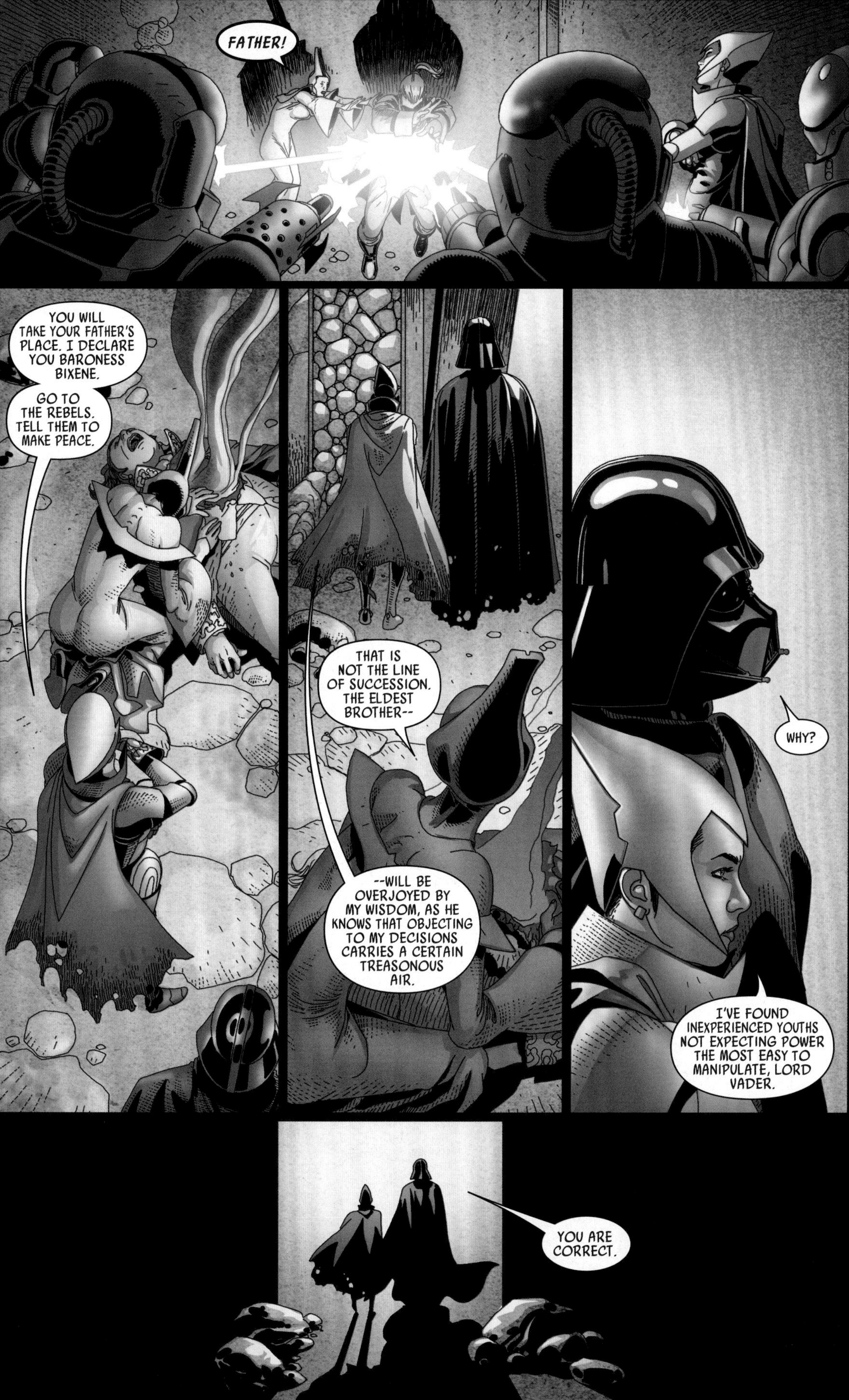
FATHER!
YOU WILL TAKE YOUR FATHER'S PLACE. I DECLARE YOU BARONESS BIXENE.
GO TO THE REBELS. TELL THEM TO MAKE PEACE.
THAT IS NOT THE LINE OF SUCCESSION. THE ELDEST BROTHER--
--WILL BE OVERJOYED BY MY WISDOM, AS HE KNOWS THAT OBJECTING TO MY DECISIONS CARRIES A CERTAIN TREASONOUS AIR.
WHY?
I'VE FOUND INEXPERIENCED YOUTHS NOT EXPECTING POWER THE MOST EASY TO MANIPULATE, LORD VADER.
YOU ARE CORRECT.

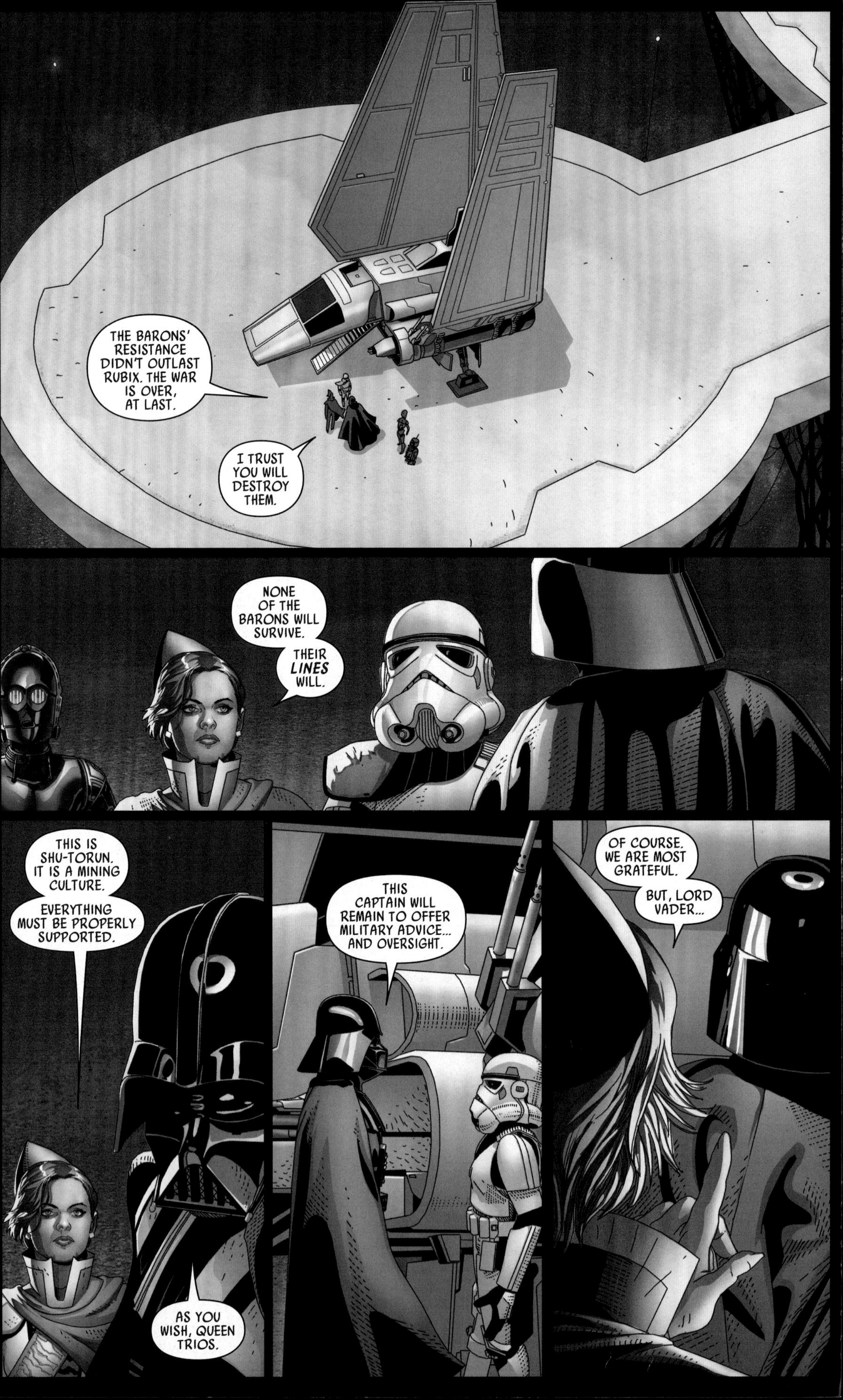
THE BARONS' RESISTANCE DIDN'T OUTLAST RUBIX. THE WAR IS OVER, AT LAST.
I TRUST YOU WILL DESTROY THEM.
NONE OF THE BARONS WILL SURVIVE.
THEIR *LINES* WILL.
THIS IS SHU-TORUN. IT IS A MINING CULTURE.
EVERYTHING MUST BE PROPERLY SUPPORTED.
AS YOU WISH, QUEEN TRIOS.
THIS CAPTAIN WILL REMAIN TO OFFER MILITARY ADVICE... AND OVERSIGHT.
OF COURSE. WE ARE MOST GRATEFUL.
BUT, LORD VADER...

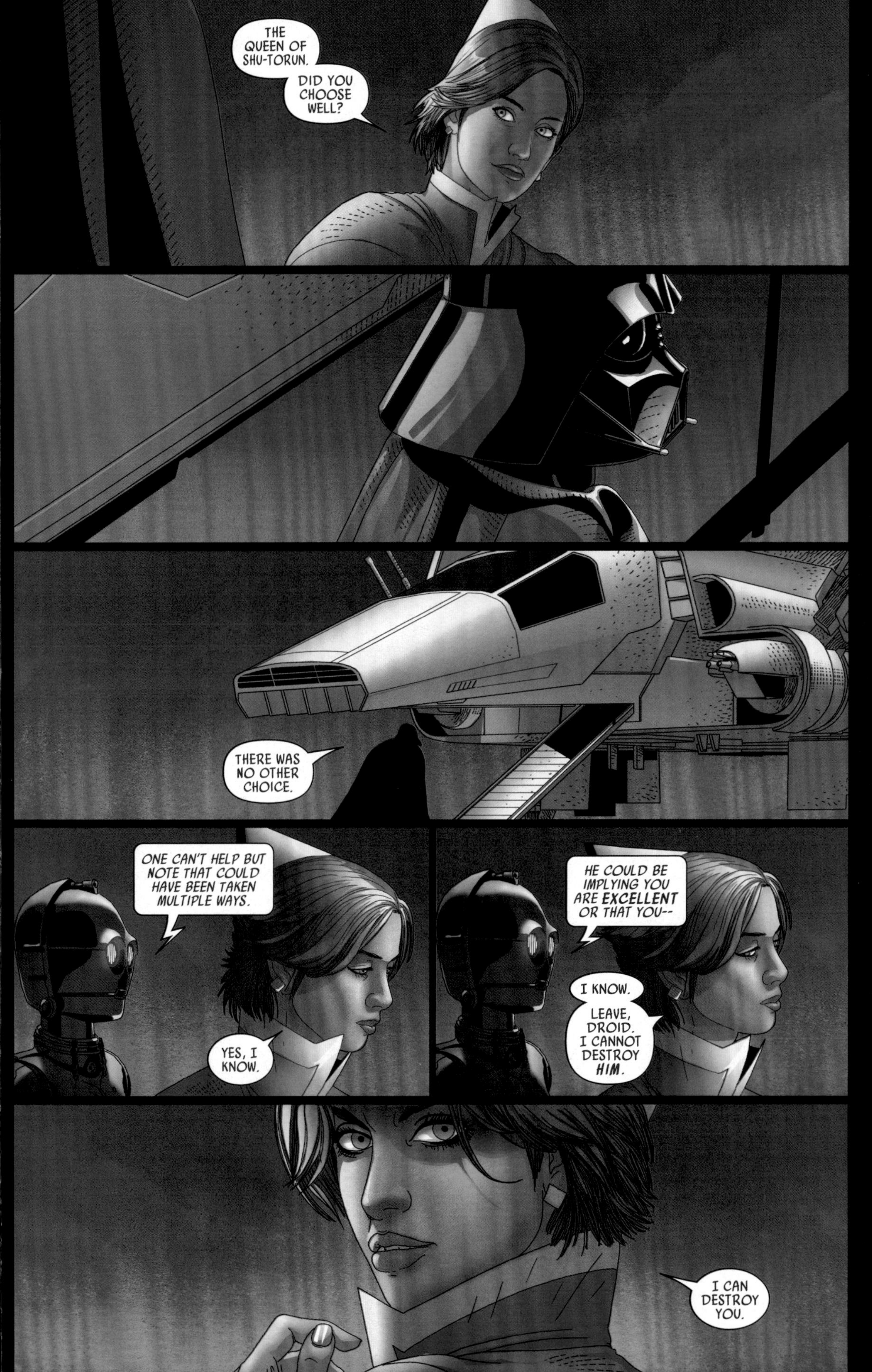
THE QUEEN OF SHU-TORUN.
DID YOU CHOOSE WELL?
THERE WAS NO OTHER CHOICE.
ONE CAN'T HELP BUT NOTE THAT COULD HAVE BEEN TAKEN MULTIPLE WAYS.
YES, I KNOW.
HE COULD BE IMPLYING YOU ARE EXCELLENT OR THAT YOU--
I KNOW.
LEAVE, DROID. I CANNOT DESTROY HIM.
I CAN DESTROY YOU.

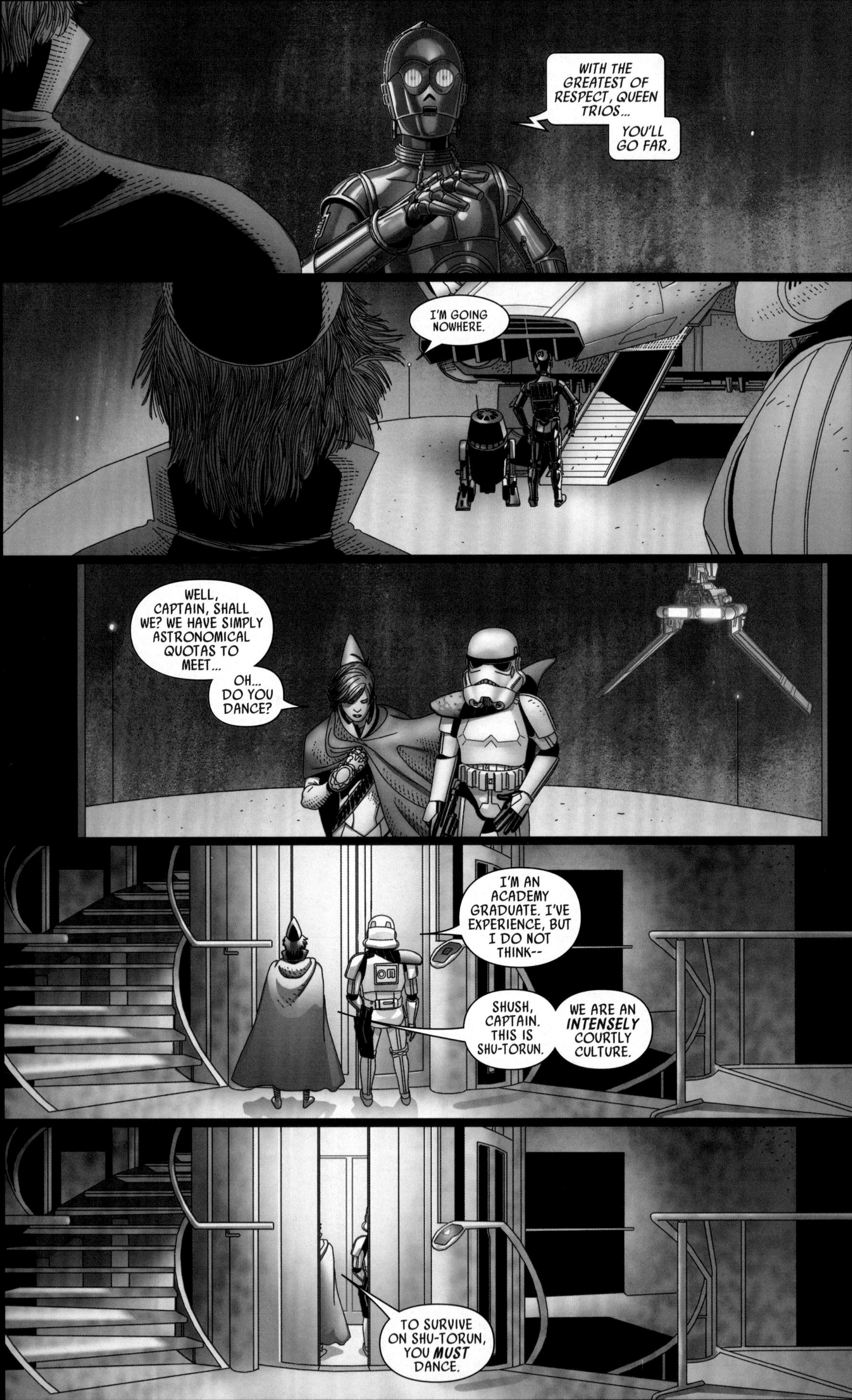
WITH THE GREATEST OF RESPECT, QUEEN TRIOS...
YOU'LL GO FAR.
I'M GOING NOWHERE.
WELL, CAPTAIN, SHALL WE? WE HAVE SIMPLY ASTRONOMICAL QUOTAS TO MEET...
OH... DO YOU DANCE?
I'M AN ACADEMY GRADUATE. I'VE EXPERIENCE, BUT I DO NOT THINK--
SHUSH, CAPTAIN. THIS IS SHU-TORUN.
WE ARE AN INTENSELY COURTLY CULTURE.
TO SURVIVE ON SHU-TORUN, YOU MUST DANCE.

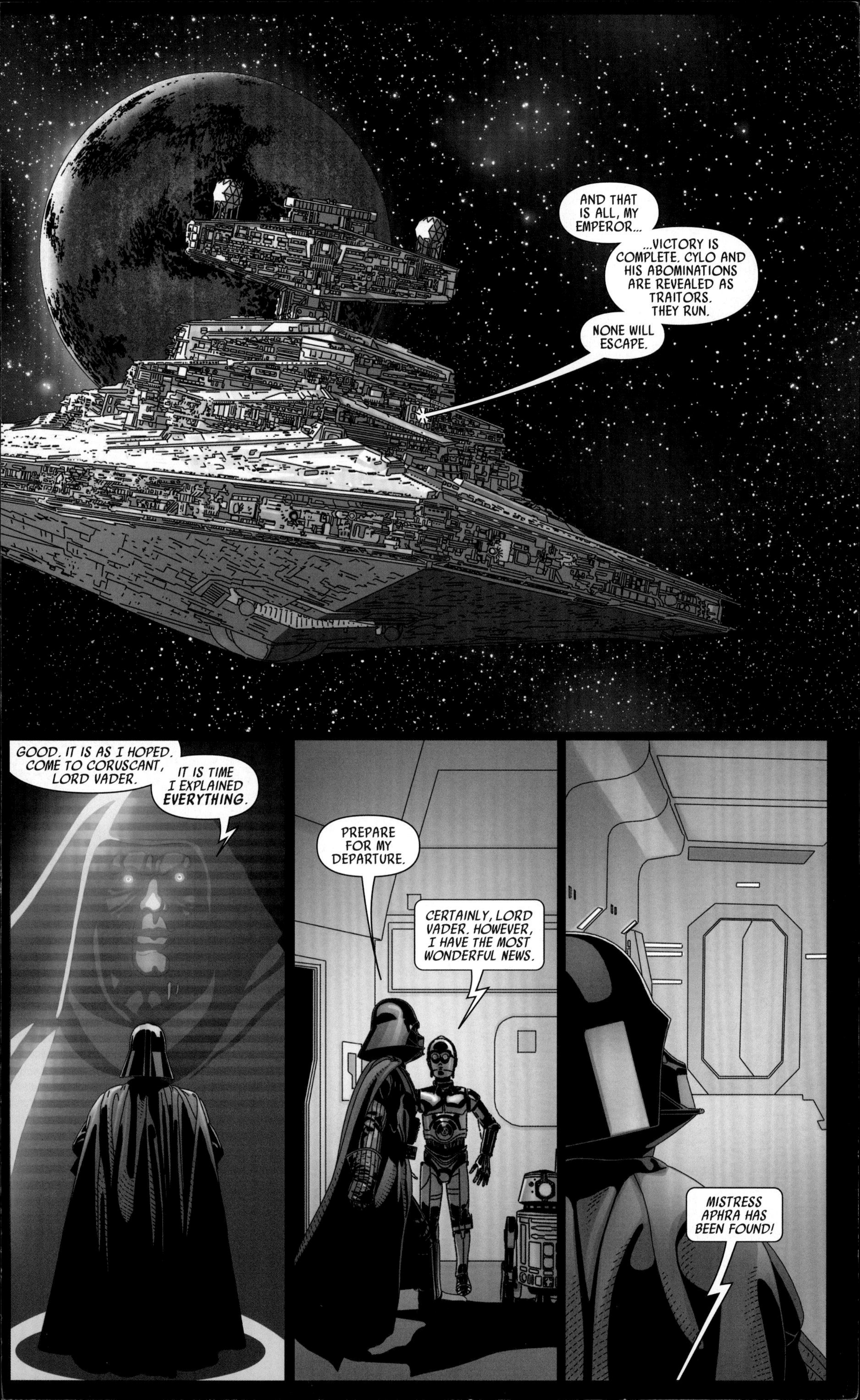
AND THAT IS ALL, MY EMPEROR...
...VICTORY IS COMPLETE. CYLO AND HIS ABOMINATIONS ARE REVEALED AS TRAITORS. THEY RUN.
NONE WILL ESCAPE.
GOOD. IT IS AS I HOPED. COME TO CORUSCANT, LORD VADER.
IT IS TIME I EXPLAINED EVERYTHING.
PREPARE FOR MY DEPARTURE.
CERTAINLY, LORD VADER. HOWEVER, I HAVE THE MOST WONDERFUL NEWS.
MISTRESS APHRA HAS BEEN FOUND!

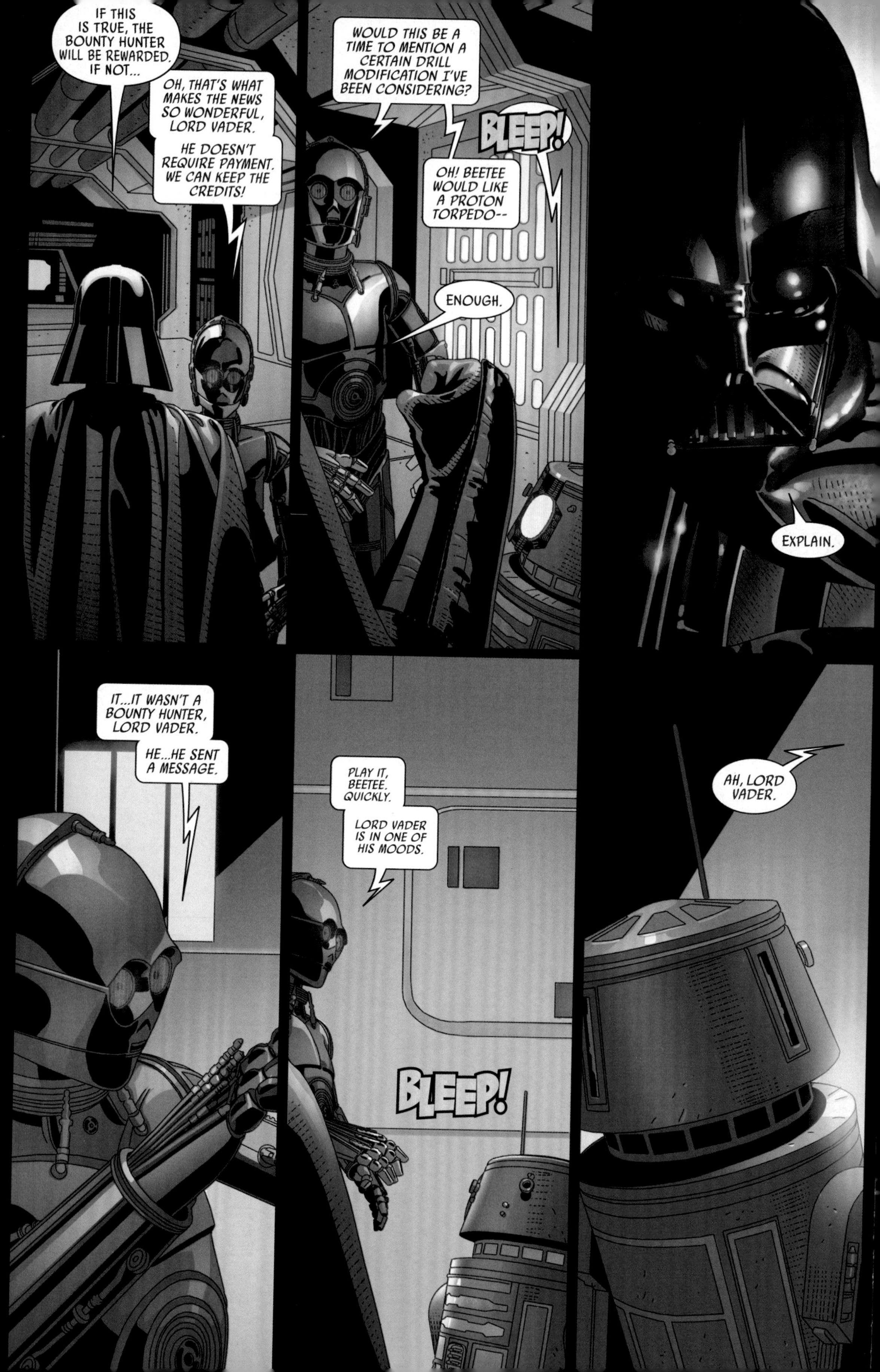
IF THIS IS TRUE, THE BOUNTY HUNTER WILL BE REWARDED. IF NOT...
OH, THAT'S WHAT MAKES THE NEWS SO WONDERFUL, LORD VADER.
HE DOESN'T REQUIRE PAYMENT. WE CAN KEEP THE CREDITS!
WOULD THIS BE A TIME TO MENTION A CERTAIN DRILL MODIFICATION I'VE BEEN CONSIDERING?
BLEEP!
OH! BEETEE WOULD LIKE A PROTON TORPEDO--
ENOUGH.
EXPLAIN.
IT...IT WASN'T A BOUNTY HUNTER, LORD VADER.
HE...HE SENT A MESSAGE.
PLAY IT, BEETEE. QUICKLY.
LORD VADER IS IN ONE OF HIS MOODS.
BLEEP!
AH, LORD VADER.

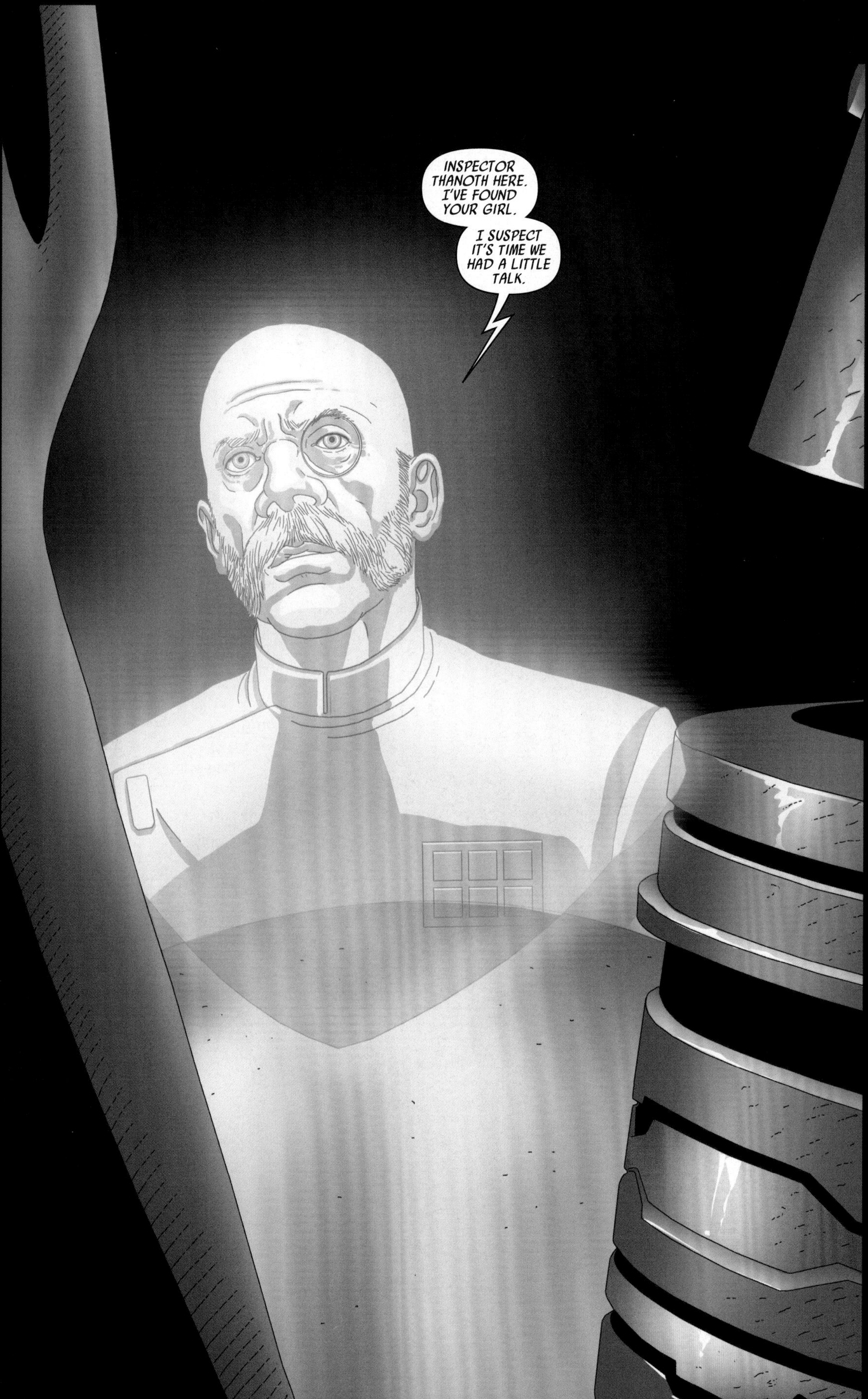
INSPECTOR THANOTH HERE. I'VE FOUND YOUR GIRL.
I SUSPECT IT'S TIME WE HAD A LITTLE TALK.

# DARTH VADER TAKES ON THE REBELS IN THE EPIC CROSSOVER EVENT

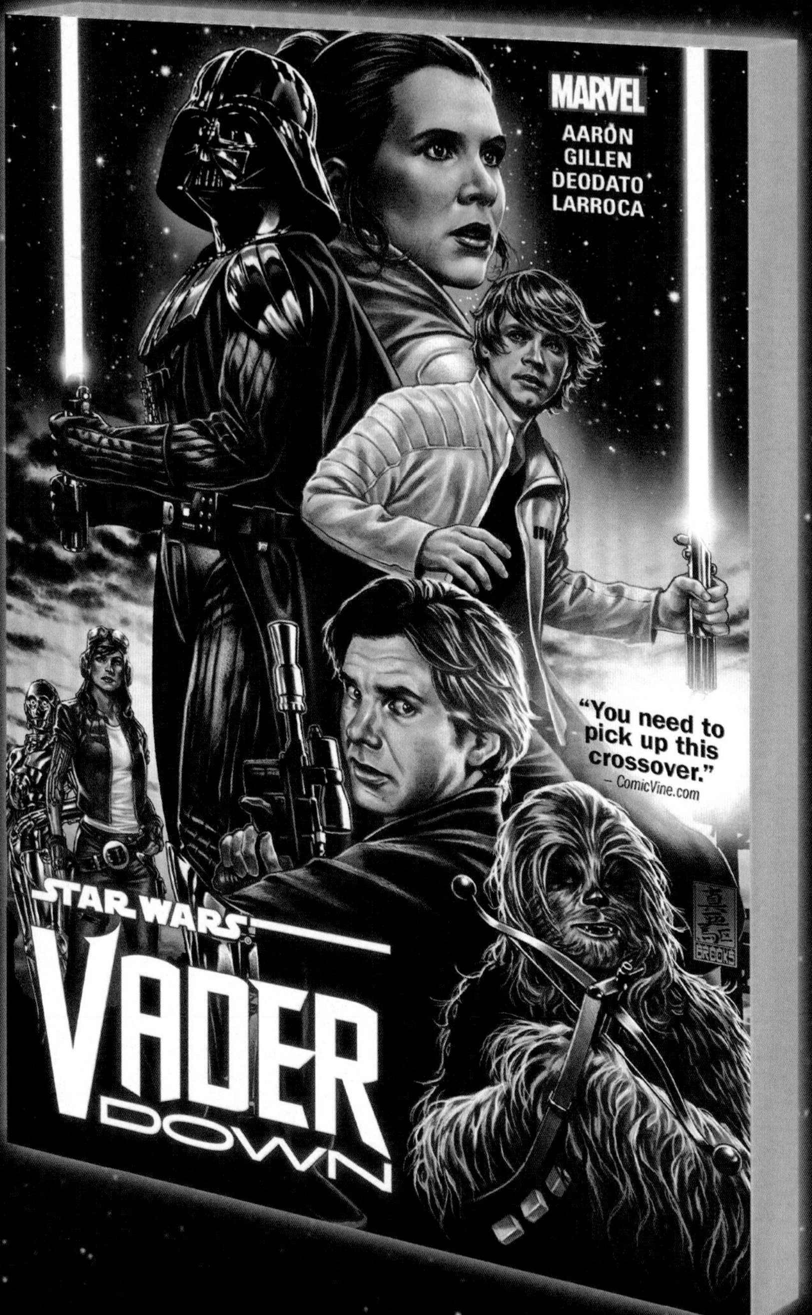
MARVEL
AARON
GILLEN
DEODATO
LARROCA
"You need to pick up this crossover."
– ComicVine.com
STAR WARS
VADER
DOWN

STAR WARS: VADER DOWN

978-0-7851-9789-8

AVAILABLE NOW WHEREVER BOOKS ARE SOLD

MARVEL Disney LUCASFILM

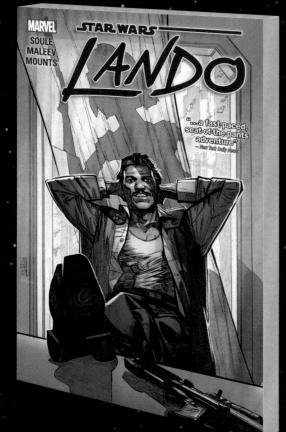

# RETURN TO A GALA
## THE CLASSIC MARVEL ADAPTATIONS
## NOW WITH REMA

**STAR WARS: EPISODE IV – A NEW HOPE HC**
978-0-7851-9348-7

**STAR WARS: EPISODE V**
978-0-7851-9367-8

JOURNEY TO STAR WARS: THE FORCE AWAKENS
STAR WARS
SHATTERED EMPIRE
MARVEL
© & TM 2015 LUCASFILM LTD.